contents

preface

Public Relations is invasive and pervasive. It is seemingly everywhere. The news media talk and write daily and nightly about 'PR exercises' and 'PR jobs'. There is an expectation that everyone understands this shorthand for implied deceit, corruption, trickery, exhibitionism, specious pleading; so much so that the mere mention of PR will provoke cynicism and disbelief about whatever it is applied to.

Why are the media so preoccupied with PR? Why do they spend so much time and effort on mentioning it? Has a sneering reference to PR become in truth the lazy journalist's easy punch line, that has little meaning except what the viewer, listener or reader chooses to give it? And why should this one occupation be so commonly reviled by another, which itself is regarded very poorly by society generally?

For any understanding of PR and its capabilities for achieving effective communication and dialogue, in whatever context, it is necessary first to peel away some of the layers of confusion, exaggeration and misrepresentation about it. There are many questions that need answers in order to achieve this. The relentless rise of social and commercial pluralism demands no less. So what is PR and what might be its practical uses, given this over-communicated, noisy world of hype and mistrust?

acknowledgements

The very many people who, intentionally or otherwise, have assisted in the production of this book are far too numerous to mention individually but nonetheless all are deserving of acknowledgement. Clients, colleagues, associates and suppliers, media contacts, City folk, politicians, lawyers, educationalists, fellow practitioners and people drawn from umpteen more walks of life have all contributed, in their many and varied ways, reflecting the typical richness and diversity of consultancy practice.

introduction

The main purpose of Public Relations is to influence the behaviours of individuals and groups of people in relation to each other, through dialogue with all those audiences whose perceptions, attitudes and opinions are critical to success. In the last two decades, use of PR has spread throughout the public, private and not-for-profit sectors. It has added new words and phrases to our language, and it has become recognized as an important modern aspect of management. Probably half a million job descriptions include some PR, in the UK alone.

Everything You Should Know About Public Relations addresses the questions so often asked about PR, from the mundane to the complex. Ever more people wonder whether they need PR, maybe to: build their businesses, help sell products and services, develop their careers, make themselves known, gain acceptance, protect their reputations, generate interest in their causes, win understanding and support to secure a result, argue a case more effectively, fight their corner, avoid creating problems they could do without or make sure people are properly informed and consulted.

They require answers to questions that they frame within their own terms of reference and relate to what they particularly have in mind to achieve. And it can greatly help to have the answers to other people's questions too. Some questions more than others will be more relevant to the individual reader's needs, just like any question-and-answer session. Some may shed light on a new aspect, while others may promote a new line of thinking about how to consider using PR for a particular purpose or in a different context.

Managers who still have little if any direct experience of using PR want to know what it could do for their operations, in terms that they can readily understand and relate to. They are thinking, for instance, about specificity, measurement and overheads. Can PR conform to conventional disciplines? How and where does it fit in? What will it involve of their time? How is it to be evaluated?

The scale and complexity of PR communication varies greatly, from meeting the needs of the individual person to those of governments and global corporations. Before embarking upon any PR activities, expectations for outcomes need to be well framed within measurable and realistic objectives. Once underway, communication has to be fully planned and managed within a close knowledge and understanding of the operating environment and its likely future development.

Guidance is offered here in a no-nonsense, down-to-earth way, based on a very firm theoretical and practical foundation. There are 501 questions, asked of me in one form or another many times. They are answered briefly, succinctly and definitively but not dogmatically, to provide a fast-track grasp of the subject before either taking responsibility for PR, determining its exact relevance and value to a current requirement or having to decide upon its future direction and purpose.

Many uncomfortable questions are to be found here, including those that journalists' tirades provoke, and, although recognizing PR's rising importance in the implementation of corporate strategy within many organizations, no particular brief is held for anyone. There is no minimizing of the PR role, to appease rivals and critics, but nor is there any attempt to elevate the status of PR practice either.

Insights into practice and explanations of much popular jargon are combined with practical examples, illustrations and thoughts about larger, broader topics such as business ethics, corporate culture, branding, globalization and technology applications. The questions are likely to inspire many more. That is the nature of PR, which continues to grow and diversify rapidly. It is a very broad subject indeed, which, once ventured into, can quickly become a captivating enquiry of enduring fascination.

Each chapter approaches PR from a particular perspective and some major topics are investigated from several aspects. The first two chapters ask exactly what PR is and is not. Then the nature of PR communication and the strategic and planning aspects are explored, followed by five chapters that examine, by turn, publicity, marketing communications, the role of PR within the organization, stakeholders and publics, politicians and government. The next five chapters address measurement and evaluation, PR practice, practical issues relating to initiating PR, hiring in-house staff and engaging consultancies. In the last chapter the questions look to the future, developing applications and emerging trends and issues.

one

dreams and **realities**

- What is the definition of PR?
- So publics are just stakeholders by another name?
- What is meant by 'That's good PR'?
- Why bother about the finer points if PR does the trick?
- Is PR about manipulation of attitudes and opinions?
- Why do people seem to respond more to PR these days?
- What is image?
- Do image and identity add up to being PR?
- Who takes charge of identity?
- What is the difference between image and reputation?
- Is PR a combination of image and reputation?
- Do people feel more confident for having a bit of PR around them?
- Do private representations come under *public* relations, or am I losing the plot?
- Would just a bit of PR make all the difference to our profits this year?
- With no formal marketing or sales, would PR be the best way to start?
- Should we concentrate on PR and keep sales and marketing for when we are bigger?
- Can PR be self-taught?
- PR starts with shifting information to those in need, correct?
- We sell business-to-business, where there is no pulling wool over anyone's eyes, so how can PR help here?
- How could PR bring us any closer than we are already to our customers?

- How does PR iron out the ups and downs of daily operations?
- Could a little PR improve productivity and contain labour costs?
- Will 'persuasive communications' sell anything?
- Can PR help raise funds for the company?
- Should we be thinking of using PR to resolve disputes?
- Do tiny businesses need PR to survive?
- Can professional services benefit from PR?
- Can PR foster social harmony to really help a voluntary body?
- What has PR got to do with education?
- Public services rely on good PR, so how large a department do we need to be sure of success?
- Is PR a cottage industry?
- How big is the PR trade?
- Do the media rely on PR?
- Isn't *press* relations really the sum total of PR?
- Can anyone do PR?
- Surely PR is for the young and lovely, not us mature managerial types?
- If we go in for PR will I have to become a celebrity?
- Will doing PR force us all to become extra smart dressers?
- PR is a state of mind in our organization. Everyone does it, so why buy PR?
- How might PR help us to achieve management excellence?

So what is PR really? What does it amount to? As a collection of low-cost, readily acquired techniques it provides accessible self-promotion for anyone who cares to take the time and make the effort. But some purists may argue that PR is solely about communication that is undertaken for a corporate purpose, that is to say, representing the organization in some way or other. Then again, practitioners are likely to emphasize the role of PR as promoter and defender of reputation, above all else.

This first chapter brings together many of the questions that are commonly asked in search of an answer to this mystery. How, for example, is PR defined, what is meant by image, corporate identity and PR culture, and how might PR contribute to achieving management excellence? Is it really only for large organizations, as some consultants might argue. Can it be effective in resolving disputes and how many people are engaged in doing it anyway? What *is* PR?

What is the definition of PR?

There isn't one, but many. Probably one of the best is: 'the management of communication between an organization and its publics'. The PR fraternity some time ago adopted the term 'publics' to describe people who matter to the organization, because one side or the other is affected by the decisions of the other side. But then that could equally well describe the 'stakeholder', and so the two terms are often used interchangeably.

This definition is, however, simplicity itself. For slightly more explanation, I offer: 'communication by an organization with people who matter to it, in order to gain their attention in ways that are advantageous to it'. This recognizes the commercial realities of most PR, but there are numerous more fulsome versions. These include the Mexico Statement, agreed in 1978 at an international gathering of PR people, which reads: 'Public Relations is the art and social science of analyzing trends, predicting their consequences, counselling organizations' leadership and implementing planned programmes of action which will serve both the organization and the public interest'.

The (UK) Institute of Public Relations had a much-quoted definition: 'the planned and sustained effort to establish and maintain goodwill and mutual understanding between an organization and its publics'. This was just about short enough to be memorable and it had a couple of elevating concepts for good measure. But times move on, and the Institute wanted change, so it added a laborious piece annexing 'reputation' as PR's own and including 'influencing opinion and behaviour' as well as goodwill and mutual understanding.

The Public Relations Society of America puts it succinctly: 'Public relations helps an organization and its publics to adapt mutually to each other. Public relations is an organization's effort to win the cooperation of groups of people. Public relations helps organizations effectively interact and communicate with their key publics'. This talks, interestingly, about mutual adaptation, as well as the organization wanting cooperation.

There are very many more definitions, so much so that in 1976 no fewer than 472 were identified. What they all boil down to, however, is communication. That is what PR *is*, in essence. The mutual understanding and so forth is about effects, outcomes. Note that in many definitions it is assumed that the communicating is being done by an organization. Usually that is so, but it should be remembered that quite often it is an individual, or his or her representative, who is sending out the PR messages, not an organization at all. This is because PR is becoming universally accessible.

So publics are just stakeholders by another name?

Not entirely. There is an argument that suggests a difference, whereby publics can be identified, or segmented, out of larger, broader stakeholder groups. These publics supposedly identify themselves by taking the initiative in singling out the organization for their attention. They tend to perceive issues, develop an interest in them and look for the organizations that they believe to be 'creating' those issues.

This activism distinguishes a public from a 'mere' stakeholder, but then what of the passive publics, those that do not conveniently identify themselves first? There is a discernible pattern here. Generally, these latent publics bestir themselves only when they come to realize that the organization is doing something that involves them. Then either: quite a few people decide 'That's life' and do nothing about it, or their curiosity is stirred and they start to see resultant problems, real or imagined. Once that happens, again, among these people some will conclude that 'There's nothing to be done about it', because they consider that they are constrained from taking action, while others will search to identify any available 'leverage' by which they may take action to counter the problem.

As publics emerge in this way organizations have no choice but to recognize them and respond. The PR effort, therefore, is based on communicating with those publics that can assist in the achievement of PR aims and objectives, and those publics that have it within their power to obstruct or damage the fulfilment of the PR aims and objectives. This is skilled work, and many times the communications effort is insufficiently focused. A company chooses its markets, but not all its publics.

What is meant by 'That's good PR'?

'It works' is the simple answer. By that it is usually meant that the PR activity has communicated effectively, but then what does that mean? We sense the presence of good PR because it gives us a favourable impression, we think well of the people and we accept the message they are pushing our way. Sometimes we have our own agenda; we approve because it confirms our particular prejudices, needs and wants of the moment. Other times we like the calculation that we see. In other words, we 'see through the PR', or at least tell ourselves we do, and admire it for its planned effect on others, not us, of course, because we are far too smart to be taken in by it.

This is the real worldview of PR, but the academics have their own, sometimes unworldly, ideas about what is good PR. It is argued by some that in a perfect world, PR would be 'excellent' if there was genuine two-way dialogue between whoever sends out the PR messages and whoever receives them. This exchange would be so agreeable that both sides would be acting as if equals, capable of exerting more or less equal influence on the other to change. This might lead to negotiation and compromise.

The probability of this happening is not high. Most PR is undertaken with absolutely no intention of making any changes to the way 'we' think or behave, the aim strictly being to effect change on 'others'. Accordingly, this notion of equality of exchange remains largely an ideal. Most times PR is a one-way exercise or at best a two-way exchange between less than equals.

Some academics worry aloud about the practical consequences if the ideal was pursued. For instance, would organizations as we know them start disintegrating under the pressure? Would there be constant turbulence, as they formed and re-formed? At its heart, PR is about persuasion. If good PR is, essentially, about persuasion that results in a benefit gained for the communicator, how does this square with negotiation and compromise? What then for good, or excellent, PR?

In the rough-and-tumble of life we judge PR by its effects, but in this increasingly pluralistic world PR has had, more and more, to take into account issues of consent, transparency, accountability, decency and respect. PR that is designed solely for manipulation is increasingly ill equipped to cope with growing adversarial public debate. Therefore, what constitutes good PR is changing too, and this is reflected in what we often condemn as poor, or bad, PR, because it does not take fully into account the realities of modern times.

Why bother about the finer points if PR does the trick?

The big thing to understand about PR is that it offers no quick fix, even when it promises to. The finest PR may sometimes look dead easy, even just plain lucky, but more often than not, that is the result of much effort; effort expended in order to look effortless. PR too has its finer points. The techniques are easy to learn, at least in principle, and most people can turn their hand to them, so 'doing the trick' depends on understanding the detail and on interpretation.

Good PR has to be well conceived, thoroughly planned and properly organized. It does not just happen, nor is it the result of an aptitude or instinct, some natural talent or 'gift of the gab'. Being personable helps, of course, but then that is far from being exclusive to PR. From a management perspective, PR needs and deserves as much care and thought as any other function.

There is a saying: 'PR never sold a bad product'. It relies on having sound material to work with and is hopeless at providing a cover up for inefficiencies, inadequacies, shoddy products and services, idle management and so on. This does not deter plenty of organizations from trying to use PR to whitewash their operations here and there, whether routinely or now and again. After all, didn't someone once claim 'There's a sucker born every minute'? That was said, however, in nineteenth-century United States about entertainment, in a very different age. Now, as then, a small dose of deceit for entertainment purposes may be harmless fun for all, particularly if we can see how it is done, but that is a far cry from PR in modern management.

Not only is PR unable to do a good job with substandard materials. It tends to expose weaknesses. For instance, lousy service is lousy service, and no amount of PR messages about, say, sponsorship of worthy causes, will wash away customers' reality. Instead, they may well aggravate feelings of discontent. Questions may arise, such as 'Why don't they concentrate on getting things right?' and 'What if they spent their money on the service and leave this sponsorship until they can afford it?' Many of these customers will think plenty and say nothing. Some, however, may decide to make clear just what they think, and who better to tell than the PR people?

It has been said that PR provides the company with its 'eyes and ears', bringing news of the outside world, some of which may be unpalatable. In historic times, the bearers of bad news enjoyed short careers, and still there is sometimes a reluctance to hear the feedback. But intelligence 'from the front' can be precious indeed, and many are the times that PR provides insights that can be turned to competitive advantage. PR, far from trying to sell a bad product, can be the impetus to getting the product right first by attending to the finer points before developing the PR policy.

Is PR about manipulation of attitudes and opinions?

The 'official line' is that it is about influencing opinion and behaviour; that much has been formally acknowledged. All the talk is about bringing harmony where there may be discord and so on, but understanding, goodwill and sound reputation have to be worked at in an over-communicated world, which certainly involves the adjustment of attitudes and opinions to meet changing circumstances and corporate objectives.

To the extent that anyone puts forward a case for or against anything, it could be said that he or she seeks to manipulate others. The obvious example is the barrister who seeks to persuade a jury of the guilt or innocence of the defendant. PR has an advocacy role too. Its messages are, above all, persuasive, however they are delivered, because any operation depends upon favourable attitudes towards it being held by all who matter to it. But PR is looking for willing acceptance, which will positively influence attitudes and behaviours, so all communications have to be tempered by realism. This does not preclude selective use of information in order to press a case, but if PR is aiming for all-out manipulation it is likely to meet with disappointment.

There is an important rider to this. Manipulation becomes more feasible when people are subjected to carefully co-coordinated messages coming at them from all around, a kind of holistic onslaught. An individual organization presents its case to the best of its abilities, but its audiences have distractions and opportunities to compare competing claims. When all the powers in the land agree an agenda and pursue it through 'saturation message bombing' of the population over a sustained period, the effects of wholesale manipulation can be very obvious. Governments and collective business interests, for example, use PR to achieve acceptance of broad concepts and conditions. Such power can be used for benign or malevolent purposes. Either way, it is not in the mainstream of PR, which strives for 'share of shout' against a welter of messages competing for attention.

Why do people seem to respond more to PR these days?

PR is both invasive and pervasive. It's everywhere, or at least it seems like it. The so-called 'profession of the decade' has injected new words into the language, filled the newspapers, inspired numerous television and radio programmes, transformed politics and persuaded even the Queen in Britain that she needs it. The constant press references serve to bring it to mind. Carping criticism by journalists, who frequently refer to anything, or nothing, as being 'another PR exercise', 'PR spin' or 'just a PR job', and seemingly endless gossip by columnists about PR and PR people can give the impression that PR is at the very heart of popular culture. It isn't, of course. That probably belongs to soccer and to 'celebrity', itself a media creation.

So is it any wonder that most people are interested? The dramatic growth in commercial pluralism resulting from market liberalization has coincided with the massive expansion in the media. Both have fuelled the growth of PR, as an occupation and as a component of management, campaigning and entertainment. This all-round sound and vision advocacy provokes, titillates, amuses and generally works hard to engage and secure a response. And it has coincided with a sustained drop in the pulling power of advertising.

What is image?

In PR, the word 'image' has many meanings, which is probably why it must be surely one of the most overused words in the language. Most people conceive image to be the opposite of reality, but then perceptions of reality can differ, so that is not entirely reliable. PR uses image as a kind of shorthand for many concepts. These include reputation, attribute, attitude, perception, belief and credibility. Image is also used more broadly, when referring to a message, communication or relationship. All this serves only to confuse, so no wonder the word is bandied around in general parlance without much regard for its exact meaning.

It can be said therefore that image is a meaningless term, but that does not prevent much time and effort being expended on the manufacture and maintenance of images. Much time is spent on their careful cultivation, like delicate, precious plant specimens. Tender loving care is committed to their creation, adaptation, projection and defence. Like plants, sadly not all images survive. Some wilt, wither, or even suffer a hideous assault upon their purity and beauty. Images have been a subject of fascination for many years.

> In 1968, the English novelist J B Priestley coined the name 'Social Imagistics' for the theme of *The Image Men*, a brilliant parody of then contemporary new-found preoccupation with images. 'They're part of the unreality that's swindling us', declares one of the principal characters, who later adds 'So if it's images they wanted, we'd give 'em images – and do it properly'. Images then, as now, were both corporate and personal.

Image, for organizational purposes, can be described as the composite perception of a company, its products and services. It is the combined result of all the impressions gained, whether in seeing a name, observing behaviour, hearing or reading about an activity or through any other material evidence. It's the current image that matters most to any organization, but a close second is the wish image, how the company wants to be seen. This is similar to the self-image of the individual, which is divided into three components: the reality, the ideal and the expectation, or aspiration.

Since image is derived from the totality of impressions gained, its management includes making sure that there is message consistency. The devil is in the detail. Images are most satisfactory, for all concerned, when they are firmly anchored on reality. Often, for instance, signs of a little humanity can work better than any amount of polish.

Do image and identity add up to being PR?

Image and identity are central to PR. They complement each other and together play a major part in any PR programme. While publics perceive images, managers deal with identity, that is, all the ways in which an organization identifies itself in pursuit of a desired image.

There is sometimes confusion about identity. It is not restricted to visual elements, such as typography and logo. For instance, the premises that the company occupies tell people something about it, and can be sending out very powerful messages. The 'total picture' is what counts. The symbolism matters a lot, certainly, and this extends to such details as uniforms, house styles and so forth, but so too do how people behave, the quality of communications and the corporate culture itself. How the company sees itself strongly influences these factors, as well as how the corporate identity serves to strengthen image and loyalty, both without and within.

Who takes charge of identity?

If identity is viewed as being solely about having a logo or symbol and the choice of typography, it can be tempting to sling the job at a graphic designer and move on. Many a business has done this, placing this terribly 'personal' (in a corporate sense) and sensitive work in the hands of a total stranger, and leaving him or her to get on with it. Some go further. Probably because they have read criticisms of large companies spending £2 million apiece on identity 'makeovers', they decide to invite the head of the local art college to nominate an inexpensive student for the job. As a laudable act of artistic patronage, doubtless this is spot on. As sound management, it does not score.

Among companies that do not shrink from spending, not a few suppose that their advertising agency is the appropriate supplier. The sheer expenditure may suggest some kind of guarantee of a 'proper' result. This is, however, another hazardous route. The ad agency may be very skilled indeed at what it does best, but should it really be invited to 'take over' the interpretation of its client's persona on those grounds?

Correctly, this is a PR responsibility. The PR people have the broad overview, coupled with an in-depth appreciation of the corporate culture and an acute understanding of the environment, in which to make sure that what results is strictly consistent with reality. There are a number of ways to approach the creation of corporate identity. These include thinking about:

- corporate values, as reflected in the way 'things get done';
- the brands, to optimize the reputation strengths;
- service characteristics, so that the identity complements them;
- age and structure of the organization, to ensure consistency and credibility;
- sponsorships, to emphasize corporate social responsibility;
- design, for coherent appearance and ready recognition.

What is the difference between image and reputation?

Reputation, like image, is based on all the impressions gained by the publics, but there is a key difference. Reputation, unlike image, is formed from personal experience, whether direct or indirect. The contact can take any form, from purchasing products or services, to reading of or hearing first-hand accounts of experiences. So, for example, a company may have a reputation based on how its staff relate, handle its customers' enquiries or how senior managers conduct annual general meetings, on the say so of a friend or relative who works there or the account of a local community welfare project sponsorship manager.

Reputation, therefore, may differ from image, which is based on beliefs developed from a distance, without the benefit of contact. There is a linkage between familiarity and favourability, between image, which is based on awareness and perceptions, and approval. This in turn may provoke an enquiry or product trial, for instance. Many are the times that such contact prompts complete reappraisal, even surprise, because it exceeds the expectations based on the image, resulting in joy unconfined. It can work the other way, of course. In any event, any significant disparity between image and reputation has to be investigated.

Is PR a combination of image and reputation?

Fundamentally, PR is about image and reputation. It seeks to create and manage both image and reputation by a variety of means, and sees its central role as the promotion and defence of reputation. However, PR does not have an 'exclusive' on this. Image can exist without PR, for better or for worse. Similarly, there can be an image but no reputation.

Do people feel more confident for having a bit of PR around them?

Certainly. We live in very competitive times, and organizations, quite apart from individuals and groups, find that having a PR commitment strengthens their managerial stance. Everyone sees goodwill as a worthwhile asset. It widens the options, strengthens scope for making connections, builds brand values and provides a surer approach to handling problems of communication. Everyone appreciates the benefit of being understood, having a sound reputation and so on. There was a memorable advertising theme for the insurance industry that likened insurance protection to a medieval castle's encircling wall. These days that could be claimed equally well for PR.

Do private representations come under *public* relations, or am I losing the plot?

PR is about self-representation, whether of the organization or the individual. This may occur very publicly or very privately, and all shades in between, depending upon the size and type of public or publics to be addressed. The aim may be to reach millions of people or a single person. So PR includes, for example, lobbying of individual opinion leaders and opinion formers. The 'significant other' could be a private person or a private body. The messages may be conveyed in the form of private discussion and presentation.

Would just a bit of PR make all the difference to our profits this year?

'Just a bit of PR' is a contradiction in terms. Like bits of anything, there is seldom much to see for the effort, and in any case, PR takes time to deliver worthwhile results. The idea that a dash of effort will avert looming profits disappointment or somehow produce a last minute rush of success is total fallacy. Surprisingly many managers still don't see this, thinking that PR is some kind of easy option that can be dragged into play when all else fails.

When a consultant is invited to do a quick one-off assignment by a company that does not usually have PR, using a specified technique known to be relatively weak in normal circumstances let alone in isolation, he or she is likely to fear the worse. Why, for example, should any marketing manager suppose that a sudden rush to assemble and place an article in a trade paper, featuring three customers eulogizing over the company's products, is going to do anything very much to convince sceptical financial analysts and satisfy the finance director's needs? It is nonsense, and the shrewd PR consultant knows it. Many such 'opportunities' have been declined by consultants, only for the company's true motive to be revealed later in the financial pages.

Only when PR is up and running, on a continuous basis, is there ever likely to be any value in 'just a bit' of PR, and then it would be not in isolation but comprise a short period of carefully timed exceptional effort. This would not depend entirely upon its intrinsic value for securing the desired results, because it would benefit as well from all that had gone before. For example, company visits for analysts or journalists might be something of a novelty within the organization but viewed by its guests as being entirely consistent in the context of the overall PR effort, resulting in greater attendance.

With no formal marketing or sales, would PR be the best way to start?

For almost all organizations in this position, the answer has to be yes. The vast majority of businesses in the United Kingdom employ fewer than 20 people, and most of those employ less than 10. There is a widespread misunderstanding among many of them that PR is only for large organizations, but the reality is that many small companies have progressed dynamically thanks to an early adoption of PR. How else are they to become known, if they cannot afford the expensive and often less efficient advertising alternative?

This is a particularly acute problem for small service providers. Their managers buy the marketing books and courses, where they read all about product distribution, and it sounds reasonable. Here is a manufacturer, say of teddy bears, and there are the retailers, selling teddy bears to consumers, like, well, hot cakes. But life for people who provide services isn't quite so simple. Many directors have to spend plenty of time 'hoofing around' to prospective customers, to secure the orders. And when their services are manufactured, often they have to be delivered personally, not just loaded into some truck and sent on their way. In other words, these businesses are necessarily sales-driven, with a vengeance.

Nor are such realities confined to those who work from desks or drawing boards. What about shops, for instance? Successful retailers know the importance of setting out each morning to achieve a target sales volume that day, and to do that they have to pull in the customers. Small traders cannot afford the volumes of advertising and other marketing used by their larger rivals. They have to think more creatively about how to optimize their chances of competing effectively as if, it can feel sometimes, with one arm tied behind their backs.

Accordingly, many organizations that have no formal sales or marketing opt for PR first, as a means of achieving growth more economically and faster. They may do it themselves, or they may hire consultancy help to get them going and only later employ someone specifically in-house. This is the usual route. Many have found that it has worked for them. A popular example is The Body Shop, which in its early years relied heavily on PR. Another brand to have greatly benefited from PR is Virgin. There are very many more such examples.

Should we concentrate on PR and keep sales and marketing for when we are bigger?

Concentration on PR to the exclusion of other marketing communications, however informal, would be unwise. Instead, making the most of opportunities created by PR's low-cost, easy-to-learn techniques while pursuing direct sales and marketing activities could well be the best way forward. In other words, the marketing is PR-led but does not exclude, say, directory advertising, and due weight should be given to the sales effort. True, sometimes the PR takes off so quickly that it can be difficult to maintain an appropriate balance, but that is not the same as placing all the eggs in the one PR basket.

Can PR be self-taught?

Yes, but patience and application is needed for sustained success. There are many 'How To' books and courses. As mentioned earlier, the techniques are easy to learn, at least in principle, and most people can turn their hand to them. Like most activities, performance and results improve with the benefit of experience. PR practice is very wide-ranging and concentration on certain areas is likely to secure satisfying results earlier than might be so otherwise.

For example, writing is the core skill, but the exact application may represent a specialization. So a self-taught person might determine to do press relations work directed solely at his or her trade or technical press initially, and see what may be achieved there, perhaps after a year or 18 months, before venturing elsewhere. Another might opt instead for producing private media, such as a quarterly company magazine or monthly newsletter. Another might prefer to concentrate initially on producing a corporate brochure and expanding the annual report and accounts.

Similarly, the self-taught person may have a specific need in mind from the outset, such as to improve their communication, presentation standards, broadcast commentary or public speaking skills. For this they seek a general understanding of PR and then concentrate on what matters most to them, and the organization, at that time.

PR starts with shifting information to those in need, correct?

PR has several strands to it, including public information, the task of telling people what they need to know. This is usually associated with government.

> In 2000, the UK government issued to every household an eight-page booklet giving advice about fire prevention and fire escape in the home. This was an admirable effort; the lack of smoke detectors, or the presence of non-functioning smoke detectors, in many homes is testament to the need for guidance.

This role as public information provider probably accounts for over 50 per cent of all PR activity, and the need to know is usually obvious, particularly in relation to the basic services of the state.

> Much PR output is of a general information nature, 'nice to know rather than need to know' but nonetheless valuable if well directed to publics that may benefit. For example, many companies produce attractive and informative booklets and posters providing general knowledge facts and figures, in direct line of descent from the warmly remembered 1950s *Shell Guides to the* [English] *Countryside.*

The key word here is 'need'. Publics are identified because they are thought to have a need to know. A public may identify itself because it has a need to know; it has a specific interest and searches for relevant companies to approach, or it believes that the company affects it in some way. However, the need may rest not with the public but with the company. Further, not all messages are as real, true or important as may be claimed for them; self-interest may be represented as being educational when in fact it is advocacy.

We sell business-to-business, where there is no pulling wool over anyone's eyes, so how can PR help here?

Many business customers look for signs of good PR being undertaken by their suppliers, just as they search for evidence of other modern management methods and techniques. Depending upon circumstances, it can be mandatory in the collective opinion of the customer company's Decision Making Unit members, a necessary confirmation that the supplier operates on the same corporate plane and is a worthy partner. So PR can certainly help there, quite apart from the actual benefits to be derived from the communication effort itself. As to 'pulling wool over eyes', it is a solid fact of life that selling to another business is tough, and the PR has to not only take full account of this but also seek to exploit it, or 'go with the grain'.

How could PR bring us any closer than we are already to our customers?

This assumes that you have reached some kind of optimum closeness that cannot be bettered. However, even with the purchaser–supplier partnership agreements, which provide extra glue for bonding interdependences in supply chains, there is usually scope for more communication, because it is the lifeblood of any worthwhile relationship. Nor should professional suppliers necessarily suppose that they know all they need to know about their clients, even in long-standing relationships forged over many years.

It has to be remembered that most people are also consumers, who continue to re-evaluate, compare, forget, misunderstand or lose interest. All the evidence suggests that they are increasingly likely to complain, protest and seek to 'hit back' against perceived inadequacies or worse. The 'silence is golden' rule seldom applies here. Time and again this closeness to the customer is not as close as might be supposed.

How does PR iron out the ups and downs of daily operations?

Through bringing greater stability to key relationships, PR contributes significantly in the constant search by managers for greater control. In this wider management context, PR helps on a number of fronts, including:

- understanding of human behaviour;
- anticipation of future trends and their consequences;
- harmonization of conflicting private and public interests;
- generation of greater goodwill internally and externally;
- avoidance of misunderstandings and disputes;
- promotion of positive corporate culture.

Could a little PR improve productivity and contain labour costs?

A little PR doesn't work any better with labour relations than with annual results. It has to be part of the ongoing communications effort, using created media, whether electronic and/or print, joint consultation techniques, information dissemination, community relations and the local public media.

PR can do much to help create a culture in which people work more willingly and productively, because they 'buy in' to the corporate vision and, particularly, sense of mission. In this, PR works closely with HRM (Human Resource Management), against specific objectives in relation to, for example, reduction of waste or absenteeism or improvement in safety or training. The primary role is to provide efficient two-way communication between management and employees at all levels. Where there are substantial numbers of employees, this also embraces their families that are resident locally, talking with them both directly and indirectly, through local associations, social groups and the media. None of this can be done effectively on an ad hoc basis now and again.

Will 'persuasive communications' sell anything?

No. For instance, some purchases are obligatory. The obvious example is provided by the utilities such as gas and water, but there are others. This does not mean that companies in this fortunate position do not need PR. Far from it, they probably need PR more than ever, to help counter complacency and maybe arrogance.

And no matter how persuasive they may be, some communications do not sell because people exercise resistances that cannot be surmounted. This does not only apply to, say, moral objections to a particular product or service. It can occur where, for example, people simply don't want to be 'bothered' or resist compliance.

Take the famous case of the great car safety belt saga. The UK government spent many millions of pounds over years in advocating the good sense of motorists to use their safety belts. It used a popular household name celebrity and a catchy slogan: 'Clunk click, every trip'. Still an estimated one in three motorists resolutely refused, so eventually an Act had to be passed, making it mandatory (something that governments, unlike companies, can do in last resort).

> Supposing that the one-third would continue to resist, a new business was launched that would involve people who would not wear belts becoming paying passengers in the cars of drivers who now had to wear them. The idea was that this would operate mainly for travelling to and from work in major conurbations. It relied on the fact that the legislation related to front, not rear, seat belts. It collapsed within days, for as soon as wearing a belt became law all the objectors took to wearing the belts, as if they had never objected.

Here what might seem like a highly persuasive message based on obviously beneficial common sense involved a particularly prestigious source, a government, no less. It might be assumed that such status would result in greater acceptance. Was the status of the source in this instance helpful or a hindrance? It seems likely that sometimes the source of the message is less important than its cogency. Could this be because people suspect they are being 'talked down to'? Just how likely that is remains questionable; the status of the sender of the message still exerts great influence, regardless of the message content. Credibility of both message and sender is the key factor.

Can PR help raise funds for the company?

Companies that seek a public quotation in their shares routinely use PR as part of their approach to the offer. Some have never used PR before, or not in the context of shareholder relations. Others have an established commitment to PR and see flotation as a natural extension of the range of PR activities and responsibilities. Once a company is 'public' it will have a formal commitment to fostering and maintaining sound relations with investors.

PR can help raise funds for the private company, but this is more likely to be indirect, that is to say, the company already has a good image and sound reputation among potential investors. This might apply, for example, where a regional motor car dealer is looking to acquire private investors from among its local customers. Similarly, a company may be looking for venture capital. All types of organization, of course, can use PR to raise funds. Perhaps the most obvious example is the charity that looks for donations and competes for grants.

Should we be thinking of using PR to resolve disputes?

Yes, in the ongoing search for harmony in industrial relations. Also, once a specific dispute has arisen, or there has been a succession of disputes, PR skills can be very helpful in unravelling misunderstandings and generally taking the emotional heat out of the situation. The 'excellence' concept of PR envisages negotiation and reconciliation of differences, and certainly PR people may be able to contribute to dispute resolution, depending upon the circumstances, when it has become an immediate problem. However, PR here is more like a sprinkler system than a fire engine, more a quiet drip, drip that spreads than a frantic dowsing of flames.

Do tiny businesses need PR to survive?

Depends what is meant by 'tiny' and what is the type of business. Every business has to make itself known, by whatever means it can, since without customers there is no business. Tiny may mean that there are two or at most three people employed. There are plenty of viable concerns, often start-ups, of this size. These small operations definitely find advantage in doing PR, which, as a set of low-cost techniques, is within the reach of an individual, and therefore should be feasible even when there are very few resources, of time and funds.

As to survival, that raises questions about the type of products and services and the structure of the customer base. Many such enterprises are heavily dependent upon a handful of customers. This can happen in both consumer and business-to-business markets. For example:

- a food manufacturer may depend upon a few buyers representing major food retailers or department stores;

- a professional services company may have half a dozen retained clients such as large companies or local authorities;
- a specialist subcontractor may work mainly for just two or three of its industry's leading names.

Some such dependencies can be very fruitful and viable, others perilous and probably unsustainable beyond current contracts.

So survival may be possible without PR, and many such micro concerns do obtain what they consider to be a satisfactory level of return without spending anything very much on PR, or marketing, year in and year out. Some may be deterred because they find that if they do try to demonstrate a proactive approach to growing their businesses their customers start demonstrating disapproval, suspecting that 'the little man who can' that they have been employing is about to charge more and/or alter the terms of supply. It is a matter of judgement for the supplier as to what extent such pressures exist or have to be tolerated, given the exact circumstances.

Nevertheless, the scale of risk resulting from heavy dependence on a few customers or clients must surely be the most compelling reason why even the smallest enterprise, particularly the start-up, should take up PR, aiming for a broad spread of customers. Additionally, it also has to give thought to how it gets on with its sources of finance, suppliers and other key publics.

Can professional services benefit from PR?

Yes, very much so. PR is a key component of 'practice development'. PR is particularly well suited to providing the relevant evidence and reassurance sought by clients in relation to their expectations. The professions' governing bodies have gradually removed many, if not most, of the traditional self-constraints relating to the promotion of professional services. In addition, there has been a steady erosion of monopoly practices. As a result there has developed a demand for PR that enables practices to grow in ways that are compatible with maintaining the good order and dignity of the professions.

The rate of adoption of PR by the professions has depended also upon the wide variety of occupations that claim professional status. Some are commercially based, and therefore 'early adopters', while others are less so and tend to be 'latecomers'. In the first category are, for example, chartered surveyors and solicitors, and in the second, dentists and veterinary surgeons. Then there are the newer occupations that claim professional status. These tend to be technology-based and quick to understand the value of PR. The old objection to PR, that 'We are not selling tins of baked beans', lacks validity now, if it ever had any in the first place.

Can PR foster social harmony to really help a voluntary body?

Volunteers are usually very sensitive to 'bad vibes' and can be fickle in their loyalties. If any organization depends upon their active involvement it most certainly needs to foster social harmony through PR that engages the volunteers and emphasizes their involvement. This is all the more valuable when volunteers are widely dispersed.

Political parties offer an interesting example of this. When a party's electoral fortunes are high, or there is a sound prospect of them improving substantially within the next few years, people readily volunteer to do all the potentially very boring jobs that need to be done. However, politics being cyclical, a party may find that its fortunes are low and its prospects bleak. At such times the volunteers flee, even some of the most loyal. It is as if they need a constant 'feel good' top up of their loyalty and commitment in order to stay on board.

Furthermore, a momentum gathers, one way or the other. Success breeds success, that is, volunteers are drawn to wanting to be associated with victory at the elections, and, conversely, they are anxious to avoid being associated with defeat. These rather extreme movements are present in other voluntary organizations, although usually they are far less pronounced. Nevertheless, they are important. Why, for instance, should anyone want to volunteer time to help run a charity shop if there is little sense of direction or purpose and the paid managers are seldom seen or heard from?

What has PR got to do with education?

Much educational material is supplied to schools and colleges, in the United Kingdom and elsewhere, and, more generally, PR has a substantial part to play in recruitment of school and college leavers. The 'milk run' annual push to attract appropriate applicants is not an isolated activity. School children and college students develop impressions of potential employers from relatively early ages and in the approach to making 'life decisions' their interest intensifies.

Most colleges and secondary schools now undertake some PR. The emphasis is on information, with copious production of materials, reports and prospectuses. This is to be expected, given the educational culture, but PR effort is also directed in three more key areas:

- lobbying of decision-makers in government and local government;

- issues management, which is probably of greatest importance internally; and
- community relations, where the emphasis is likely to be on support for parent-orientated events and interests.

These are not optional bolt-ons, for competition at all levels has intensified sharply and is likely to increase in the future, with the government-led drive to university graduate half of all UK school leavers and the introduction of specialist status among state secondary schools, of which there are approaching 1,000 already designated. The continuing controversy over public examination standards reflects the growing ferocity of competition, both within and between the public and private sectors, at university, college and secondary levels.

None of this comes as news to the long-established private schools, where the early adopters of PR gained massive advantage over their more conservative rivals in developing image and reputation. Nevertheless, the PR responsibility was usually run in with teaching and pastoral duties, perceived as being a relatively less time-demanding activity. Now many such schools have long since employed PR consultancy, but in state-funded education such 'outsiders' can still have difficulty in advising unless they intimately understand the institution's 'delivery capacity'.

Further education colleges led the way in appointing internal specialists, but more generally, appointments have been made as and when needed, perhaps without much conviction, probably in response to perceived difficulties or inadequacies in dealing with the media.

On an international scale, PR contributes to, for example, the marketing of postgraduate degree courses, such as the new Surrey University MBA, which has secured substantial media coverage for its inclusion of a laptop computer in its course materials. The UK has a well-established international reputation for education at all levels and PR is particularly in evidence where there is saturation or approaching saturation of domestic demand or a high proportion of pupils are the children of foreign nationals.

Public services rely on good PR, so how large a department do we need to be sure of success?

The Audit Commission, a UK government agency that evaluates the performance of the public sector services, published a report during 2002 into PR in local government. The main conclusion was an assertion that the optimum size of a PR department was five people and that any more than that was wasting taxpayers' money.

This is certainly likely to have a ring of truth to it for PR people working in the private and not-for-profit sectors, where three to five people staff many PR functions. Some public sector bodies have developed large in-house departments, so presumably they were the ones that the auditors had in mind. A favourite figure seems to be 12, although there does not seem to be much evidence of why this is so. It is certainly a neat figure that perhaps may appeal to the empire builder's spirit of adventure. There are some doubts about this scale of commitment among some of the authorities, however, since one or two have staffed up, only to staff down again.

There is no denying that the public services need good PR and they should be under constant pressure to explain their tax-financed expenditures, so wanting to be sure of success is understandable, but what exactly is meant by this? Since it is difficult to be sure, a gradual approach to developing the PR is probably the most advisable way forward.

Maybe this could be undertaken along the lines of a long-familiar pattern seen among many medium-size and larger organizations coming fresh to PR. They tend to hire outside consultancy first, to obtain practical insights, identify and focus on needs and take advice about how to build an in-house capability. Later, a department replaces the consultants, usually initially no more than two people strong. Gradually it grows, and at some stage, typically when there are four or five people doing the PR, outside consultants are hired again, selectively, to provide specialist expertise.

Is PR a cottage industry?

If cottage industry means small, the answer has to be no. The PR trade in the United Kingdom is recognized by the government to be one of the most highly developed in Europe. That seems a modest assessment. For many years it has been widely thought of as being second only to that of the United States in scale and complexity. Like many other occupational categories, it has a small number of large consultancies, a few medium-sized ones and very many small and micro ones. Accordingly, there are some of the world's largest firms based in the United Kingdom. There are also very many talented self-employed freelancers.

Similarly, the larger the firm the more likely that it has a broader spread of industry- and sector-specific experience and a wider range of specialisms. Very many well-established national and regional suppliers serve particular industries or sectors and/or offer specialized services, such as lobbying. Furthermore, it is estimated that about one-quarter as many people again are employed in-house, particularly in large companies, the public sector, government and the not-for-profit sector. These people tend to have specialized knowledge of their employers' particular sectors.

How big is the PR trade?

Current estimates suggest that in the United Kingdom, over 50,000 people are employed in PR. There are some 1,400 PR consultancies and self-employed freelancers, supported by probably as many suppliers, and during the 1990s the trade experienced very rapid growth in revenue. However, it is vulnerable, probably more than most other occupations, to changing economic conditions and to the influence of world events that affect business sentiment. There is uncertainty about the numbers of people employed, owing to the use of various job titles and apparent confusion among some employers.

> South Somerset District Council (an English form of local government) advertises for a Public Relations Officer, whose primary skills are as a computer operator, with a dash of journalism, some design capability and preferably but not essentially some familiarity with local government. PR as such is not mentioned, just 'a fresh approach to the media and our corporate publications'. At the very same time, next door neighbouring Dorset County Council (another, larger, form of local government, one tier higher) wants a professionally qualified Marketing Officer, who 'will be expected to have experience of a range of marketing techniques and to be able to provide public relations coaching for Unit staff'. Although the title is marketing, the reality is a combination of marketing and PR.

In addition, there are many more people, including chairpersons and chief executives, who 'do' PR as part of their non-PR specific jobs, and a veritable army of voluntary PR people who work for a broad mass of groups, associations, clubs and so on. Where two or more are gathered together in order to share an interest, apparently one of the very first consequences is more PR. All manner of institutions have heeded the call to PR.

Do the media rely on PR?

They would hate to admit it, and might deny it, but the answer has to be: largely yes. The media have grown dramatically since the 1960s;

just think of all those television and radio stations, for example. The growth has been brought about by the massive leaps in technology that have facilitated rapid improvements in news gathering, sourcing of material and dissemination. The result is that vastly increased output is being achieved with far fewer people needed to achieve it. In consequence, journalism is a trade in decline, even, ironically, as there is more space and airtime to fill than ever before.

This has worked exceedingly well for PR, which provides, directly or indirectly, the greater part of the source material. Much of what appears in newspapers and magazines, in the United Kingdom and often elsewhere, is PR-sourced, as is a substantial, and growing, proportion of what is broadcast. PR is also now beginning to impact on the Internet. Media owners need fewer journalists, because PR is subsidizing the traditional tasks of journalism. In consequence the overall character of media output has changed. The 'news values' are increasingly less likely to be determined by journalists and more so by PR. For the PR person who can recall the difficulties of 25 years ago in, say, 'placing' an article in a magazine or the virtual impossibility of securing a television programme, the modern dependence of the media represents a remarkable, not to say unbelievable, turn around.

Isn't *press* relations really the sum total of PR?

It may seem like it, but no. PR used to be very heavily concerned with addressing the print media, but as it has grown it has diversified. The media are now more varied, and PR has developed heavily in other areas too, such as sponsorship and its own 'created' media. Many of the core skills required for press relations have been adapted for application in other areas of activity. It is likely that PR people on average still spend about 40 per cent of their time on media relations, as a whole, and probably three-quarters of that involves the print media. Typically one-third of budgets are allocated to media relations. However, there are some PR people who seldom if ever have any dealings with the media, and others who do little else but media relations.

Can anyone do PR?

Yes. Anyone can set up in business as a PR consultant. Anyone can act as the PRO for his or her pressure group, local social club, informal 'grumble gathering' or any other such crew. Anyone can do PR in hope of becoming famous. Anyone can use PR to seek redress for a perceived wrong. How *well* anyone can do it is another matter.

Among the professionals inevitably standards vary, largely based on depth of training and experience. Among the amateurs much may depend upon the exact circumstances and how readily the simpler techniques may be applied.

Surely PR is for the young and lovely, not us mature managerial types?

Despite many if not most of the people who earn their living solely from PR being in their 20s and 30s, much PR is undertaken by older people, notably chairpersons and chief executives, and includes very many senior managers who act as spokespersons for their organizations. 'Mature types' can be better suited to the work than some young full-time practitioners. Any 'ageism' should be discounted; it is to become illegal in the EU by 2006 anyway.

If we go in for PR will I have to become a celebrity?

No, unless you would like to be a celebrity. True, some greater personal recognition may arise if, say, you are involved with presentations or speeches, maybe as part of local community contact, but you are unlikely to have to dodge autograph hunters in the street. There seems to be a widespread belief that 'celebrity' somehow automatically occurs. Most people in PR toil away quietly, have low profiles and seek to avoid becoming 'part of the message'.

> Should they find themselves the subject of the message, PR people recognize a problem and often depart quietly, as occurred with Charlie Whelan, the Chancellor of the Exchequer's (UK Finance Minister's) PR spokesman, now an outspoken critic of his former employer's communications.

Of course, there is nothing intrinsically wrong with being something of a celebrity, if the job calls for it. Leadership skills necessarily include a degree of corporate representation that involves stepping forward to meet and greet, what might be called 'Doing a Richard Branson' (a leading UK businessman noted for his publicity-seeking stunts) in its more extreme forms. This should not be confused with the celebrity hype of nonentities that fills the popular press.

Will doing PR force us all to become extra smart dressers?

People who think themselves to be a bit scruffy might decide wisely to smarten up for the big occasions, but surely they do that already for the sales pitches. Those that customarily dress well should stick to what they know and not start worrying that they may look too smart. It is true that PR people tend to dress well, but that does not imply formality necessarily, and they are pretty good at knowing what level of formality works best in different circumstances.

The popular advice is to 'be yourself' because then you don't think about your appearance and concentrate on matters in hand, but this can be a mite bit dodgy because it all depends upon how 'being yourself' is interpreted. It is reckoned that words account for only 7 per cent of the speaker's effect on an audience. A massive 55 per cent of the speaker's impact comes from visual appearance, while 38 per cent of his or her impact comes from voice. Appearances do count heavily, more than probably they should, and most people prefer to keep it simple because of that, so that the risk of visual distraction is minimized. When it comes to matters of dress, the requirements of PR are no different from any other 'front office' activity.

PR is a state of mind in our organization. Everyone does it, so why buy PR?

If the PR culture has taken root to that extent, you are presumably already committing a lot of time and effort within the business to PR. When everyone really understands its value and becomes 'ambassadorial' for the company you are collecting extra dividends on a scale that may make buying in any PR seem unnecessary. However, many companies with substantial PR commitments do indeed look outside for particular expertise, such as government lobbying. Maybe it is their very commitment that leads them to keep refining and expanding the function. Smaller organizations can generate remarkable results across a wide range of measures by imbuing everyone with an appreciation of the value of PR to them, as individuals and collectively.

How might PR help us to achieve management excellence?

As an organization seeks to manage its relationship with its environment, through identifying pressures, responding to them and making necessary adaptations, PR contributes as the corporate eyes and ears for managing environmental interactions. In addition to report-back and commentary, the PR function seeks to confirm and clarify the stakeholders, identify the publics among those stakeholders, anticipate the issues as they are developing, or may develop, and prepare solutions to meet them.

This environmental scanning and analysis is central to the task of assessing various corporate strategy options against probable and possible political, economic, social, legal and technical outcomes. PR provides the key linkages between central and subordinate strategic development, through its 'boundary spanning' between the organization and its outside world, between units internally and between those units and externally. The PR strategy, in turn, is driven by the need to focus on the issues that may help or hinder the organization in its performance.

PR has been described as being the essential 'glue' that holds the organization together and links the strategies at the corporate, business and operational levels. Perhaps a better metaphor is 'lubricant'. Either way, this is a powerful, if often 'hidden', strategic role that contributes to organizational excellence. In addition, the internal role of PR and its contribution to marketing help significantly towards the achievement of excellence.

two

myths and **mysteries**

- Isn't PR just common sense?
- Why should we need PR when we have no direct dealings with the public?
- Isn't PR all about knowing the right people?
- Isn't PR just a glossy add-on cost that makes no difference to the bottom line?
- PR 'never sold a bad product', or did it?
- How does PR differ from what senior managers do anyway?
- Isn't the job of PR like that of the harlot: power without responsibility?
- Isn't word-of-mouth always the best PR?
- Surely it is PR's job to confer credibility?
- Why do we need PR when our competitors do not?
- Isn't PR just for the 'big boys and girls'?
- Isn't PR really a safety valve, to be blamed when anything goes wrong?
- Why should I believe anything I read or hear that is the result of PR?
- How can I expect anyone to believe us if they know we are into doing PR?
- If we start doing PR now, after all these years, won't that look obvious, and risk making us look foolish?
- A lot of PR is just about wining and dining, isn't it?
- What is meant by 'just a PR exercise'?
- Aren't professional people above using PR?
- Doesn't PR complicate telling how it is, plain and simple?

- Who are the hidden persuaders and why do they hide?
- Isn't PR a weapon of mass distraction by another name?
- Does PR-created fame wither with age?
- Isn't PR really free advertising?
- Surely the less we tell the less we risk information abuse?
- Why should we ever want journalists prying into our affairs?
- Why do journalists keep disparaging PR?
- Aren't PR people and journalists in a cosy huddle, making 'mugs' of us all?
- Why do so many journalists go into PR?
- If PR is all so valuable and so important, why does it have such a poor reputation itself?
- We are results-driven and time-short, so can we do PR as well?
- Our patients are glad to have our services, so why waste money on PR?
- Does PR use different names for concealment?
- How does PR differ from propaganda?
- Is propaganda easier than PR?
- Why bother with PR if propaganda will do just as well?
- Why would anyone on TV or radio ever be interested in us?
- Isn't PR just muckraking?
- PR is sales promotion by another name, isn't it?
- PR is publicity, isn't it?
- Surely there's no such thing as bad publicity?

Now is an appropriate moment to address the popular assumptions, misapprehensions and claims made about, and sometimes on behalf of, PR; in other words, what it is not. This chapter's questions arise out of various influences, including:

- widely-held hostility and cynicism fostered by the media;
- managers' reservations based on their observations and impressions in business;
- prejudices of professionals towards promotion of their services;
- public sector managers' distrust and resistance to market concepts and practices;
- confusion over the exact nature and purpose of PR, compared with other management functions.

Isn't PR just common sense?

Much of the purpose of PR can be seen as common sense, but PR adds up to a lot more than 'just' common sense, if by that is meant that anyone can do it by simply trusting his or her instincts and outlook. Old hands may tell you that it all boils down to common sense, because they expend much skill in making it look easy and uncontrived and wouldn't want you thinking otherwise. In reality, much care and attention to detail may lie behind making some message look like simplicity itself. But then this could be said equally well of many other occupational activities. It seldom is, because we live in an age when making much of the simplest task seems to be very popular.

Why should we need PR when we have no direct dealings with the public?

You may not have any direct dealings with 'the public', but what about your publics? Every organization has them. Care is needed to not slip into the popular misconception of thinking in terms of 'the general public', which is meaningless in PR terms. It is useful to recall, in this context, that 'public opinion' is the preoccupation of politicians, who hunt for signs of what the mass of people appear to want at any given time. Organizational PR wants much more precision than that. As to whether dealings are direct or indirect is immaterial; PR is about optimizing the environmental conditions in which the organization functions.

Isn't PR all about knowing the right people?

Depends what is meant by 'all'. Since identifying accurately the various publics and issues and then addressing them necessarily involves also identifying individuals, such as influential opinion leaders, or formers, 'knowing the right people' can be useful. However, PR is not some quick fix networking routine, even if sometimes its messages are indeed delivered in private. It has broader and deeper objectives than is suggested by this, and there are practical considerations to be borne in mind too. This is not the deferential world of yesteryear, and opinion leaders come and go rapidly. Everyone is entitled to an opinion, and much of the time most people seem to have one on just about everything. Grumble and intolerance are rife; acceptance without questioning is in decline. Awareness and understanding are on the up; indifference and disinterest are on the down.

Isn't PR just a glossy add-on cost that makes no difference to the bottom line?

Measurement and evaluation methods have evolved in recent years that can demonstrate when PR is or is not pulling its weight, so the idea that it adds nothing can be proven nonsense. No, PR is not a superficial addition and there is an abundance of evidence provided by many organizations that have succeeded very well while depending substantially or even mainly on PR, rather than, say, advertising. The contribution to the bottom line may depend upon individual circumstances. Some companies, for example, are probably better placed than others to benefit, owing to some characteristic of the business, its products or services, its markets and/or its people.

Take two examples of how this may be:

> Any long-established manufacturing business that produces industrial products for a relatively small number of customers may rely largely on PR for its communication needs, whereas any department store that has several million people living within a 50-mile radius may also use extensive advertising, for example, particularly in the critical pre-Christmas period. The one is working in business-to-business markets, while the second has a large number of consumer customers, drawn from within a geographical region.

Two more illustrations may be useful:

> A small computer consultancy with a range of corporate customers and a handful of consumer clients may rely entirely on PR, while a leisure centre that attracts thousands of visitors on summer weekends may place its emphasis on marketing. The first offers knowledge-based specialist services that require a high level of interaction and communication with customers, whereas the second offers entertainment with mass appeal to certain consumer publics, maybe coming great distances or from abroad.

PR 'never sold a bad product', or did it?

'Never' is impossible to confirm, but PR is no substitute for a substandard product or service, nor even for one that is just poor or inadequate, or plain unconvincing. Equally, PR cannot stand in for a product or service that simply does not exist. This may sound odd, but it happens all too often that, for some reason or other, the PR effort runs ahead of the reality. A common occurrence is the missing new product at the exhibition stand. Everyone, probably above all the competitors, awaits the unveiling, in vain. The PR effort may have been excellent, but the damage is likely to be long-lasting, because credibility has suffered a severe blow.

How does PR differ from what senior managers do anyway?

Senior managers have their specific responsibilities to discharge. Some have an element of PR in their job specifications, usually in the context of the leadership role. However, styles of management are also relevant here. Everyone at work is kept busy trying to understand what 'the boss' *really* meant. It's a popular preoccupation, which calls for strong management communication skills. Some managers are very adept at communication and set the tone for higher standards for everyone else. In this sense they may be perceived as doing PR although they may not recognize it as such.

Isn't the job of PR like that of the harlot: power without responsibility?

Doing PR is not a recreation. It carries responsibilities. As to how the job compares with that of the harlot could be the subject of some structured research, without which we have to rely on very limited available hearsay. The question asserts immorality in PR, as if this is unknown in other commercial activities or occupations, which seems a mite bit exaggerated. PR is not, by any reasonable measure, harlotry. For one, it is not routinely paid for in advance.

Isn't word-of-mouth always the best PR?

Word-of-mouth can be very valuable, but it benefits, or suffers, from the credibility of whoever is speaking, in the perception of the listener, so it cannot be 'always the best PR'. Furthermore, the message may bear little relationship to how it started out or what was intended. It cannot be assumed that 'word-of-mouth' equates necessarily with accuracy or favourability.

Surely it is PR's job to confer credibility?

PR, whether communicated direct or through a third party, confers credibility only where credibility is earned. If the source or the method used lack credibility the PR cannot confer it. Credibility is not like some all-weather paint in an agreeable durable colour, that PR can spread evenly and easily over all disagreeable cracks and crevices for everlasting permanence and concealment.

Why do we need PR when our competitors do not?

PR is not a 'me too' activity that has to be undertaken because 'they' are doing it. Similarly, because 'they' don't do it should not, of itself, determine that PR is unnecessary. And, in any case:

- How certain *are* you that the competition does not use PR?
- Have you checked this out with some journalists or trade contacts, for instance?
- Are there no telltale signs, like trade gossip about people or events?
- Are they never seen at the trade shows?

It may be that the competitors are really quite busy on the PR front, but are not making a fuss about it, perhaps even preferring to give you the impression that they are inactive. Better maybe, therefore, to decide about PR needs closer to home.

Isn't PR just for the 'big boys and girls'?

No, every organization has communication needs, wants to be understood, benefits from goodwill, aims for a good reputation and seeks a positive image. Every organization wants to create the best possible circumstances in which to flourish. There seems to be a lingering suspicion that PR is something the smaller operation should aspire to, rather than engage with, which is entirely at odds with contemporary culture. On the contrary, when viewed as a set of low-cost, easily accessible techniques, PR is particularly well suited to the needs of the smaller concern.

Isn't PR really a safety valve, to be blamed when anything goes wrong?

Maybe this idea comes of PR people being too professionally nice and therefore vulnerable to being 'dumped on' when the going gets tough. PR can be cheery at times, when it brings evidence of success, particularly when there hasn't been that much lately, but it lays no claims to being a collective therapy for corporate angst.

Why should I believe anything I read or hear that is the result of PR?

PR-sourced messages are not deceitful as such, if only for purely practical reasons. Further, choosing to believe anything is still optional, even in these ironic, doubting times. From personal observation and experience, we can probably agree that we live in a world where many voices are raised in self-interest, aiming to assert various differences and objections or rejections. It truly is a more adversarial society, the cost of which, measured in terms of compensation claims, has now topped £10 billion a year in the United Kingdom alone.

Given that, we may expect to encounter the skills of the advocate, who selects his or her words carefully. As to what is written rather than spoken, that, presumably, has first passed through the editorial filter, which is intended to wash out any supposed impurities and cleanse messages of their hyperbole and verbiage. Since this may be relied upon as providing some sort of guarantee of probity, a proportion of the scepticism might well be usefully directed at the filter as well as at the source.

There is, of course, the type of 'branded editorial' that sets out to make clear its marketing purpose. Many people rather enjoy this kind of PR-led material, which informs them about a vast range of products and services. Again, believing is optional. Some of these messages go through an editorial filter first. Some do not. Quite apart from helping to determine such major life decisions as knowing where next to go on holiday or buy a car, there are also many more serious matters to be found in PR-generated messages, among which there are likely to be at least some that repay the time taken to listen to or read them.

How can I expect anyone to believe us if they know we are into doing PR?

This implies that all PR is lies, treacherous and shameful, an activity that is to be undertaken in dark corners by stealth of night. It isn't. Indeed, people who know you are doing PR may rather approve. For instance:

- Many corporate customers expect to see their smaller suppliers demonstrating modern approaches to how they run their operations.

- Many members and donors of charitable bodies want to see positive efforts made to promote the cause.
- Many taxpayers require seeing public service organizations demonstrating a commitment to communication.

If we start doing PR now, after all these years, won't that look obvious, and risk making us look foolish?

PR does not, contrary to hearsay, build reputations overnight, nor, for that matter, save or rescue them. Since you have been around for all these years, you have a reputation, and an image, evolved over a sustained period. Unless you are anxious to make substantial adjustments in the hope of a neat, fast outcome, it is difficult to see how those who know you would think your adoption of PR to be foolish. More probably you intend to make gradual and carefully considered adjustments to your reputation and image.

People who know that you are making this move will see this as a message in its own right and will adjust their perceptions accordingly. The fact that you have not done PR until now may be taken into account. The probability is that many contacts may not notice the change. Just because it is an important move for you does not make it so for them. Unless it heralds disturbances in established relationships, the introduction of a more constructive approach to communications is likely to be viewed as being a natural progression and probably beneficial. Adopting PR in a long-established organization as a measured innovation should be construed as a continuum, not a threat.

A lot of PR is just about wining and dining, isn't it?

There is an element of social contact and sometimes discussions are held over meals, often because it uses the time more efficiently, since we all have to eat. The perception of PR being focused on three-hour-long lunches in luxurious dining rooms and restaurants probably owes more to wishful thinking and satire than reality. In the past decade the 'business lunch', or for that matter, breakfast, tea and dinner, has contracted dramatically in importance.

One-to-one meetings take some beating for quality of communication, but these days PR people tend to skip lunch in favour of hurried snacks and use many more communications channels than were available to them only a few years ago. Probably this industriousness has restored some of the impact of entertainment. So no, sadly PR is not 'just about wining and dining', although this perpetual urgency to achieve more output with the available time has not yet, thankfully, destroyed observance of common courtesies in those countries where social etiquette remains a key component of doing business.

What is meant by 'just a PR exercise'?

This is a term of disparagement much loved by journalists, who use it indiscriminately to describe anything they dislike and much else besides. They seek to infer that whatever they mention is disreputable, but unfortunately they wildly misapply it, often accompanied by a knowing post-modern ironic sneer. As a result some remarkable distortions can occur, as where, for example, an announcement that distracts media attention from another coincidental occurrence may be interpreted as a deliberate 'damage limitation' ploy, when the two were in reality totally unconnected.

The term is based on the presumption that anything connected with PR is disreputable and designed to mislead the journalistic pursuer of truth. The addition of the 'just' is inserted to suggest that the matter complained of is but the latest in a succession, inferring that nothing better could be expected from such a source. There are, of course, many PR activities that might well be described as 'exercises', just as some other military terms are commonly used, such as campaigns, 'putting to safe', officers (as in PROs), logistics and briefing. These activities may attract the opprobrium of the journalists, but most do not. In the sense used by the media, they are not 'just PR exercises'.

Aren't professional people above using PR?

Time was when the professions could rely on their patients, congregations, clients and customers to seek out their services, but no more, except for the privileged few, such as barristers and surgeons. Most professional people have to be proactive in attracting custom, and there is an element of competition in all of them. So no, professional people are not above PR, or, put it another way, PR is not below professional people. In fact, many professions have been strongly committed to doing PR in the past two decades, gradually liberalizing their restrictive practice regimes to allow their members to adopt a more positive stance towards their publics.

Doesn't PR complicate telling how it is, plain and simple?

PR is not concerned with spreading confusion, with whatever motive may be imputed. The aim is quite the contrary, to achieve levels of understanding, and for that clarity is required. PR people often go to great lengths to reduce complex messages to simple, understandable ones. In this there is a recognizable and ever-present risk of distortion, which has to be guarded against. Effective communication requires factual accuracy, reasoned argument and the identification of sources. The process of preparing the message may be complicated, and often is, but the message itself has to be without complication.

'Telling how it is' often takes time and is sensitive to location and the method of communication. Again, these factors have to be taken fully into account. There are some circumstances, for instance, when this is wholly inappropriate in a given time and place. The timing of messages is designed to avoid any potential confusion or misunderstanding. These considerations can be portrayed as complications in themselves, but from that it does not follow that the resultant communications serve to complicate otherwise understandable messages.

Who are the hidden persuaders and why do they hide?

This memorable description was used by Packard in 1957 to describe the US advertising industry's use of motivational research, which he called mass psychoanalysis, in the middle of the last century. Almost all of his polemic was focused on the 'admen', persuaders who appeared to be not at all interested in hiding from anyone, and whose efforts were for the most part very public indeed. He reassuringly concluded that 'We still have a strong defence available against such persuaders: we can choose not to be persuaded.' It was a memorable, if much misunderstood description, with sinister overtones, that retained popular appeal and is still sometimes used in reference to PR people in general. They see themselves as being in the business of persuasion but deny the charge of being the hidden persuaders.

Isn't PR a weapon of mass distraction by another name?

This journalistic phrase, cleverly coined to disparage the allegations about weapons of mass destruction held by the 'wrong' people being used to justify military attack, applies no more and no less to PR as to any other communication activity. PR can be used for many purposes, from providing entertainment to telling painful truths. Communications are focused and not in the mass, except on those relatively rare occasions when entire general publics within a given geographical locality or region need to be contacted about a matter of general relevance and application, as in, for example, an emergency relating to a natural disaster or contamination of food or drinking water.

Does PR-created fame wither with age?

Fame that comes about through PR does not have a distinct intrinsic quality of its own that clearly distinguishes it from fame that emerges by any other means, for example, resulting from a disaster at sea. All fame that is shallow rooted tends to wither. Some has been said to evaporate after only 15 seconds. PR is hard pressed to sustain much of the manufactured celebrity fame of current times, and in all probability many of 'the famous' are quite glad of that.

However, well-earned fame of the more solid kind is usually (not always) enduring. PR that creates such recognition, for example, by communicating outstanding achievement in some field of endeavour, can serve to maintain the fame over decades. Furthermore, we are all 'never so good as when we are dead', it is said, and PR may continue to maintain fame beyond the grave, in the service of our need for heroes.

For the organization, fame is a precious commodity that rides with image and reputation. The need to make known and be known goes to the heart of attracting goodwill and understanding resulting in support and kinder operational conditions. Probably 'never heard of them' is the most damning condemnation of all.

Isn't PR really free advertising?

Very little in this life that is worth having comes free, and that includes PR; unless they are working in a voluntary capacity, say for their local tennis club, the services of PR people have to be paid for, just like any other occupation.

Nor is PR advertising by another name. Advertising aims, whether in the short or long term, to generate sales through achieving optimum persuasiveness. PR, by contrast, has a broader remit. When, like advertising, it is working in support of marketing, its focus is on customers, indirectly seeking sales through educating markets, often ahead of advertising or other marketing or sales activities. Beyond this Marketing Public Relations (MPR), however, PR seeks to engage with many other types of publics for a variety of purposes. In doing this it may use advertising as a PR tool, as for example in announcing financial results, recruiting volunteers, attracting potential employees or promoting public services.

PR also differs from advertising in how each appears in the print and broadcast media. Advertising space or time is bought and the advertiser determines exactly how that space or time is to be used, within certain limits defined by statute and self-regulation. Advertising agencies live largely on commissions based upon the cost of space or time that they purchase on behalf of their customers. PR seldom buys space or time but instead submits matter for consideration by the media. It may appear largely or wholly as supplied, or it may not. The PR source has no comparable control in the details of media presentation, position, layout, heading, timing and so on. PR consultancies earn fees and when occasionally they use advertising in the service of PR they usually rebate any commissions they may receive in consequence.

So editorial content that has been based on one or several PR sources, or maybe PR and non-PR sources, has to earn its appearance on its merits, as these are judged by the media personnel who are employed to research and write what appears. In some countries however, editorial in newspapers is purchased, so this principle is not wholly universal, although it applies throughout most of the world. What little editorial that is purchased in the United Kingdom, like advertising, is marked as such, to make this clear.

Surely the less we tell the less we risk information abuse?

Presumably if you don't tell anyone anything you eliminate any risk of information abuse, but in PR there is a presumption in favour of communication rather than against it. As in all communications, there arises the need to determine what, in the circumstances, amounts to a need to know and what is merely nice to know. The risk of a 'snow job', or information overload, is often real enough, which is why much time and effort is spent on trying to simplify the complex and focus on its core content.

All communications have to take their chances, and an appearance of excessive secrecy can itself convey unintended messages. The source that considers it has much to hide is never likely to be forthcoming and may find itself repeatedly placed in a defensive posture, trying to deflect the inquisitiveness or interrogation of outsiders about what it perceives to be sensitive matters. PR is always positive in its approach. That does not mean that it is some sort of conduit, down which has to flow every morsel of available information, regardless of the circumstances.

As to leaks of internal information to the press, UK newspaper editors have come to realize of late that, however courageous or high-minded their intentions, they cannot expect judges to protect them from the consequences of publishing leaks. Furthermore, the UK's Financial Services Authority has power to compel editors to hand over leaked documents.

Tougher measures have resulted from incidents such as the leaking of a document that had been doctored to suggest that the Belgian brewer Interbrew was preparing for an imminent £4.6 billion takeover of a named rival. Shares in the supposed target soared in value on the news. Interbrew's lawyers tried unsuccessfully to persuade three UK newspapers and a news agency to hand over the leaked document, which had done great damage.

Why should we ever want journalists prying into our affairs?

This view of PR as the 'stalking horse' for unwanted and unwarranted press enquiries is based on a mistaken understanding of media relations. Journalists ask questions of people and organizations that they find interesting, from their particular perspectives, and that they expect will interest their readers, viewers or listeners. They try to steer well clear, therefore, of those that do not qualify, that is to say, are of no real interest or are downright boring.

Organizational PR is therefore likely to be proactive in seeking to attract the attention of selected journalists through having something interesting to say to them. Such contacts fostered through this are developed, so that with time the journalists initiate contact, rather than the organization. The PR is purposeful and constructive, within a policy framework that determines the range and type of information that could be made available should the organization wish to disseminate it or a journalist request it.

Journalists are paid to ask searching questions, although remarkably few do. Just how uncomfortable or disconcerting an enquiry may be has to be a matter of judgement at the time. What is demonstrable is that no organization can sensibly expect to have worthwhile 'on/off' relationships with journalists, whereby they expect interest to be shown when it suits them and not when it does not. Such attitudes are one of the principal sources of complaint by journalists, particularly among specialist and trade/technical writers who would expect to have steady, reliable ongoing contact.

As to intrusion into private lives, this very rarely affects managers, who are not usually considered to qualify for the journalists' general rule, that only people who are already 'in the public eye' are vulnerable to being intruded upon against their consent. Doing PR for the organization may result in a personal public profile, within an industry or sector perhaps, but usually for the press this does not rate the manager as interesting when compared with the likes of politicians and actors. It should be added that sometimes managers provide the press with insights into their private lives, but that hardly qualifies as intrusion.

Why do journalists keep disparaging PR?

Why indeed, particularly since so many journalists later go into PR and quite a few help train PR students. What can be said with some certainty is that PR is not truthfully represented by journalists to their audiences. Perhaps the contraction of journalism, coinciding with the expansion of PR, has more than a little to do with this. Journalists' sense of security of employment has been generally undermined, and they fear the erosion of the distinction between what they perceive to be, on the one hand, journalism and, on the other, PR in the service of marketing and politics. Furthermore, they worry that in some circumstances PR people are gaining recognition as more reliable news sources than journalists, which threatens to challenge their entire *raison d'être*.

Journalists also see PR as a challenge to their self-proclaimed absolute right to 'objectively' determine what is and what is not news. Their problems are compounded by the colossal expansion in the amount of time and, particularly, space to be filled, which inclines them to accept much more PR-sourced material than hitherto. Perhaps not surprisingly, many journalists appear to be fascinated with what they call 'spin' and some appear to have difficulty in thinking about much else.

Aren't PR people and journalists in a cosy huddle, making 'mugs' of us all?

It may seem so at times, when journalists apparently fail to do any more than serve as post offices for PR input. Thankfully, from the PR perspective, even 'branded editorial' usually goes through some sort of editorial filter, which adds credibility to what results. Certainly there is a strong interdependence and the two trades work together closely, but members on each side value their personal credibility and guard it as an important asset. Friendships there may be, but there is no likelihood of a mass conspiracy to defraud media consumers, as implied by the suggestion of a 'cosy huddle'. On the contrary, there is usually a creative tension between the two, and values differ widely, across the divide and within each camp. Many journalists perceive themselves to be superior to the PR people, who tend to dismiss their insults with disdain.

Why do so many journalists go into PR?

Most that do cite improved earnings and prospects, although salaries in PR are generally a bit on the low side when compared with similar occupations, the result perhaps of there being an excess of demand over supply in PR employment. Some see it as an escape from what they perceive to be drudgery into what they conceive, all too often mistakenly, to be an exciting, glamorous and 'fun' world.

They are usually ill prepared for the exceptional levels of stress and long hours of work in PR, well in excess of what they knew in journalism. Nor are their prospects of employment security much improved; both trades are notably vulnerable. Better rewarded, more secure people like solicitors often express difficulty in understanding why anyone would want to do it; 'PR people work *so hard*' is a typical observation.

If PR is all so valuable and so important, why does it have such a poor reputation itself?

It is deeply ironic that PR has a low reputation, since it is, by its own account, 'the discipline that looks after reputation'. Not that everyone in PR acknowledges that it does have a problem, or, if it does, that it matters.

> Consultant Chris Lewis, writing in the *Financial Times* (30 October 2001), after delivering a blistering attack upon a 'bitchy, back-biting industry' and its representative bodies, declared 'let's stop worrying about PR's image and get on with doing a good job and adding value'.

The charge is, however, that the trade of PR does itself no favours, and in consequence it has a low standing; that how it performs is discreditable and deserving of contempt. It shares this opprobrium with a number of other occupational groups that include journalists, politicians, lawyers, financial advisers and estate agents. The nub of the perception is that PR is about trickery and misrepresentation.

Why, or how, this came about is particularly interesting, since much the same could be alleged of many other trades, which nevertheless appear to escape the same depth of rebuke. It seems probable that the relentless public 'rubbishing' of PR by journalists has taken its toll. This has injected various disparaging terms into general usage, which have then been applied with uninformed abandon. For instance, anyone who appears in public to air a grievance is likely, sooner or later, to allude to 'a PR job' in describing some statement or action that is not agreeable to them. Such aspersions are cast repetitiously, like popular slang and bad language, and are usually accepted without question, often accompanied by ritualistic knowing nods and winks.

Another major factor may be the unflattering depiction of PR in films and novels. That this is entertainment does not appear to deflect assumptions that it truthfully depicts real life. Film makers and novelists, after all, are allowed plenty of poetic licence and the exaggerations of the entertainer are gradually absorbed into perceptions of reality.

Such a low level of esteem does not appear to have impaired the demand for PR, from all quarters, perhaps itself also deeply ironic. Those who employ or commission PR may disapprove and people generally may suspect sleight of hand, but the rush to use PR for promoting every conceivable cause is undeniable. Rather as the hotelier Conrad Hilton famously spoke of location, location, location in accounting for his success, PR people tend to talk much about reputation, reputation, reputation. Perhaps this also fails to help their cause; after all, when last did, for example, the estate agents want to keep 'banging on' about reputation, or, for that matter, the journalists?

We are results-driven and time-short, so can we do PR as well?

Yes you can, but it has to be properly allowed for and given a fair opportunity to prove its worth. Managers who are new to PR as part of their responsibilities invariably think it is something they can turn to at the end of the day, when all the 'real work' is done. They are too busy attending to what really matters, they explain, usually past 6 o'clock in the evening, on the telephone to their PR consultant, who is meanwhile just getting into stride with the evening work session.

There is a saying that 'The busiest people have the most time' and it applies to PR work, which should be accorded its fair share of available time. It is about achieving results too, and is not some fanciful extra, or tiresome burden, depending upon viewpoint. If it is denied adequate commitment and attention it tends to 'hit back'. For instance, a press statement may be produced hurriedly and dispatched, as if with optimum efficiency, but have unforeseen consequences that more patience and attention to detail would have avoided. So it was done after 6 o'clock, and sent out first thing the next morning, but what scale of achievement was that if it raises problems later?

Similarly, just because *now* is not the time allocated for dealing with PR matters does not mean that other people know this, or care. For example, the important press enquiries have a way of coming through without regard to meetings schedules. Invitations and opportunities do not always wait patiently in a pending tray for attention. Crises that invoke the need for swift communications are seldom predictable, and never orderly. PR is an ongoing commitment, not a hobby.

Our patients are glad to have our services, so why waste money on PR?

Patients are consumers of medical services and deserve 'customer care' by the supplier, as with any other supplier. Doubtless they are glad to have the services, but then that is so of other services too. They may be *gladder* to have these particular services, because all personal services such as surgery and dentistry tend to have a high priority, but that does not diminish the entitlement to customer care; far from it, it probably *increases* it.

PR spent on delivering enhanced service is never wasted in these conditions, because the patients have exceptional opportunities to become aware and form judgements. Often they have little else to think about. Patients pay for what they receive, whether directly or indirectly. Monopolies in supply appear to be in significant decline in the United Kingdom, and patients also have access to alternative foreign providers.

Furthermore, patients have families and friends who form a critical public and directly affect reputation. Those that visit the patient in hospital, clinic or home have a *heightened* awareness of customer care and can be influential in exerting change. It is unsound, therefore, to suppose that a patient is without influence and cannot retaliate. Nor should it be assumed that, where services are provided by the State, further 'purchases' are determined by the natural course of events, not the wallet or purse, therefore rendering PR irrelevant. On the contrary, PR has much to contribute in securing the grants and funds of more earthly powers, the lifeblood of most services.

Does PR use different names for concealment?

It is unlikely to be for concealment. Although most PR people prefer to occupy a back position, and not be 'up front', they are not temperamentally suited to being invisible, which in any event makes no sense for the consultants and the executive high flyers. True, there has been a tendency towards finding alternative titles for PR. This may be motivated by a desire to be more explicit or in order to escape the drag anchor of the trade's low reputation. There are several alternatives used, of which the most common is communications. This has its problems, though, because it is also a favourite of telecommunications companies and just about everyone else who has some connection with communication in the broadest sense.

> Interviewed in *PR Week* (19 October 2001), an elderly doyen of the trade, Harold Burson, said 'The term communications has become synonymous with PR but this does a disservice to our profession by making it tactical. The term "perception management" was contrived. The best term for what we do is public relations.' In this he criticized his former firm, which adopted 'perception management' in 1996. Earlier, talking to PR undergraduates, he had remarked that 'we PR people do a poor job explaining what we do'.

How does PR differ from propaganda?

Propaganda invariably relies upon an element of self-praise and tends to be very dismissive of all opponents. The ultimate purpose is to secure an uncritical following, which is usually achieved through arousing emotions and evoking spiritual responses. It is usually associated with causes, politics and religions, and its use can be well intentioned, as with the US 'New Deal', or ill intentioned, as in Nazi Germany during the same period.

PR is always positive in tone, aims to avoid 'puffery', or self-congratulation, and is directed towards achieving willing agreement, acceptance and support. The declared aim is two-way dialogue, although clearly much PR falls way short of that, and it endeavours to be as factual and relatively unbiased as is consistent with its content.

This is designed for the very practical purpose of giving messages the optimum prospect of being received and accepted.

It is probable that the fundamental difference, when all is said and done, is one of degree. Propaganda tends towards being overbearing, dogmatic, assertive and disinterested in debate; PR tends towards a more engaging, milder advocacy that admits of discussion. The first can demand simple belief, extending to obedience; the second supposedly tries at all times to engage in reasoned dialogue and persuasion.

Interestingly, much, probably most, PR output is simple dissemination of basic facts and figures, unadorned by any argument or elaboration. Sometimes the propaganda versus PR difference is confused by the use of 'propaganda' as a pejorative term, typically to describe trade sales literature, usually intended with a degree of ironic good humour, as in: 'That sales brochure is all just propaganda!'

Is propaganda easier than PR?

Depending upon its intentions, almost certainly propaganda is easier to undertake than PR. Maybe when, as with the New Deal, it is designed for positive purposes, and it therefore depends upon a willing and ready acceptance, it may be more difficult because, presumably, it has to take greater account of how it is to be received.

Why bother with PR if propaganda will do just as well?

Quite apart from the ethical inhibitions relating to propaganda, as the mass management of opinion, there are the practical drawbacks. In communications-rich societies there is much wariness of anything that is suggestive of propaganda and widespread condemnation and rejection of it once it is identified, or even suspected. It may have limited success, with the gullible or uncaring, but it is not likely to achieve anything of significance except to corrupt and eventually destroy reputation.

That does not stop politicians, in particular, from using propaganda, but liberal, democratic, educated peoples tend to be better able to resist and think for themselves. Propaganda for various '-isms' is also ever present, but generally this tends to be cause-related and usually tolerated provided it is contained within the confines of 'campaigning' and clearly labelled as such.

Writing in *The Guardian* (22 April 2003), researcher David Miller suggested that the BBC's inclination to follow UK government propaganda in its domestic television and radio news on the US/UK military invasion of Iraq may have damaged its reputation within the United Kingdom for reliable impartiality. He reported that when the *Frankfurter Allgemeine Zeitung* commissioned research into media coverage of the campaign in five countries, the BBC was found to have reflected the widespread popular dissent substantially less than any other media: just 2 per cent of its total output, the next lowest being 7 per cent on ABC, the US network. Miller cited other aspects of the BBC's output, some of which was admitted to be 'wrong' by the BBC, including frequent use of admittedly false military stories and eager depiction of the fall of Baghdad in terms very similar to the UK government's version of events.

Why would anyone on TV or radio ever be interested in us?

Because you have something interesting to say or show, you are qualified to contribute your opinions, you have 'made news' or you have come up with a brilliant idea for a programme. Also, you understand that neither television nor radio are the preserves of a performing elite, long-serving pundits or insider hucksters. That is not to say that all three types are not found there, of course, but nowadays they have to let a few others in as well, including people who have something responsible and/or serious to contribute. The question implies awe of the broadcasters, which is entirely misplaced.

Isn't PR just muckraking?

No. PR people leave that to the journalists. US President Theodore Roosevelt coined the term 'muckraker' to describe early investigative journalists in the 1900s who made damaging disclosures of corruption in the New York Police Department when he was its Commissioner. These days the term is often used to describe elements of popular journalism.

PR is sales promotion by another name, isn't it?

PR is often mistakenly confused with Sales Promotion (SP), since they both have the ability to communicate with individuals and relatively small groups. SP is directed towards obtaining short-term results, over weeks or a few months, the aim being to affect a particular market quickly, by stimulating sales or product sampling. It is a means to achieve market changes, always with the objective of stimulating sales. By contrast, PR is committed to obtaining results that take a lot longer to achieve, over months and years, and is not solely concerned with sales. SP can impinge on PR: any disappointments among business customers or consumers that arise from offers that fail to deliver on their promise invariably affect reputation.

PR is publicity, isn't it?

No: publicity is a part of PR and comprises a range of techniques used sometimes. Publicity is about drawing attention and creating awareness by means that are credible and relevant. It is relatively easy to draw attention through stunts and so on, mostly events designed to be noticed and remarked upon, but not so easy to communicate intended messages by this means. Publicity can be viewed as a result, which may be controllable or uncontrollable, and it can create a favourable or an unfavourable image.

Sometimes publicity arises in consequence not of some contrived occurrence but some information becoming known, possibly unintentionally. Occasionally bad publicity is sought, in the belief that it will be beneficial. PR, unlike publicity, is not only interested in creating awareness and it concentrates solely on gaining favourability. Most publicity is harmless in nature, but historically it is associated with exaggeration and trickery.

Surely there's no such thing as bad publicity?

Oh yes there is. And it is best avoided. This saying is attributed, incidentally, to one Phineas T Barnum, the US showman who also introduced the world to his 'Greatest Show on Earth' in 1871, alias the Barnum and Bailey Touring Circus of performing animals and artistes. That was a while ago now but the saying endures.

three

is there **anyone there?**

- What is the 'communication loop'?
- Where does PR fit into the loop?
- Can PR improve the quality of feedback?
- Does PR encourage people and organizations to adopt different values and behaviours?
- Isn't all this talk of two-way dialogue just blue sky?
- There isn't *really* any theory behind PR, is there?
- What is really meant by the 'media-ization of society'?
- Do people believe what they see and hear?
- What's the difference between PR and communication?
- Why do some people talk about communication yet others about communications?
- What exactly is corporate communication?
- Why do people call PR 'communications'?
- Exactly *what* boundaries does PR span and why?
- Does PR always aim for change through persuasion?
- Can PR communications result in changes to each side, Them and Us?
- Are PR messages always self-interested by definition, or can they serve a wider interest?
- What is meant by 'public information'? Surely *all* PR is?
- Are pressure and cause-related groups hostile to the notion of two-way communication?
- If we do live in an over-communicated world, when is silence still golden?

- Why does everyone grumble when there is so much communication?
- What is Newszak and can it be turned off, like music in public places?
- What is infotainment?
- What are red tops?
- So what are broadloids?
- All media have to originate somewhere, so what is created media?
- What is the total newsroom?
- What is contract publishing? Surely anyone who works in the media has a contract?
- Don't the journalists fix all the news anyway?
- What if this company never has any real news to tell?
- Are journalists routinely hostile?
- What is meant by an information subsidy, since there seems to be no shortage?

This chapter explores the nature of communication and what is necessary for it to be effective. An attempt is made to unravel some common misconceptions, about news, journalism, the media and the role of PR in communication, both internal and external to the organization. Some of the practicalities and jargon used are also considered.

In addition to examining how communication works, topics here include such propositions as silence is communication, journalists alone decide what is news, communication is not communications, two-way dialogue is plain wishful thinking and communication fosters discontent.

What is the 'communication loop'?

There is a theory that when people communicate this can be depicted as forming a 'loop' between the sender and the receiver. There are several more components to this:

- the *message* itself;
- the *medium*, by which the message is sent;
- the *code*, by which the message is put into a format that is reckoned by the sender to best fit the circumstances; and
- the *feedback* in reply.

This last completes the loop, but very often there is no feedback, or it is partial, and frequently when there is feedback it is not noticed by the sender. This is tricky, since silence itself can be construed as feedback in some circumstances.

There are plenty more problems in the process. The message has to be 'properly' *encoded*, using, for example, the correct language, the appropriate choice of words and symbols and making sure any technical terms are likely to be understood. This can be fraught with difficulties.

> The Camping Club of Great Britain and Ireland (now The Camping and Caravanning Club), aiming for increased use of its camping and caravanning sites, sent sales literature to Germany that had been translated into German by a professional translation agency. Months later there came a call from the BBC World Service. 'We have been tossing a coin here to see who among us would volunteer to tell you about the hundreds of our German listeners contacting us to thank you for giving them such a good laugh. The translation is terrible and we felt we ought to let you know'.

Which brings us to *decoding*, another delicate matter, since receivers often have their own 'agenda' when deciding what they think of messages. Nor is this assisted by *noise* and *distortion*, being any interference that impedes understanding. Noise is of three types:

- environmental, such as over flying aircraft 'drowning' conversation;
- internal, as where thirst causes distraction and breaks concentration;
- psychological, when attitudes and perceptions colour reception.

Distortion can be physical, as where post is physically damaged or shredded by the deliverer, or in the mind of the recipient, where, for example, an existing relationship affects how that person interprets the message.

Where does PR fit into the loop?

When feedback is poor there is said to be a two-way asymmetrical process, that is, although both sides are communicating, there is an imbalance; the sender is making most of the effort, while the receiver is not making much effort at all. When the effort becomes more equal it is getting closer to the two-way symmetrical ideal, where two sides of relatively equal power are engaging each other in a dialogue in which the possibility may arise that either side persuades the other into change.

In PR there is commonly a heavy one-sided emphasis. The organization usually wants to persuade the receiver, who may not be much interested in trying to reciprocate, not at least in that way or to any great extent. The need for a more balanced exchange arises, usually, in proportion to the complexity of the message. PR thrives on feedback, but the most strenuous attempts to secure a more balanced exchange can go unrewarded.

Sometimes PR can result in a need to make adjustments to the organization's stance, offering and so on as a direct outcome. When that occurs, should a stalemate arise it is PR's task to facilitate a solution that satisfies both sides. Obviously if negotiation and compromise became commonplace the flow of communication activity would be slowed very substantially, for lack of time if no other reason. Presumably also there would be some practical limits to how much and how often organizations would be willing, and able, to change in order to satisfy external demands.

Can PR improve the quality of feedback?

Most definitely yes, because it aims to take the fullest account of the receiver's standpoint and values. PR people also understand and appreciate the importance of the three overriding reasons why messages may not be decoded and understood as they were intended:

- selective *attention*;
- selective *distortion*; and
- selective *recall*.

PR aims to overcome all the many hurdles by using combinations of carefully designed and directed messages.

Does PR encourage people and organizations to adopt different values and behaviours?

Yes. In planning to achieve two-way communication, completing the loop, PR people endeavour to achieve the greatest possible degree of change in both attitudes and behaviours. The greater the symmetry the more likely that there may be changes on both sides and over time values are adjusted. There have been great changes in values in recent decades, brought about gradually, relating to, for example, the environment, consumerism and multi-ethnicity.

Isn't all this talk of two-way dialogue just blue sky?

No, but it has to be worked for. Even all-out public confrontation in the media between two 'PR machines' such as the government and a striking public sector workers' trade union usually ends in some sort of dialogue. True, in less extreme conditions a lot of exchanges are lopsided. However, the allegation by critics that PR often does not want a response reveals a gross misunderstanding; since obtaining information from the front is integral to improving communication effectiveness.

There isn't *really* any theory behind PR, is there?

Oh yes there is. Some might say there is rather too much, most of it borrowed and adapted from the social sciences. PR people generally have tended to be dismissive, preferring empirical learning on the job to theorizing, but that is gradually changing as ever more PR-specific graduates enter the trade. The allegation that PR is some kind of hit-and-miss affair, that cannot be explained or measured properly, largely misrepresents reality and is usually made by rivals who prefer it to be seen that way.

What is really meant by the 'media-ization of society'?

It is a way of describing the growth and diversity of the media and their influence on us, how most people willingly look to the media daily for information, entertainment and gossip and how the media exploit that captive interest in the service of dominant power groups, particularly in politics, bureaucracy, business and the professions. It is said that more newspapers are read per head of population in the United Kingdom than elsewhere in the world.

Do people believe what they see and hear?

People may accept messages that they consider to be credible. The status of the sender influences acceptance but does not assure it.

A UK politician, Clive Soley, wrote in *The Times* (31 July 2002) that 'There is one stark statistic that should concentrate our minds. Only 18 per cent of the population thinks that politicians are trustworthy and 15 per cent believe that journalists are trustworthy'. His article was addressed primarily to journalists and suggested that politicians and journalists together should seek greater credibility.

By way of explanation for this lamentable lapse from grace, Mr Soley added that 'many people think politicians and journalists are two of a kind. We sound the same, we talk the same language, we seem unable to talk about the things that affect the lives of ordinary people.' By 'ordinary' he appears to mean anyone who is not a journalist or politician. His comments might equally apply in many other countries.

What's the difference between PR and communication?

PR has been described as:

- the management of communication;
- an art and social science;
- a planned and sustained effort to establish and maintain goodwill and understanding;
- an effort to win cooperation;
- help for achieving interactive communication;
- establishing and defending reputation;
- influencing opinion and behaviour; and much else.

PR in practice is principally, some might say mostly, concerned with communication as a tactical means to a PR end.

Why do some people talk about communication yet others about communications?

The term communication was adopted by social scientists in their research of behaviour, and therefore it tends to be used specifically in connection with communications *within* the organization. In consequence it may sound more meaningful. Most PR people tend to use both words without distinction and for all practical purposes, but those that do should know better, because there is a subtle difference, which deserves to be observed. Without the 's' describes a management tool embracing all intentional forms of communication both within and outside the organization, whereas with the 's' describes means of communication, for whatever purpose, such as telephone equipment.

What exactly is corporate communication?

Most people suppose that corporate communication means any communication emanating from a company, or occurring within it. The word 'corporate' refers however to 'the whole body', or *corpus*, and applies to any kind of organization, regardless of whether they are in the private, public or not-for-profit sectors. True, companies have tended to set the pace in worrying about images and reputations, but non-commercial bodies are also interested in corporate communication. Corporate communication can be divided into three components:

- communication by managers, commonly thought of as being corporate communication, because it is driven by the need to favourably influence stakeholders and publics;
- marketing communication, which is directed at achieving sales;
- organizational communication, engaging those publics with which there is interdependence, by implication the major groups such as investors, employees and suppliers.

Why do people call PR 'communications'?

Depends who the people are:

- Many PR people think it spells out more clearly what they actually do, because it is assumed that most of us know what communications are, whereas we might have difficulty with PR.
- Cynics say that the use of the word by the PR trade in substitution for PR is because it too has difficulty; in other words, there is an attempt to avoid any connection.
- People outside PR may use it because they are having such difficulty disentangling editorial journalism and comment from PR that it is 'all communications' to them, together with, for example, advertising, messages on the 'voicemail' and 'junk mail' through the letterbox.

Exactly *what* boundaries does PR span and why?

The boundaries are both between the organization and its external environment and within the organization, between interacting parts or subsystems (units) within the organization. PR's boundary-spanning role comprises:

- communication between the organization as a whole and external publics and individuals;
- assistance to other subsystems in their communications with components of the external environment; and
- facilitation of communications between subsystems internally.

Does PR always aim for change through persuasion?

Persuasion is always present, as with legal advocacy in a court of law, even in compromise and negotiation. There is an argument that persuasion overwhelms and is coercive, denying freedom of action for the respondent, but in reality persuasion is present in all dispute resolution. In any case, PR messages are open to acceptance or rejection. They do not have the power of, say, law or regulation, even when they are about such matters.

Can PR communications result in changes to each side, Them and Us?

Yes. PR seeks responses, it wants to complete the communication loop and do it as efficiently and effectively as possible. If the messages coming back suggest to the sender that some adjustments may be needed by the sender, these have to be taken into account and may result in some adjustments being made to his or her previous position.

The Brent Spar saga in 1995 provides an outstanding illustration of communications resulting in changes. Royal Dutch/Shell wanted to sink a defunct North Sea oil storage platform in a deep Atlantic Ocean site. This provoked one of the most high-profile environmental protest campaigns ever, led by Greenpeace, a campaigning group. Demonstrations were organized in several countries, Shell brand petrol was boycotted and a German petrol station was fire bombed. Shell changed its plans. The Brent Spar was dismantled and recycled instead, rather like old cars returning as new clothes washing machines.

Coincidentally, in the same year, Shell found itself accused of 'complicity and collusion' with the Nigerian government, with which it had a joint venture, over the executions of nine environmentalists. Given Brent Spar and then this, the company concluded that 'reputation management was something that was now a global issue' and it embarked on protracted soul-searching, which it called *Society's Changing Expectations*. This led to its adoption of a framework of three campaigns, entitled Business Transformation, Profits and Principles and Living the Values.

As for Greenpeace, the oxygen of publicity propelled the group forwards, to become a byword for environmental protest and a formidable organization. It is adept at PR and uses it to generate favourable public opinion in support of its activities. It is active throughout the world and exerts substantial influence.

Global and multinational companies are, perhaps, more likely to find themselves making substantial adjustments, but although this is often asserted it is not proven. Indeed, it could be argued that small and micro organizations are more capable, inclined and likely to do so. For every one long-remembered headline-grabbing example there are surely countless more, probably much smaller, that go publicly unrecorded.

Are PR messages always self-interested by definition, or can they serve a wider interest?

Some PR output is without self-interest. Probably the most obvious example is that of attempts to persuade particular groups of people to claim payments by the state to which they are entitled. All government and related pronouncements of the 'this is good for you' type are presumed to be made on behalf of and for the benefit of all citizens, or subjects, however they are grouped into publics, but this has to be tempered by the knowledge that we live in a highly competitive democracy.

The 'public sphere' supposedly provides an accessible platform for articulation of reasoned argument that is persuasive but not necessarily self-interested. Here, in theory, the messages are factually accurate and everyone, whether as individuals or organizations, can join in. Some contributions are PR-sourced, others are not; some are self-interested while others are relatively or entirely disinterested.

Amongst all this there may be some PR messages that are devoid of self-interest.

What is meant by 'public information'? Surely *all* PR is?

Public information is what governments, government agencies, regional and local authorities and most of the rest of the public sector disseminate. For example, government departments give information about policies, plans and achievements and seek to inform and educate about legislation and regulations. That, at least, is the theory.

The glamorous end of the public information spectrum is responsible for but a small part of the total output. For instance, local authorities issue shoals of material that supposedly informs 'the public' (in general) about all manner of matters, from how to pay tax to the topographical features of the countryside and renting videos from the public library. All of this is made 'public' in a broad sense, although publics apply here too, say, with council taxpayers, walkers and video entertainment buffs.

Are pressure and cause-related groups hostile to the notion of two-way communication?

Intemperate language, violent demonstrations, sabotage, hostage-taking, and similar, give the impression that for some groups at least two-way dialogue is their very last desire. However, the vast majority of groups are more temperate, law-abiding and subtle. They are not paragons of virtue, but most of these do *seem* to prefer reasoned argument and discussion. An organization that finds itself engaging with such a group should take comfort from the growing recognition around the world of the importance of negotiation and dialogue. Many groups appreciate the value to them of trying to get into a constructive dialogue and know that any outcome worth having, from their perspective, is likely to be based on mutual compromise.

If we do live in an over-communicated world, when is silence still golden?

This might be a question about ethics, for there are plenty of times when 'the least said the soonest mended'. In PR, remaining silent in response to others is seldom an option, however much it may be preferred. Silence is readily interpreted as guilt. But knowing when to initiate communication and how much to communicate often requires fine judgement.

It is commonly supposed that PR is all about throwing out the messages, but it is not. There is a torrent of material bearing down on the media's newsrooms, which might suggest the need for urgency in gaining attention, but the pursuit of quality instead of quantity in PR message output has its rewards. The same rules apply here as in human relations more generally.

As for keeping quiet, with its implication of having something to hide: better to consider what it might be like for the organization to have a reputation for being human than to needlessly opt for adopting an unnecessarily defensive posture. Sometimes well-intentioned preoccupations with credibility and reputation can colour decisions to the disadvantage of the organization.

Why does everyone grumble when there is so much communication?

It is possible that grumbling is the direct result of so much communication by so many. This does seem a contradiction, since the more we know the more, it might be supposed, we would consider that we were 'in the picture' and thereby satisfied, or at least more, rather than less, satisfied. The problem may lie in all the argument and conflict that necessarily arises when there is intensity of competition to be heard. It is noticeable that greater affluence appears to have little effect on this trend.

According to MORI research in 2002, reported in *The Daily Telegraph* (26 August 2002), people in the United Kingdom aged 35–54 have become 'the grumpy generation', displacing older people as the most dissatisfied. Explanations offered include 'being so fed up with their lifestyle and the way the country is run', 'the pressures of modern life' and 'the sterility of popular culture'. Furthermore, 'The 35s to 54s are of prime working age, in the most over-worked nation in Europe'. Maybe it is research like this that is helping to create the grumble culture.

What is Newszak and can it be turned off, like music in public places?

The term Newszak is based on the more familiar Muzak, a branded broadcast music system commonly found in hotels and other public buildings, whose name has entered the English language because it is associated with aged melodies sung by past popular singers to lush orchestral accompaniments. The problem being that, quite apart from its attempt to entertain all tastes and thus relatively few, this music is often broadcast loudly just about everywhere and can seem inescapable. It can be turned off, but usually this is done only during the night.

The implication, therefore, is that Newszak is some kind of similar all-pervasive environmental pollution, based not on music but news. Newszak was coined to describe a product 'designed and promoted to gain market share for the media business, with an emphasis on entertaining, unchallenging, personal items'; a kind of 'Strangers in the Night News', to soothe away reality, maybe.

Some journalists both recognize this description of modern media output and are prepared to go public about it, writing about the growing popular perception of news on radio and television and in the press as synthetic interpretation of 'pure information' and about the cynical use of distorting emotion and pathos. It is asserted that the time-honoured journalistic enquiry, 'What happened?' is being supplanted by 'How do you feel?' as the primary question asked.

Like canned music, this Newszak could be turned off, but that seems unlikely. The media dedication to 'infotainment' and other such concoctions seems unassuaged and, indeed, unabashed. Just how much PR is complicit in all this is uncertain. It definitely has understood very well the media requirements in order to disgorge Newszak on the world, and is probably the originator of a substantial amount of it.

What is infotainment?

This describes a blend of information and entertainment, both content and presentation, that now pervades broadcast news and current affairs and much of the printed media. Accuracy and truth are vulnerable to being distorted or corrupted, presumably owing to the apparent media belief in a need to distract and trivialize in the pursuit of larger audiences and readerships. The idea seems to be that people cannot handle anything too serious for very long.

Editors and other journalistic luminaries blame the development of trivialization on youth, rather than on commercial pressures. For instance, in *The Times* (4 December 1998) Brian MacArthur reported the editor of *The Guardian*, Alan Rusbridger, as saying 'They're post-modern, post-serious, post-literate... and post-broadsheet. We either adjust to meet them halfway... or become extinct'. The veteran radio current affairs interviewer John Humphrys is reported by Magnus Linklater, in *The Times* (2 September 1999), to have remarked that 'Soft, cosy journalism intrudes everywhere because it is assumed that the listener prefers news pre-digested rather than delivered straight'. Linklater complains of 'spoon-fed news for couch potatoes'.

What are red tops?

This describes how many popular newspapers prefer to display their names using red ink across the top of their front pages, often with the name reversed out of a red rectangular flag-like background. The term is used to imply triviality and sensationalism. Recently, a leading mass circulation daily newspaper in the United Kingdom, *The Mirror*, decided to become 'more serious' and one of its changes, designed to give that impression, was to abandon its use of its red masthead. Reportedly, sales have risen.

So what are broadloids?

The larger broadsheet size newspapers are supposedly 'quality' newspapers, as opposed to 'popular' ones that appear in the smaller tabloid sheet size. The term broadloid is used to imply the inclusion of triviality and sensationalism in the broadsheet size publications, that mixture of the serious and inconsequential that presumably *The Guardian* editor sees as a halfway compromise.

All media have to originate somewhere, so what is created media?

Also referred to as private media, this describes all the media that are created, and owned, by organizations for their own communications purposes. They include house journals, which may be in the form of a newspaper, magazine or newsletter. These are usually printed and may be available electronically on the intranet; they may be produced only for people within the organization or for publics outside, typically customers and opinion leaders. Publications also may include:

- annual report and accounts for financial publics and media;
- abridged annual report and accounts edition for employees;
- annual report or review of activities;
- recruitment brochure;
- sponsored book;
- technical bulletins and manuals;
- booklets, leaflets, induction packs, etc.

What is the total newsroom?

In the total newsroom editorial content, editorial promotions, advertising and circulation (distribution) are handled and coordinated together. This differs from the traditional arrangement, comprising a discrete editorial newsroom and separate advertising, promotions and circulation departments.

What is contract publishing? Surely anyone who works in the media has a contract?

Contract publishing describes all the many magazines that are produced for organizations, mostly companies, under contract by specialist suppliers, who provide a total service, including sourcing content, writing, editing and production. Many are produced to a standard that is comparable with any paid-for magazine in the newsagents. They may be supplied free or charged for, and their central purpose is to build and maintain strong brands. Probably the most familiar are those provided by the leading grocery supermarkets and motoring associations.

Don't the journalists fix all the news anyway?

Yes, in that they decide what is published and what is not, but much depends upon what is meant by 'fixed'. The media has 'hard' news to handle most days, such as natural disasters, of which there are said to be more now owing to climate change. Then there are other 'hard' news events, such as terrorist attacks, kidnapping, deaths of famous people, coups d'etat, invasions and so on. There is seldom much shortage in this category and they have to be, or should be, reported.

They have greater discretion in deciding what to include of the 'soft' news, which is frequently contrived by the media themselves, unassisted by anyone, usually in pursuit of 'celebrity fiction' or crime reportage. And there is all the PR-sourced material, both 'hard' and 'soft', that is used by the media. This may account for as much as 50 per cent of total output, allowing for the contributions from politics and business.

What if this company never has any real news to tell?

Don't worry, you will. It may take time for the PR to dig out the nuggets from scratch, but you would be surprised how many organizations have started by thinking they are of absolutely no interest to anyone, only to discover that there is a world of publics out there to be addressed. PR is certainly not about modesty, false or otherwise, but measured communication with purpose.

Are journalists routinely hostile?

They are paid to enquire and check, so an encounter with an on-duty journalist could become hostile, but that is not to say that it is some routine they all enact ritualistically whenever the opportunity arises. True, quite a lot of them, particularly when they are newer at the job, tend towards the hostility end of social graces, in the mistaken belief that it is expected of them and gets them results. The shrewder, usually matured, variety, however, incline more towards adoption of the wise old bird approach, which time and experience has taught them can be more rewarding and less exhausting for all concerned.

From the point of view of the PR novice giving an interview or briefing, both ends of the spectrum can be equally treacherous. One way may seem like an attempt to put words into your mouth while the other may be deceptively cordial. Every encounter is therefore strictly on the record at all times. That's fine by the journalists; they just want a story, and the quicker the better.

What is meant by an information subsidy, since there seems to be no shortage?

This term refers to the 'subsidy' that is represented by PR material, destined to fill space and airtime that otherwise would have to be filled at the expense of the media. The cost of this is borne not by the media but by those who supply to the media. Unequal output among competing providers may result in less competition in consumer and business-to-business markets, although this is improbable, for a host of practical reasons, but substantial differences *may* result in distortions. For instance, in the United Kingdom the large national real estate agents dominate the PR-generated residential property writing in the national press, but this is roughly balanced by regional and local agents' domination of press editorial within their regional markets, where the properties for sale are located.

four

fit for **purpose**

- What types of objectives can be set?
- What is the likely short term for setting objectives?
- When is PR *strategic*?
- How does PR tie in with corporate business strategy?
- How can PR be our eyes and ears?
- What's ethical about PR?
- When should PR be used to generate interest in business ethics?
- What is a 'positioning statement'?
- Should we have a formal PR strategy?
- Would we be better off with general aims and clear, firm objectives for our PR and keep the strategy simple?
- Could we have a PR strategy without a formal business plan?
- Would a PR strategy provide the basis for developing a business plan?
- Are there different types of PR strategy?
- How could we structure a PR strategy?
- What are *strategic* communications?
- Should PR take its strategy lead from the marketing strategy?
- Would the PR benefit from having its own strategy that then links in with marketing, sales and other functions?
- Could we have more than one strategy at the same time?
- How much flexibility should we aim for in our PR?
- Isn't PR really all about tactics?
- Do PR people really know the difference between strategy and tactics?

- But could we be more effective with PR tactics alone?
- Should we rely on tactics to give us the flexibility to exploit changing conditions?
- Do we need an action plan?
- Why try to plan what must remain flexible, responsive and creative?
- What plans should we make to protect our reputation?
- Could journalists give us a few useful tips about reputation?
- What is issues management and could PR help us to advance an important issue?
- What does being 'on message' really mean outside politics?
- How do we go about planning for a crisis?
- What does PR contribute to crisis management?
- What should we look out for in trying to avoid crises?
- What makes a 'good' crisis?
- What can go wrong?
- If anything blows up we have the internal systems to cope, so why PR?

Much PR can seem unplanned, even fortuitous, probably because it may be carefully designed to look that way. In reality, there is as much need for careful planning and execution as in any other activity, probably more so. Here strategic communications management is explored for its purpose and relevance, potential contribution to overall management and impact on corporate culture. Thought is also given to ethics and reputation and a number of questions ask about crisis management, including how to plan for one, the warning signs and what can go wrong in a crisis.

What types of objectives can be set?

Objectives usually fall within four broad categories:

- recognition and status;
- goodwill and understanding;
- reputation;
- organizational performance.

Objectives may be long term or short term, and they must be SMART: specific, measurable, achievable (or actionable), realistic and timed. In particular, they must be measurable in terms that make sense financially. PR objectives have to satisfy these criteria. For instance, general statements about goodwill are just not good enough. How would extra goodwill be likely to translate into measurable gain, and how would that be measured?

Increasing awareness is often stated to be a PR objective, yet without being SMART it remains a broad aim. The role of goals is also frequently confused. Sometimes goals are seen as being aims, a means to describing larger purposes, indicating intended direction, other times they are considered to be short-term objectives, yet again they are used as subobjectives, to be met as part of fulfilling greater objectives. In PR it is advisable to keep it simple: goals are aims unless they fully meet the SMART criteria.

What is the likely short term for setting objectives?

Three to six months is the usual duration for fulfilling short-term objectives. They may be buried within the business plan, which is likely to be written to last three years, maybe five, or they may arise between times, as where, for example, there is a company takeover battle, a merger of public authorities or a consolidation of subsidiaries. Accordingly, these short-term objectives may be taken fully into account in current PR programmes or they may need discrete campaigns to be constructed and implemented, usually at short notice.

When is PR *strategic*?

It is often said of PR that it is 'all tactics and no strategy'. This is because, probably since PR has so many dimensions, activities can very easily begin to look like a succession of tactics, with no obvious strategy behind them. There is, however, one acid test that indicates whether the activity qualifies for being called strategic: does it *contribute substantially* to the corporate vision, mission and objectives? Yes or No, for there cannot be any equivocation about this.

Asking this question can raise some uncomfortable questions about the vision, mission and objectives, but that's probably no bad thing. It follows that the PR should be involved actively with helping to define and refine the corporate *raison d'être*. The organization that excludes PR from the so-called 'dominant coalition' of managers that decide such matters is neglecting a valuable resource.

How does PR tie in with corporate business strategy?

The largest single contribution of PR is in its gathering and interpretation of information, the eyes and ears function, and in the translation of this into usable intelligence that can materially assist in strategy development, for example, by determining changes or identifying publics to be addressed. In addition, the possibility arises that the PR people may have a broader contribution worth making, similarly to other functions. The problem seems to be that many dominant coalitions of senior managers deliberately exclude or minimize the PR contribution owing to preoccupations with status rivalries between differing occupations and a desire to retain power and authority.

How can PR be our eyes and ears?

PR people get about; they talk with a lot of others, inside and out. They are skilled listeners, or should be, and they move up and down through the organizational hierarchy and side to side, across its boundaries. They aim to hear what folks are thinking. Outside the organization, they make plenty of contacts, with, say, opinion leaders, journalists, customers, suppliers, parents and patients. They spend time with these publics, often sustaining an ambassadorial role for extended periods with people that in the normal course of events neither they nor anyone else in the organization would be that likely to meet, much less pass the time of day with.

Over and above that, PR people undertake formal research, either to secure statistically valid results or to gain insights for guidance. Surveys, using questionnaires, in-depth interviews, focus groups and quality circles are the most commonly used techniques, and much of the work is contracted to specialist researchers.

In addition to this primary data there is the secondary research that is gathered from the 'desk' rather than 'in the field'. PR people tend to do a lot of this, which is the usual starting point, because it identifies the gaps to be filled, with primary research that is either commissioned or undertaken discretely or is syndicated. Syndication describes research done as part of a larger exercise, as where questions are included in regular surveys, across a range of subjects that are conducted by research companies or in work being undertaken by another function, such as marketing, within the organization.

What's ethical about PR?

Trust is a precious asset, a lubricant of relationships. Lack of it can bring communications to a standstill, because organizations have to be perceived to be trustworthy if they are to turn their environments to their optimum advantage. Unfortunately, too many have, at least in part, forfeited the trust of others in recent years, and this is making life a lot harder for the rest. In consequence, a presumption of mistrust is widespread and is almost certainly damaging the economy, because it reduces levels of commercial activity and increases costs of communication.

> The aspirational character trait of the moment, for business and politics, is trustworthiness, according to Ann Treneman, writing in *The Times* (29 November 2002). 'Suddenly, they all want to be trusted – by us. This is because they have discovered that after Enron and WorldCom we no longer trust them (or their auditors). Nor, after the Roman Catholic Church abuse fiasco, do we feel kindly about big religion'. She recommends that in order to regain public trust first government and business must 'work out ways to acquire certain traits, such as openness, honesty, accountability and transparency'.

In addition to being trustworthy, organizations need to be viewed as responsible and soundly governed. It is the job of PR to communicate these values in an ethical manner consistent with them. In trying to see that this is done appropriately, the trade relies mainly on self-regulation, which emphasizes the ethical dimension, although enforcement is weak, compared with established professions and some other trades. However, PR practice is also influenced to varying degrees by a vast amount of statutes and regulations.

When should PR be used to generate interest in business ethics?

PR seeks credibility for its messages, and telling the truth, plain and unvarnished, can do more for credibility building than all the most carefully calculated selective truth telling. This is not to say that a) truth is absent from PR messages per se or that b) all PR messages are carefully prepared concoctions of deliberate deceit. However, there will be times when the PR function should be prepared to 'stand up and be counted', not because the PR people fancy martyrdom in a fanatical cause, but out of sound good sense.

It is axiomatic that if you want to be a good liar you need at least as good a memory. Some organizations' managers would do well to heed this. PR can be used to tell highly selective truths, and probably succeed at that many times over, but what about the 'credibility thing'? Telling the truth when it is uncomfortable to do so can win a lot of understanding, goodwill and credibility. Trying to avoid the truth with weasel words or silence can have a damaging effect on image and reputation. This truism should not have to be the subject of managerial histrionics, outstanding bravery by the PR people, intense emergency debate or the destruction of careers; it should be part of the corporate culture, 'the way we do things around here'.

PR may also routinely generate interest in business ethics, when it raises questions about the use of reasoned persuasion, correct identification of information sources, explanation of accuracy factors in data, emotional appeals and influences and comment dressed up as reportage. Internally, it can act as a respected check on corporate enthusiasms or a critic of mendacious intentions. Externally, it can seek to promote genuine public debate, invite comment and criticism, foster participation, take a lead and thereby 'raise its game' among its publics. This is not heroism, but practicality.

> According to Shoshana Zuboff, a Harvard professor, and James Maxmin, former boss of Volvo-UK and of Laura Ashley, 57 per cent of people in the United States say they do not trust corporate executives or brokers to give them honest information. In *The Support Economy* (2003), they also report that two-thirds of people in the United Kingdom say they do not have faith in corporations, whereas 30 years ago two-thirds said they did. There has also been a simultaneous erosion of trust in doctors and teachers.

What is a 'positioning statement'?

A statement that says, succinctly, the organization's purpose, function, aims and aspirations, so that the reader can understand, quickly and easily, just exactly what it is all about. The position that is spelled out in this neat way provides a central point of reference for management and a strategic tool for the PR, which has to be wholly consistent with it. Positioning statements are quick to read but can take plenty of time to compose. They should be model examples of how to write with absolute precision and economy.

Should we have a formal PR strategy?

Yes, if the alternative is informality. In this respect it should stand favourable comparison with all other functional strategies within the organization, not scribbled on the back of an envelope, or expressed so vaguely that it is capable of misinterpretation. Sadly, much PR appears to be lacking in any strategic backbone, often because it is reactive rather than proactive.

Would we be better off with general aims and clear, firm objectives for our PR and keep the strategy simple?

Formality is preferable, because informality risks insufficient focus and clarity. That does not imply rigidity, just plenty of active maintenance and being prepared to review whenever necessary to anticipate and meet changing requirements and circumstances. There is no obvious correlation between simplicity and complexity. That is to say, for example, a micro business with a handful of people nevertheless might need a fairly complex PR strategy.

Could we have a PR strategy without a formal business plan?

Yes, provided the vision, mission and objectives were clear. Some smaller organizations prefer to decide on a PR strategy as a preliminary to detailed business planning, because the work necessary to do this generates much of the thinking necessary for later. Companies may decide to take this approach with marketing, but of course that is solely concerned with customers.

Would a PR strategy provide the basis for developing a business plan?

The PR strategy could be a major resource, because it is based on a specific positioning for the organization and that is the result of research and analyses, taking into account all of the currently identified publics.

Are there different types of PR strategy?

There are four types of PR strategy:

- creative, to develop image and reputation;
- expansive, to increase competitive advantage and performance;
- adaptive, to embrace change and extract value;
- defensive, to counter inaccuracies and hostility.

How could we structure a PR strategy?

Here are the basic stages:

1. vision and mission: knowing what these are;
2. internal evaluation, to profile competencies and capabilities;
3. external scanning, of the whole operational environment;
4. competitors: depth analysis of all available intelligence;
5. opportunities: identified through comparison of internal and external data;
6. options, being opportunities that satisfy the vision and mission;
7. long-term objective, compatible with selected options;
8. strategy needed to fulfil the selected options;
9. short-term objectives, to specify measurable achievement;
10. short-term substrategies, in support of the strategy.

Thereafter attention turns to the detailed planning of programmes, deciding about resources, tasks, people, technologies, structures and timescales, measurement and evaluation.

What are *strategic* communications?

Communication that is intelligent, intelligible, consistent, relevant and reflective of sound policies and procedures.

Should PR take its strategy lead from the marketing strategy?

Yes, when it is working in support of marketing, but this supposes that marketing public relations (MPR) is the sole dimension of the organization's PR. True, if you look at all PR activity the signs are that most of it is in support of marketing, but there are many more publics, other than those comprising customers; those also require attention. One last point: the marketing strategy is likely to be a major consideration in framing PR strategy for a marketing-led company.

Would the PR benefit from having its own strategy that then links in with marketing, sales and other functions?

Yes, most certainly, particularly owing to the boundary-spanning nature of PR.

Could we have more than one strategy at the same time?

The PR strategy informs the substrategies that are based on the objectives for each public and determines the communications requirements, with a view to achieving total integration and consistency throughout. This requirement for integration means that there has to be a single, central strategy, which is then interpreted with high specificity, in a cascade effect.

How much flexibility should we aim for in our PR?

Plenty: time and again PR delivers best when it is thinking ahead and worst when it is 'bringing up the rear'. The first often throws up cost benefits too, whereas the second invariably adds costs.

Isn't PR really all about tactics?

The tactics are critical to the outcomes, but they have to be based on strategy and planning. Otherwise they risk becoming driven by passing opportunism, without direction, sending out contradictory messages and breaking the fundamental PR practice rule of total integration.

The impression given to observers that PR is all tactics and not much else is understandable. Much of the communications content looks decidedly tactics-driven, and PR people mostly run around each day in exuberant preoccupation with the minutiae of the minute.

They call this being a 'self-starter', which might imply action over thought but that is far from the truth. In this respect they are similar to sales people, and deserve to be admired for their energetic daily self-renewal, always keeping at it, whatever 'it' happens to be at that moment.

Do PR people really know the difference between strategy and tactics?

This is a popular question, or is it a vocalized doubt? Rather too often, it seems, the perception is given that they do not. Many PR people who should know better manage to give a fair impression that they would not be able to recognize a strategy if it hit them, and quite a few seem to not much care either. This has to change, for the trade's sake, and probably will.

But could we be more effective with PR tactics alone?

Depends on what is meant by 'alone'. PR supports and complements other activities, notably marketing, but PR tactics can carry an organization a long way forwards. Witness the way toiletries retailer The Body Shop grew so successfully in its early years, when it relied heavily on low-cost PR, an achievement that financial journalists commented on when it went public. Companies find that PR lends itself more to some situations than others and there are plenty of 'horses for courses' decisions to be taken.

Should we rely on tactics to give us the flexibility to exploit changing conditions?

The tactics are framed to take full account of current circumstances, based on the strategy. Knowing when to change a tactic and having a viable alternative is a key aspect. For example, the general who fears his men are outnumbered and out-equipped by the enemy hesitates to engage directly, although that was his intention, usually preferring instead to find a way of drawing fire more on his terms, perhaps through use of guerrilla tactics. Translating this into PR, maybe, for example, the organization that is being denied 'share of shout' in key trade press by its larger competitors decides to launch an all-out push for coverage when the journalists' heroes are off on holiday or otherwise distracted from maintaining their usual dominance of the newsprint.

Do we need an action plan?

For PR, yes, most certainly you do need a plan of action. PR is a structured, purposeful activity that has to be carefully planned, with designated actions and who is responsible for what. Charging in on a sudden fit of enthusiasm is ill advised.

Why try to plan what must remain flexible, responsive and creative?

True, trying to deal with unstable environments is tricky and calls for plenty of fresh thinking and prompt action. This makes planning very difficult. Nevertheless planning there has to be, of a different order, because how the organization sees its world may have to change quickly. What is needed, therefore, is planning that combines both the 'traditional' and 'extraordinary' approaches.

The first is based on a number of certainties and assumptions, relatively settled conditions and gradual change, which provides the planning bedrock, while the second creates the degree of flexibility and scope for innovation needed to cope with turbulence. PR operates both within the conventional hierarchical structures and in the informal groups that form and re-form in order to address change. It works with the 'givens' and at the same time asks a lot of 'What if… ?' questions.

PR people are not always given sufficient scope to anticipate, monitor and exploit change to full advantage. After all, this can be a scary activity and not wildly attractive to organizations that can fondly recall when they sailed in calmer waters, so the PR function may be required to approach dealing with change within a fairly timid, restrictive regime. Sometimes changing senior managers can be more appealing than giving turbulence its due. Creating an innovative culture can be very challenging indeed.

What plans should we make to protect our reputation?

When concerns arise about corporate reputation it is usual to start by re-examining internal policies and procedures, wherein valuable clues may be found for what is wrong, or simply not good enough. For instance, a company that has a reputation for being inefficient, or non-competitive, or apparently not very keen to chase new business, may have a tendering process that handles all enquiries on a 'first come, first served' basis that fails to prioritize in accordance with tendering deadlines or potential contract values. The intention to be 'fair' is resulting in missed deadlines and giving wrong impressions.

Could journalists give us a few useful tips about reputation?

Probably, but to what extent their comments were valid would need to be taken fully into account. The nature of their work tends to encourage gossip and hearsay.

What is issues management and could PR help us to advance an important issue?

Issues management is about identifying a growing concern, when it may be no more than a small black cloud on the distant horizon, perhaps some interest of literally a handful of people to start with, that is gathering support and developing its own momentum. It also involves analysis, really understanding what is 'the issue', setting priorities for how to address it, considering the options, developing and conducting a programme and assessing the results.

Issues have a way of flaring up unexpectedly, but some can take a long time in gestation and be difficult to detect. What makes an issue is variable, and can be complex, often the result of socio-economic factors. Knowing what is a trend and what is a passing fad is valuable to their detection and analysis. The key point is that issues should be handled proactively, and not reactively. Unfortunately, neglected or untraced issues can develop into crises. Just as many external issues are fostered as a result of PR, so too the organization can use PR to develop an issue that is *its* concern.

What does being 'on message' really mean outside politics?

There has to be consistency in all messages. This is not to say that everything said and done in the name of PR has to be identical or even similar, but it does require that there are no contradictions. The term 'on message' was coined to describe this, when Labour politicians in the United Kingdom embarked on training to make sure that all their pronouncements were consistent with current policy, a process that was greatly aided by the fortuitous and timely invention of text messaging. The scale of risk of inconsistency is likely to be greater in politics, but the on message rule applies outside as well.

How do we go about planning for a crisis?

Firstly, you need to have some idea of what risks you are taking. For instance, if your office is down the street from a government building, is there a risk of a terrorist bomb blowing out your windows? If you have confidential documents stored, what chance is there the nearby river that flooded the town in 2000 will do it again? If you rely heavily on computer systems, what damage could a recreational hacker inflict in an evening?

Secondly, what would such a crisis, in each scenario, involve in communications terms? For instance, what if part of the building is alight, the cars are all inaccessible in the car park, the power supply to essential equipment is withdrawn and the last call you received before all the telephones failed was from a blackmailer to mention that there is glass in your food products? How would you communicate and with whom?

Thirdly, you then need to develop a plan, within which there are clearly stated procedures designed to cope with each realistic possibility. This is more than just knowing where the staff would assemble in the car park. Ideally, nothing should be left to chance. It involves anticipating disaster striking at night as well as during the working day, at the weekend maybe, when everyone is on a public holiday, when all the senior managers are attending the annual general meeting, and so on. It needs to be robust, capable of being tested to destruct.

Lastly, and by no means least, you need to train the people who will be implementing the communications plan and to rehearse them in what is needed. This includes senior managers who are designated to act as spokespersons, as well as the people who run with the messages, not an enviable task, because the news may be bad and the risk of panic may be real. This is the part that many organizations become a bit squeamish about. They think they know what would happen, but they do not care too much to enact it. Better, though, to go through the pain of preparation and emerge more confident than to try not to think about it.

What does PR contribute to crisis management?

PR aims to make sure that an issue does not become a crisis and that there is a positive attitude to dealing with crises. Often issues management and crisis management are thought of as being one and the same, because each shares a number of features. What can be said with a degree of certainty is that the first usually allows time enough for some measured evaluation and planning, the second seldom does. There are three main aspects to crisis management:

1. The PR has to communicate positively the organization's credentials for not deserving a crisis.
2. Potential crises have to be identified and avoided if at all possible.
3. There has to be detailed planning for handling all types of possible crises.

These three dovetail with each other. PR has a big hand in the second and third, as well as the first, because of its environmental scanning and the vital part played by communication in any crisis.

What should we look out for in trying to avoid crises?

Aim to avoid:

- anyone who says that there will never be one;
- anyone who says crises are strictly for the others, not for us; and
- anyone who says planning for a crisis is a waste of time anyway.

All these people may be perfectly well intentioned, personable and 'drenched' in their certainty, and their contributions are always appreciated, as a matter of course.

What makes a 'good' crisis?

Nothing, of course, makes a crisis 'good', but the PR people can win new laurels surprisingly quickly if they show firm leadership, calm and all that when all about them are 'losing their heads', particularly if that includes the chairperson and/or chief executive or managing director. The kernel of the job is to explain, plain and simple:

- what happened;

- what is being done about it; and
- the organization's concern and understanding.

No gush, or synthetic tears, are called for, just unadorned, straight communication.

> Probably the best recent example of straight communication in the eye of media interest was when the then Mayor of New York, Rudolph Giuliani, addressed the media several times during 11 September 2001, when the World Trade Center was destroyed. He is said to have displayed extraordinary qualities of leadership at that time. Later the UK government awarded him an honorary knighthood for his services to the British deceased and to Britons resident in New York. He is reported to have jokingly instructed His Royal Highness The Duke of York, during a visit to see him: 'Don't call me Sir Rudy'.

It is also important to get the priorities right. In a crisis the financial implications should come last, after people, environment, property, disruption to services, wider consequences and so on.

Depending upon the nature of the crisis, it can be a great help to be able to call upon a few sympathizers who are prepared to say some words in support, for, although an organization and not an individual person may be at the centre of the storm, it is remarkable how lonely a crisis can be and how quickly people form impressions if they see that. What the public in general, and publics in particular, may be thinking always needs to be kept much in mind.

Again, last but not least, the job involves making sure the employees, and if necessary their families, are kept fully in the picture and do not feel neglected. Crises offer ample opportunity for bonding or disaffecting employees, who may be concerned and involved in numerous ways, from simple inconvenience to serious injury, or worse. It is at such times that each and every employee has the potential to be an ambassador, or not.

What can go wrong?

There are a number of problems that can arise on the spot, including:

- mass panic, making nonsense of the best-laid plans;
- too many people wanting to be spokespersons, for whatever reason;

- wanting to run away from media enquiries;
- getting angry with the intrusiveness of the media;
- speculation about causes to satisfy media demands or personal motives;
- underestimating the genuine level of public interest;
- not being prepared to ask for help;
- not listening to friends who want to help;
- allowing the lawyers to dictate how to deal with the problem;
- giving the impression of 'making a meal of it' for gain.

If anything blows up we have the internal systems to cope, so why PR?

If the systems exclude PR presumably the situation is one in which communication will not play any part in handling a crisis, but that seems unlikely.

five

look at **us**

- Does publicity have any serious purpose?
- Do publicity stunts have any value?
- Do the media respond to publicity?
- Are the media interested in all sorts of events?
- Is publicity worthwhile without media interest?
- What do professional publicists do?
- Isn't publicity an old-fashioned concept?
- Should business avoid seeking publicity?
- What part do gimmicks play in publicity?
- Is PR a smarter name for publicity?
- We have done well enough without publicity, so why seek it now?
- Isn't publicity used to conceal shallow performance?
- How long does the benefit of publicity last?
- So publicity can be a two-edged sword?
- Does successful publicity depend upon celebrity endorsement?
- Isn't publicity a blunt instrument for increasing sales?
- What happens when publicity goes horribly wrong?
- Can counter-publicity help to deflect the damage?
- Is there any danger in believing your own publicity?
- What if our publicity unintentionally bears an uncanny resemblance to someone else's recent effort?
- Surely everything we do by way of promotion is publicity?
- Can any competent manager handle publicity?
- Have charities reached the point of diminishing returns on their publicity?

- Why should we graduate from publicity to PR?
- Is publicity correctly even part of PR?
- Is publicity an unnecessary expense for a public sector organization?
- Is all publicity good publicity?

A lot of people think publicity is another name for PR, and vice versa, including some leading marketing authorities. Some publicists call themselves image-makers, others simply agents. The role of publicity is explored in this chapter, to untangle the confusions, identify publicity correctly and explain how it can fit within the overall PR framework. Some popular apprehensions about publicity are explored: for instance, that it is a 'two-edged sword', lacks serious purpose, is old-fashioned, entirely about celebrity, an artful distraction, overdone in the voluntary sector and not suitable for the public sector.

Does publicity have any serious purpose?

Publicity is intended to draw attention and create awareness by any means that is both credible and relevant. Whatever the activity or nature of the publicity, it must not detract from the underlying purpose of the message. Amateur publicists frequently congratulate themselves on achieving publicity that is neither credible nor relevant. Often what appears to be successful, on the face of it, lacks one or other essential ingredient. This is because publicity can be relatively simple and inexpensive to obtain if it is sensationalist. A sound use of publicity is consistent when it is anchored within a PR programme; then there should be no risk of sending out contradictory messages.

Do publicity stunts have any value?

Contrived events that interrupt the normal flow of life are a major method of securing publicity. They are well worth the time and effort provided they convey a message that is easily understandable and are obviously connected to an overall publicity purpose. When that connection is clear, stunts can be very effective and even admired, for their ingenuity and creativity.

Some pressure and cause-related groups are adept at using stunts and they have been well rewarded with media interest, on which many a stunt depends heavily for success, and resulting increased public support. Often what they want to publicize lends itself to visual interpretation, which is a key factor in conceiving most stunts.

Problems can occur through over use of stunts, because what looks like a 'stunt dependency' can damage image. An occasional stunt should create awareness and receptiveness to further communication, but successive stunts can begin to progressively lose their impact and value.

Do the media respond to publicity?

You bet they do, so much so that they hunt daily for publicity and publicity proposals, often with a particular set of requirements. In other words, the media are in the 'publicity business'. They calculate that most publicity has news value, as they see it. This, of course, can result in some contradictory interpretations of what is deserving of coverage and what is not. Publicity provides valuable sources for journalists, who sort the wheat from the chaff according to their needs.

Are the media interested in all sorts of events?

There are many reasons why some events fail to attract media interest. For instance, they may be considered dull and worthy, irrelevant, ill timed or 'just not us'. A typical example is where local civic dignitaries, officials and hired celebrities attend a ceremony and reception to open the company's new office building. The local newspaper sends a photographer to collect a quick captioned pic because all famous visitors qualify for this treatment fairly automatically. The trade newspaper does not attend, because new offices blocks are '10 a penny' and the stars of the show are irrelevant to its interests.

Hours afterwards the regional television interviews one of the hired celebrities, quite forgetting to mention the company or the event, and a whole month later the trade paper runs an interview with the chief executive, pegged to, or based on, the opening, about the company's expansion plans. The lesson learned from this is that perceptions of credibility and relevance can vary greatly between different types of media and between each news outlet.

Is publicity worthwhile without media interest?

Any attempt to obtain publicity that will rely solely on media reporting for its success should be thought about very hard indeed. In many cases publicity is directed at a particular person or group, so the public in question is small and clearly defined. Then the message can be delivered without an intermediary.

> A protest at the site of a proposed building to which there are local residents' objections, held to precede or coincide with the local council's planning committee site inspection, may be directed at only a handful of people, who are members of that committee. Press reporting of the demonstration is nice to have, but the message can be delivered very effectively and efficiently without it.

However, when the aim is to create wider awareness among a much larger public, or publics, the involvement of the media becomes that much more important, because of the extra reach and credibility provided.

> A demonstration outside the embassy of a country to which there are objections relating to human rights may be noticed by a couple of staff inside and a few passers by, but otherwise may go unremarked. If the demonstration appears but fleetingly on television with about 10 words of explanation its impact has multiplied many thousandfold. The difference was made by a brief media visit that probably lasted no more than 20 minutes, just long enough to obtain sufficient time for a brief item with presenter commentary; transformation was secured.

What do professional publicists do?

Professional publicists specialize for a living in promoting the careers and causes of 'celebrities', people whose career prospects substantially depend upon continually being famous. Much of their efforts are directed at communicating with large publics via the media, which invented celebrity in its modern form.

This celebrity culture is a highly specialized field, sometimes described as being a particular subset of PR. The fame is highly worked at, many of the celebrities being famous simply for being famous. They are manufactured in seemingly never-ending succession, drawn largely from entertainment, politics, sport and the arts. They come also from academia, the sciences, catering, fashion and just about anywhere that produces people wanting to appear, by some means or other, in the highly illustrated pages of consumer and glossier business magazines.

A welter of events and 'insights' has to be contrived to provide the platform for fame. The work bears closer similarity to theatrical and literary agency than PR and much of what appears in the media is the result of commercial negotiation.

The doyen of the trade in the United Kingdom is Max Clifford, a self-described image-maker, who provokes a rich variety of descriptions, both insulting and flattering. He comments frequently in public as an expert witness of the publicity process and is credited with 'one of the most famous headlines of all time', 'Freddie Starr Ate My Hamster', which provides a fair indication of his work.

Isn't publicity an old-fashioned concept?

The attempt to draw attention for commercial advantage began in the United States in the 1860s, so it is long established. Yes, it is beginning to look old-fashioned, but the people who specialize in it for a living demonstrate that they can keep reinventing it to the amusement of many and the considerable gain of their clients.

There is a little black cloud on the horizon, however. This intense outburst of celebrity culture may be heading into decline. The major newspapers were primarily responsible for its current incarnation, but there are signs that public appetite is waning from over-sufficiency. One UK title, *The Mirror*, claims to have turned its back on celebs and their 'café society' antics, wanting instead to be taken more seriously again by newspaper purchasers, presumably because there is more commercial value in this.

The problem for many such publications is that there are basic confusions created by the contradictions inherent in trying to combine entertainment passed off as news with serious reportage of 'real news', something more akin to orthodox journalism, and editorial comment on current topics. The new *Daily Express* description of itself as a picture newspaper may indicate a way out of this dilemma for editors and provide a portent of the future, in which popular daily papers will be largely visual, probably more akin to the weekly news magazines that are so popular throughout much of the world.

Another interesting trend is towards newspapers being sued by the celebrities, who want as much publicity as possible but strictly on their terms. They protest about invasion of their privacy when it has not been negotiated for and purchased, and they appear to be meeting with some success.

In the well-reported case of Hollywood stars Michael Douglas and Catherine Zeta-Jones, the couple sold an exclusive right by one British magazine, called *OK*!, to photograph their wedding in a New York hotel in 2000. 'Realizing that the demand for photographs of the ceremony would greatly increase if no unauthorized ones were available', according to celebrity lawyer Keith Schilling, writing in *The Guardian* (14 April 2003), they 'allowed *OK!* to publish selected pictures'. In the event a rival title, *Hello!*, also took and published photographs, without prior agreement. The UK's High Court supported the actors' claim for breach of confidential information over any public 'right to know' and freedom of expression, thereby strengthening the right of the individual to privacy.

From publicity there have developed other marketing communications that may make some publicity efforts look decidedly transparent and unsubtle, but this does little to detract from the continuing value of well-planned and executed publicity.

Should business avoid seeking publicity?

Most times the decision to seek publicity is optional. If the purpose then is carefully considered and the outcomes are plainly stated, it can make a valuable contribution, provided, as always, that it is credible and relevant. Sometimes, of course, making known is absolutely required on legal or public policy grounds.

Exactly what can be classified as publicity for an organization may present some confusions. For example, it may look more like corporate hospitality, not publicity as such, in the sense of there being some event or action solely designed to draw attention for advantage.

Take that old favourite that features in many a company calendar, the annual Golf Day. This is for customers and contacts who are probably very well known to the hosts and vice versa, but that does not exclude the possibility of using the event to publicize some of the company's activities or interests to the audience formed by the guests, maybe in a speech or ceremony over lunch. Then the publicity is but a small element, with the event providing its platform.

What part do gimmicks play in publicity?

As little as possible, since 'gimmick' is a derogatory term used to describe activities that are thought to be insubstantial, inconsequential or simply trivial. Sometimes, surprisingly, the very people who hand them out often describe promotional gifts as gimmicks. In reality these (usually) low value tokens can play a useful part in raising awareness and aiding recall. Gimmicks are best avoided.

Is PR a smarter name for publicity?

No, although PR is often referred to as being publicity, even by leading marketing authorities who should know better. PR is about striving to achieve and improve two-way communication, whereas publicity seems to be mainly about one-way communication, not seeking any kind of dialogue or exchange much beyond awareness and recognition.

We have done well enough without publicity, so why seek it now?

Publicity, as such, is neither necessary nor desirable for every organization, even in these highly competitive times. There are, for instance, some businesses that have no obvious need to deliberately seek publicity, because they enjoy sound existing trading relationships and they are communicating effectively with all of their publics anyway.

Isn't publicity used to conceal shallow performance?

It is no substitute for performance, but certainly there are occasions when publicity is sought by way of distraction, maybe to gain more time or reposition, rather like the military commander who seeks the means to re-form the troops. Probably the question is fair comment about some organizations, however, particularly those that appear to have something of an advanced addiction for publicity.

How long does the benefit of publicity last?

This seems to be entirely dependent upon the quality of the publicity. Some publicity is forgotten within the week, while some is remembered for years, usually because it was particularly well received or memorably notorious.

> There was a time, in 1993, when the UK (Conservative) government repeatedly told journalists that public disapproval of what it did was of no consequence because people forgot everything they read and heard about within a week. At the following election, in 1997, the Conservatives suffered their greatest election defeat ever, since 1832. Still, according to subsequent polls and opinion research, the vast majority of UK voters have not forgotten what they were expected to forget within a week.

So publicity can be a two-edged sword?

Publicity is designed primarily to draw attention and create awareness. It yields an impression that can be favourable or unfavourable. It can be viewed as being a *result*, the consequence of some contrived occurrence or of some information becoming known, and this may be controllable or uncontrollable. Not all publicity, therefore, is sought, but escapes, perhaps through an indiscretion or leak.

Does successful publicity depend upon celebrity endorsement?

No, but having a celebrity involved certainly can help. Then, though, there has to be an alignment of the image and reputation of the celebrity used with that of the organization and the circumstances. A mismatch could prove to be less than beneficial, and expensive as well. Surprisingly, this mistake occurs remarkably frequently.

When prominent UK television presenter Anthea Turner remarried in August 2000, the bride and groom sold their 'wedding rights' to a magazine that published a picture of them at their reception eating Cadbury's Snowflake chocolate bars, which were being given away to its readers in a sales promotion. According to the *Daily Mail* (23 January 2003), 'the couple were ridiculed for the tacky stunt in an affair jokingly dubbed "Flakegate"'.

Isn't publicity a blunt instrument for increasing sales?

To the extent that publicity lacks precision in its message, content and direction, it certainly is a blunt instrument for generating sales. That does not prevent many charities using it to raise donations in volume, and well-produced publicity has done much for many brands.

What happens when publicity goes horribly wrong?

A hard lesson has to be learned, quickly followed by the realization that publicity deserves to be taken seriously. Relying on memories to fade is inadequate; some substantial remedial work may be necessary to hasten a cure. Usually this needs to be prompt, as where attending to a genuine grievance can largely neutralize the damage. 'Horribly wrong' may imply personal injuries, but could apply just as well to grievous injuries inflicted on image and/or reputation.

Can counter-publicity help to deflect the damage?

It is almost always worth the effort to correct damage done by earlier publicity, most particularly if there are material facts now to hand that were not available before or there are people who are now willing and able to come forward. The main aim is to avoid giving the impression of a fumbled attempt to correct an earlier impression, because that may simply serve to refresh and reinforce memories. It may also imply dismissal of critical judgements as being worthless, suggesting a bad dose of corporate arrogance.

Counter-publicity in reaction against a competitor can be very effective. No company wants to be a forgotten also-ran or 'me too' that was never given any thought. In corporate acquisitions and mergers, a particularly effective response to a hostile attack might be provided through use of publicity.

Is there any danger in believing your own publicity?

Not if your publicity is credible and relevant. This question implies that the publicity has created a false and deliberately misleading representation of the organization that in time will come to be accepted as being truthful by its creators. Such self-delusion may be harmless enough, or it may prove a hindrance, say in understanding realistic capacities and competencies.

The expression 'believing your own publicity' originated as a reference to Hollywood film actors, who held powerful sway over the collective public imagination through carefully cultivated images. Some still do, to a lesser extent. Apparently, as their careers matured, some, and maybe all, of the earlier stars gave the impression that they thought rather better of themselves than did their adoring fans.

What if our publicity unintentionally bears an uncanny resemblance to someone else's recent effort?

This is a perennial problem. There is, usually, no copyright in ideas, and successful publicity relies on creative interpretation. Similarities do arise, and are therefore a risk of trade. Probably the only solution is to aim for greater creativity, which is easier said than done. Indeed, creativity is a cornerstone of publicity, and PR work more generally, and it seems to be absurdly underrated. There are very few 'big ideas' in this life – for instance, there are said to be only nine basic literary plots – and therefore the effort lies in the interpretation of the idea to the exact circumstances for which it is intended.

Publicity can fail owing to extraordinary coincidence, as when, for example, the UK press heavily covered, as a photo story, a new collapsible lightweight German bicycle making its appearance at a big London exhibition, suggesting an economical alternative to motoring during a current fuel crisis. Just that same day Senator

Edward Kennedy's disabled son was photographed by the US press bicycling around Central Park, New York. As far as the British press was concerned, the almost identical story in the United States won out over the UK one: the combination of fame and the human factor was universally judged to be of stronger interest than sensible but boring alternative cheap travel to work.

Surely everything we do by way of promotion is publicity?

This is using 'promotion' and 'publicity' very broadly. Certainly all 'making known' is publicity in the broadest meaning, but not, of course, in the context of publicity being a function of PR.

Can any competent manager handle publicity?

Probably not, unless his or her competence is relevant. Sometimes managers find themselves 'dragged into', as they see it, a publicity effort, perhaps because it touches, maybe only lightly, on their function, or there are simply not enough available people needed to implement it. Then often misery prevails and they dearly wish they had not had anything to do with it. Publicity work is really best left to those who have the relevant skills, whether within the PR function or outside it.

Have charities reached the point of diminishing returns on their publicity?

It may seem so at times, particularly after a hot and hectic summer weekend, not being much noticed at yet another crowded country show in some unshaded field. In reality, charities thrive on publicity and some folk in the media – among them journalists, producers, editors and commercial people – are extraordinarily cooperative. Given the ferocious competition among the charities, there appears to be little practical alternative to sticking at it.

Some are blessed with ample scope for developing interesting and attractive publicity, owing to the nature of their interests and activities. Some may be tempted, more out of desperation than calculation, into frenetic and haphazard efforts that smack of poor direction and purpose. Then, sadly, the point of diminishing returns is indeed likely to be within sight. Apart from bonding the volunteers, such publicity is of little value; the charities that have drifted in these directions usually know this very well.

Why should we graduate from publicity to PR?

Publicity is not in some way inferior to PR, but part of it. True, the further dimensions of PR may seem a bit daunting if simple publicity has been relied on to date, but to think in terms of graduation, or stepping up, can be misleading.

Is publicity correctly even part of PR?

Yes, and its development over the years has been chronicled as being one of the main strands of PR, described as 'press agentry'.

Is publicity an unnecessary expense for a public sector organization?

The criteria for deciding when publicity is needed are likely to differ from those of either the private or not-for-profit sectors. Well-conceived and implemented publicity, which is proactive and not reactive to outside pressures, can be a powerful tool. The emphasis lies in doing it well. There is seldom a shortage of volunteers, particularly if the project has the right feel to it, and the very fact that it often has to be done economically only serves to emphasize the need for careful attention to detail.

Is all publicity good publicity?

Publicity as such is not always good, regardless of its content. True, not having been heard of by your publics is damning; then sometimes even notoriety may seem preferable. Indeed, in some carefully defined circumstances a bit of bad publicity can work wonders, for example, in popular music or 'alternative' entertainment. But the list of commercial activities where this applies is short indeed. The general rule is: in almost all situations bad publicity is just that, bad, and best avoided.

Those organizations that think 'So what?' have an uncanny tendency to suffer unwanted consequences, often when they initially suppose that they can ride out the bad publicity and emerge unscathed. There seems to be a belief among some that they can face down everyone, presumably relying on the 'in your face' cult, but some customers, shareholders and others are telling these organizations that they think otherwise.

six

getting on with the **relations**

- Why do marketing and PR people see things differently?
- All PR is *really* marketing by another name, isn't it?
- What is 'marketing public relations'?
- When is marketing part of PR?
- Why don't marketing and PR people 'speak the same language'?
- Why should marketing take PR seriously?
- Why do so many marketing people despise PR people?
- Why do PR people generally live in awe of marketing people?
- What might PR do better than marketing?
- Would you agree that brands are far too valuable to be put at risk with PR?
- What can PR contribute to the development of the marketing plan?
- How does environmental scanning differ from what marketing does anyway?
- What does PR contribute to customer feedback?
- What is the difference between market and marketing communications?
- What are 'mediated marketplace communications'?
- What is viral marketing?
- What is integrated marketing communications?
- What is the difference between market research and marketing research?

- What is the difference between a PR manager, a marketing manager and a marketing communications manager?
- Should anyone doing PR have had experience of writing marketing plans?
- Is PR cheaper than advertising?
- Why does advertising always have the larger allocations and PR is the poor relation?
- Is PR the clever joined-up writing and advertising just the 'eye candy'?
- Is PR the froth and marketing the serious stuff?

The relations here are in marketing. In this chapter the questions explore the relationship between PR and marketing, to identify the potential synergies and practical contributions that PR can make to marketing. How use of PR's 'eyes and ears' can provide market insights to benefit marketing planning, how PR's generation of mutual understanding between an organization and its publics can benefit marketing communications.

There are some direct enquiries about all aspects of the relationship, and questions about important topics such as integrated marketing communications, viral marketing and advertising in relation to PR, as well as confusions about whether PR is really marketing or separate from it, when might marketing be part of PR and what is the difference between market and marketing communication.

Why do marketing and PR people see things differently?

- Marketing is solely concerned with customers, whereas PR is about creating the most favourable overall conditions for the organization.
- The first is highly focused on delivering sales, while the second scans the entire operational environment.
- The first aims to identify, anticipate and satisfy its customers' requirements profitably, whereas the second embraces all communications designed to best serve the organization's interests.
- The first directs its energies towards external markets, the second works both outside and inside the organization.

All PR is *really* marketing by another name, isn't it?

No, although it may seem like it at times, particularly when marketing people claim PR as their own. Within the context of marketing, PR is one of the main marketing communications tools used by marketers under their umbrella term of Promotion; the others are direct sales (sometimes referred to as 'the sales force'), advertising, direct marketing (often called 'direct mail', which is a major component) and sales promotion. Marketers speak about 'communications' when referring to any and all of these, and sometimes they also identify elements as being other, discrete tools under Promotion.

What is 'marketing public relations'?

This describes PR when it is part of Promotion within the marketing mix, aimed at fulfilling marketing objectives, as against PR relating to, say, finance or HRM. However, PR also has a keen interest in and may be involved with other aspects of the marketing mix as well: particularly in Physical evidence (corporate identity), People (customer-contacting employees) and Process (service production and delivery). The remaining 'seven Ps' are Product (or service), Price and Place (distribution).

When is marketing part of PR?

Many PR people employed in public sector and not-for-profit organizations, such as colleges, schools, hospitals and clinics, government agencies and local authorities, are engaged in 'social marketing' designed to foster or change social behaviours. These are identified as being either desirable on grounds of public policy, or anti-social and likely to have undesirable consequences, which may be personal to the individual and/or of wider significance, perhaps extending to the future provision of social services. For example, marketing campaigns are mounted to encourage parenting, school attendance, personal hygiene and safe food preparation or to discourage cigarette smoking, alcohol abuse, drug abuse and unsafe sex. PR people engaged on social marketing may be expected to have some additional formal marketing expertise and/or qualification.

Why don't marketing and PR people 'speak the same language'?

Often they do, but the differences between each trade are reflected in their use of language. There is also a degree of competitive rivalry involved. For instance, whenever budgets are due to be pruned, the tendency has been to start with the PR and save marketing costs for later. PR people have argued tirelessly that what they do is cheaper and can be more effective, so PR deserves more, rather than less, expenditure at such times. With PR gaining in recognition, this is an argument that is being heeded more, resulting in economies in, say, advertising, instead. This rivalry can be expressed in claims for the supremacy of one over the other. Marketing people talk about the 'marketing concept' to describe orientation of all company activities towards the customer and claim that any function that has a connection with customers should be viewed as being part of the marketing function. PR people talk about a 'PR culture' that prizes the tenets of good PR practice and infuses the attitudes and behaviours of everyone within the organization, regardless of function.

Why should marketing take PR seriously?

There are many important publics, in addition to customers and potential customers, which can impact very seriously indeed on performance. The task of communicating with these lies not with marketing but with PR. Further, MPR supports marketing in many powerful ways. These include:

- educating markets ahead of marketing activities;
- maintaining and strengthening brand loyalties;
- generating direct sales leads;
- identifying and evaluating potential markets;
- motivating the sales force and distribution chain;
- reviving and sustaining mature and declining products.

In this and other ways, PR has the happy ability to secure more return for existing marketing budgets, a key point that accounts significantly for MPR growth.

Why do so many marketing people despise PR people?

Marketing people have been taught in the past that PR is a relatively humble technician's task, lacking intellectual rigour and incapable of measurement and evaluation. In short, they have been taught to be highly dismissive. Criticisms have tended to be in the way of sweeping generalizations, without much specificity. However, some of the more extreme examples met with formal censure by teaching authorities.

Lately there has been a significant turnaround. In the past decade, as marketing has intensified its efforts of persuasion, PR has been embraced as a marketing communication, and detailed aspects of PR practice are taught as part of marketing. As a result, newer marketing people are rather more respectful of PR and some appear to see little difference between marketing and PR.

This is reflected in the educational materials, where some marketing courses could read just as well as PR training. It is estimated that upwards of three-quarters of all PR practice is now undertaken in support of marketing and presumably the traditionally hostile attitudes of marketing people towards PR will cease over time.

Why do PR people generally live in awe of marketing people?

The historic hostility of marketing towards PR was responsible for much of this. PR people knew that they handled much smaller budgets and had much greater difficulty in explaining and justifying what they did. They knew that there was a substantial and growing body of research relating to marketing but precious little comparable work being done in PR. They found the criticisms often stuck and they had no ready means of countering.

Now the awe has largely subsided, although it still lurks in the collective subconscious of PR people. They are employed in a burgeoning trade and they see the marketing people wanting their skills. The tides of opportunity that swept marketing to the fore have moved on and are now benefiting PR. Advertising, the marketing communication of first choice for many decades, is having to concede ground to PR. Sponsorship, which advertising tossed disdainfully at PR three decades ago as being not worth its bother, has become a major activity, so much so that it now often stands alone as a discrete function.

What might PR do better than marketing?

Firstly, there are those tasks that PR does for marketing that it is unable to do so well for itself. PR is much better at explaining complexities, whether they relate to products, services, issues, policies or anything that requires a little bit more of the customer's time and attention. Also, through fostering goodwill and understanding between customers and suppliers, PR is very well equipped to undertake positioning and repositioning of corporate and product brands.

> PR was used to relaunch 'Mr Brain's Faggots' (a savoury pork meatball) in the United Kingdom. Sales of this long-established product were falling to the point where its future was in doubt and a new sales director had been recruited to generate a major improvement. Reported on *Trouble at the Top* (BBC2 television, 23 April 2003), a real-life family, claiming to be devoted to the product, was recruited, amidst substantial media coverage and participation, in exchange for expenses and holidays, to participate in a touring sampling 'road show', accompanying media interviews and a one-week long in-store promotion at 23 supermarket food stores within five of the six major national chains. The genuine family that 'lived the brand' was integral to the repositioning of the product: consumers identified strongly with 'real people' (of the right kind) in preference to actors or celebrities (who would have cost a lot more). In the event, sales far exceeded best targets, by some 1 million units, and the sales director won promotion.

Secondly, there are those communications commitments that lie outside marketing, which PR is better experienced to handle because they come within its specialized practice. These include, notably:

- investor relations;
- political lobbying;
- internal communication; and
- engaging with cause-related and pressure groups.

Would you agree that brands are far too valuable to be put at risk with PR?

No. On the contrary, PR has much to offer in building brands, both organizations and products, and is primarily responsible for many of the most successful. It is particularly appropriate in some cases, such as where there is a strategic differentiation of a product or service that is focused on a market comprising knowledgeable and informed publics. Specifically, PR can support a brand by, for example:

- providing greater credibility via third party endorsement by an opinion leader;
- generating involvement through participation in brand-based activities;
- creating relevance by connecting with current news, fashions, trends and fads.

What can PR contribute to the development of the marketing plan?

PR can:

- provide market intelligence;
- assist in gathering data;
- identify any potential inconsistencies in messages, as between customers and other publics;
- indicate potential communications synergies; and
- offer a view based on a broader experience of the total operating environment.

How does environmental scanning differ from what marketing does anyway?

PR seeks to identify issues and trends, analyse them, determine their likely development, predict their consequences and plan action accordingly. This scanning includes markets. Marketing, by contrast, concentrates on studying, very closely, the activities of customers, potential customers, competitors, potential competitors, suppliers, distributors and all other detectable market forces. Both PR and marketing scan the environment to identify and evaluate the likely effects of political, economic, social, technological, legal and environmental factors on current operations.

What does PR contribute to customer feedback?

PR energetically engages with customers and potential customers in support of marketing, such as providing additional information about products, services and their use, addressing consumer issues and running customer relations contact schemes. It seeks feedback to complete the communication loop, and can provide a welter of information from the front about attitudes and perceptions to corporate and product brands. This comes directly and indirectly, from the public and through intermediaries.

What is the difference between market and marketing communications?

Market communications comprise information relating to markets that is supplied by observers such as government departments, industry regulators, business data providers and a variety of commentators, critics and consumer interests. This information may encourage or discourage sales, whereas marketing communications are about encouraging sales.

What are 'mediated marketplace communications'?

This is an umbrella term to describe all market and marketing communications, including marketing public relations (MPR), within the market that are sourced other than by word of mouth, alias gossip, or 'the grapevine'.

What is viral marketing?

This term is used to describe recommendation of World Wide Web sites to 'visit' and is therefore a potentially most valuable element in trying to gain interest in a site. The problem to address is that most people prefer to spend their time online at sites that are already known to them and not to investigate much further. 'The point about viral campaigns is that they have got to be arresting enough to prompt friends and colleagues to pass them on to each other', wrote Dawn Hayes in *The Guardian* (24 March 2003), reporting on viral games that friends and work colleagues e-mail to each other. 'They therefore need to be raw, edgy and funny'.

She illustrates her point with a Web advertisement for John West canned fish, which featured a salmon fisherman fighting a bear beside a lake, which is said to have attracted up to two million people world-wide. 'When you've got communities passing information around, it's much stronger, because it brings with it endorsement and credibility that a traditional advertisement doesn't have', according to its creator. 'But it has got to be something people latch on to and love because it's funny or surprising in some way'.

There are strong implications for e-PR, which is all about making and exchanging direct contact with publics, through Web sites, e-mail messages and discussion groups, cutting out the media that are so strong a feature in most other PR practice. The potential offered to engage with publics on any topic and to foster viral communication among them represents a significant advance.

> Lastminute.com, an online booking company that sells inspiration and solutions for 'last minute' purchases, typically entertainment and flight tickets, was among the first to adopt viral marketing, using teasing e-mail messages that recipients then forward to others for their amusement or interest. Their early e-mail campaigns included an 'office flirt test', linked to the company's Web site, which contained suitably themed offers. It provoked some 1 million responses just before St Valentine's Day (14 February) in the United Kingdom, which is associated with romance. Writing in *The Times* (12 May 2001), reporter Nick Wyke quoted the company's UK managing director: 'People like sending messages and playing games with each other. It's all good affiliation to the brand and a great way of sending traffic directly back to the site'.

What is integrated marketing communications?

IMC is a big name for a very simple concept with major implications. All forms of communication must be wholly consistent one with another and integrated, so that they complement each other in order to achieve best effect with greatest efficiency. In other words, 'the sum is greater than the parts'. Integration of all the elements within the marketing mix is designed to achieve optimum clarity and impact with target audiences. This is not confined to marketing of products and services, but also embraces the marketing of corporate brands.

In addition to integration of the various communications tools being used for promotion, there is integration of all activities horizontally across all elements of the marketing mix and across each department and unit within the organization. This requires harmonious collaboration between, say, production, finance and marketing, so that messages to customers are consistent. And between, for instance, customer service, stores and despatch, so that data is shared and accessible.

There is also integration vertically, so that marketing and communication is consistent with corporate vision, mission, objectives and strategy. And that all internal communication ensures that everyone who needs to know is kept informed on all the key issues, such as upcoming advertising campaigns, products, joint ventures, new service standards, procedures and marketing initiatives. And that all external communication ensures the closest collaboration between partners and suppliers engaged on every aspect of marketing.

IMC has a simple purpose as well: to envelop the potential customer in a totally consistent, fully integrated communications web that propels him or her towards purchase. As part of that process IMC should achieve measurable economies as well as greater revenue and profitability. PR, of course, has interests that additionally span the full range of corporate concerns, and so may at a given period be directed primarily at enhancing corporate reputation instead of achieving sales, but the same central principle of integration in all communication applies; indeed, it is a central tenet of PR practice.

What is the difference between market research and marketing research?

Market research examines markets, including, for example, size, characteristics, trends, customers and competitors. Marketing research scrutinizes the effectiveness of marketing communications, taking in such matters as choice of media used, the content of advertisements and broadcast commercials and the organization of sales territories. Sometimes it is called advertising research, but it is by no means limited to advertising. Incidentally, separate research is also undertaken into products, sales forecasting, pricing and distribution.

What is the difference between a PR manager, a marketing manager and a marketing communications manager?

Any confusion is understandable, since both titles and practices vary:

- Typically, a PR manager heads the PR function, possibly within the marketing department and answers to the marketing director. If PR enjoys greater status in the organization it is more likely to be a discrete function, headed by a PR director or director of PR.
- A marketing manager has a similar role and status, and therefore is likely to be found alongside the PR manager in the organizational hierarchy.

- A marketing communications manager usually has operations responsibility for sourcing materials needed by the department and answers to the marketing manager.

Should anyone doing PR have had experience of writing marketing plans?

It would be a great advantage for any PR person engaged in marketing support. The occupational training programmes for PR include 'entry level' advertising, marketing, media and behavioural studies, designed to give a broad understanding, and these marketing components are expected to be strengthened in the next few years. The full marketing qualification includes detailed marketing planning and a small but growing band of graduates has been following this by also obtaining a PR diploma. There are also university marketing graduates working in PR.

Is PR cheaper than advertising?

Since some PR consultancies claim annual revenues of £20–40 million, it might seem that PR is the more expensive, particularly when advertising expenditure has been falling while demand for PR services has been growing. Historically, PR has always been cheaper and it continues to offer a set of relatively low-cost techniques.

No such comparison should neglect effectiveness. Advertising offers greater precision, in what it says, how, when and where. It can focus on market segments like a laser beam, or not. It is often expensive, there is an awful lot of it around and receivers are adept at not seeing it. PR benefits from editorial credibility, to the extent that receivers rate it several times more believable than advertising. However, media credibility is declining, there is a clutter of PR-led and branded editorial, many messages are filtered through intermediaries and timing in delivery is less certain.

Often PR or advertising is used alone, but a combination may produce best value, with each complementing the other. Typically, for example, the last 10 or 20 per cent of the advertising allocation could be reassigned to PR, to provide value well in excess of that which would have been derived from leaving it where it was with the advertising.

Why does advertising always have the larger allocations and PR is the poor relation?

Advertising began earlier and for decades there have been 'hard' markets in advertising, owing to high levels of demand, resulting in high costs of entry for prospective advertisers. Markets for PR remain relatively 'soft' for the most part and purchasers continue to enjoy greater flexibility. Advertising also involves substantial ancillary production costs, while comparable PR expenditures are for the most part less expensive. In consequence the 'spend' on advertising is usually much greater, but this is not an immutable law. Some campaigns are now 'PR-led' and the fall in the effectiveness of advertising is having an effect on charges.

Is PR the clever joined-up writing and advertising just the 'eye candy'?

PR is better at dealing with complex issues and offering greater explanation, while advertising excels at arresting the attention and commanding interest, telling simple messages powerfully. They both make best use of visual communication tools.

Is PR the froth and marketing the serious stuff?

Allocating respective degrees of seriousness is impractical. Sometimes PR and marketing activities can look less than serious, and often this is carefully contrived, but there is always an underlying serious purpose, however well concealed.

seven

making the **connections**

- Is PR a management function?
- Where does it fit in the structure?
- What are corporate affairs?
- How do corporate affairs relate to PR?
- Does the PR manager enjoy special access to the chairperson?
- Don't middle managers who handle PR gain unwarranted access to confidential senior management thinking?
- Should PR be a specific responsibility within senior management?
- Does the PR become a type of agent for the company spokes-person?
- Can any competent manager handle PR, apart from publicity?
- Why do quoted companies get so hung up on PR?
- Are some listed companies more likely than others to benefit from PR?
- Does a company need to be listed on the Stock Exchange first for PR to be of any real value to it?
- How do investor relations differ from PR?
- What is financial PR?
- Can PR help cyclical stocks?
- What is a company visit?
- What is a facility visit?
- What are the main areas where other departments would or should consult with the PR function?
- Can PR compensate for any weaknesses in other activities?

- How does PR relate to the legal function?
- Are departments likely to adopt different attitudes towards PR?
- Isn't PR just another self-serving function that looks to grow by attaching to other areas already handled perfectly well?
- What are common failings in employee communications?
- Is there a standard, one-size-fits-all way of handling employee communications?
- How does PR relate to Personnel, or HRM?
- Isn't all internal communication best left to Personnel?
- How can the grapevine be controlled, or at least anchored in the real world?
- Should the intranet now be our communication channel internally?
- How do structure and culture interrelate?
- To what extent can employee participation benefit management?
- What contribution can PR make in developing corporate style?
- How do we know if we are making the most of our PR function?

In addition to marketing, PR interrelates with other internal functions, such as HRM, finance and sales. In this chapter, the role of PR within the organization is examined, since guardianship of reputation and image brings wider responsibilities and potential for purposeful collaboration with others.

Questions here explore the advantages of PR awareness in operational thinking and performance, the function linkages and internal communication. A number of questions ask about PR for publicly quoted companies. Behind most lie further questions. Can large organizations effectively persuade all employees to take PR seriously? Why do many smaller enterprises appear to thrive on positive internal attitudes to PR? What factors may be significant in creating the best conditions for PR to flourish internally? Are different types of organization better suited and, if so, why?

Is PR a management function?

Yes, because PR has various management responsibilities, including environmental scanning, identifying change and predicting its consequences, advising senior managers accordingly and guarding corporate image and reputation.

Where does it fit in the structure?

Because PR 'spans boundaries' in all directions within the organization and between the organization and its publics, probably where it is located does not matter that much, apart from considerations of status and self-worth. In the majority of cases it is found in the management 'camp', particularly when a substantial amount of time is allocated to corporate affairs, but, where MPR accounts for much of the effort, it may be part of, or alongside, marketing, in the disposal subsystem.

This boundary spanning gives PR its unique character among the functions. It belongs to management because what it does is consistent with control and integration, conflict resolution and needs reconciliation. However, it works to support all subsystems, including those that are concerned with production, maintenance, planning and change management. PR people:

- liaise between the organization and the external publics and individuals;
- assist other subsystems within the organization in their communications direct with the outside world;
- assist other subsystems in their communications one with another.

In consequence, PR is to be found at any given time working throughout most of the organization, to a greater or lesser extent.

What are corporate affairs?

This term embraces all matters that affect the organization as a whole, in its operations and future development.

How do corporate affairs relate to PR?

PR scrutinizes commercial plans and operations against what it knows about the external environment, with a view to warning of any developments that are likely to impinge on, or indeed aid, the organization's progress. In particular, PR scrutinizes political and social trends that are likely to adversely affect operations and the perceptions of its publics towards the organization, both current and likely, in relation to the detected changes. It seeks to differentiate between sustained trends and passing fads and advises on how best these trends may be addressed.

Does the PR manager enjoy special access to the chairperson?

The PR manager is rarely some kind of 'special adviser', sitting in a small antechamber, waiting to be summoned, although it has been known in a few large companies. However, at least half of all PR managers report to their chairperson or chief executive/CEO. About 10–15 per cent report to their managing director and about as many again report to the marketing director or manager.

Don't middle managers who handle PR gain unwarranted access to confidential senior management thinking?

Viewed from the perspective of other middle managers, it may seem unwarranted, but of course it is necessary in order for the PR manager to be able to do his or her job. A key characteristic of PR is the ability to work alongside people at all levels within the hierarchy and to both gain and respect their trust and confidence. To a fellow middle manager, this may look like unfair competitive advantage, in relation to 'hobnobbing' with 'them upstairs', but it can be a waste of time and not at all enviable in relation to 'mixing it' with the support staff elsewhere.

Should PR be a specific responsibility within senior management?

Senior managers have plenty enough to think about, certainly, but the answer surely has to be yes. The dominant coalition, that is, the management group that gives direction to the organization, needs the presence of PR in its strategic planning deliberations and processes in order to enhance its effectiveness. The popular alternative, of simply asking the PR people to advise about best presentation of policies only after they have been arrived at, is to miss the point. Increasingly, PR people are being recruited at board level.

Does the PR become a type of agent for the company spokesperson?

In so far as the PR manager secures platforms for the chairperson, chief executive and any other company spokespersons, he or she acts as a kind of agent. This does not, usually, involve negotiation of a fee, but it does require persuasive presentation of the reasons in favour of the 'appearance', including background, outline content and purpose.

Can any competent manager handle PR, apart from publicity?

This is a good question that is often asked. Much depends upon what exactly is meant by PR, in that there are elements of PR practice that any manager should be able to pick up readily, particularly when they relate directly to his or her function. For example, the head of a company's research and development department might be competent and confident about running an open day with laboratory demonstrations and talks to explain and illustrate the work to prospective employees and their families.

There are, though, the more complex, technical and/or demanding elements of PR, which call for varying degrees of specialist training and experience, much of which deliberately go relatively unnoticed by managers outside the PR function unless they have direct interest in them. These are, therefore, probably best left to the dedicated PR people. That is not to say that competent managers are unsuited to specialize in PR; some turn to PR as a career change and become very successful, particularly where they benefit from a long-standing previous operational experience within the same organization.

Why do quoted companies get so hung up on PR?

Offering shares in a company on the stock market can be a fairly hair-raising experience. The business, and those who run it, is brought under close scrutiny, on a scale unfamiliar to anyone who has not run a public company before. PR plays a most important role at such times, and thereafter there is an ongoing need to consider matters relating to image and reputation in relation to investors, because they have a direct bearing on market confidence in the company, its share price and asset value. Directors may seem 'hung up' about this, but really it amounts to simple prudence.

Are some listed companies more likely than others to benefit from PR?

There are some 3,000 listed companies in London, the largest European financial centre, although levels of trading in individual stocks vary greatly. When the London Stock Exchange's main market, sometimes referred to as The Big Board, is operating normally, much of the dealing is concentrated in the stock of relatively few UK companies, surprisingly few, probably no more than about 125 companies, plus a handful that are in the news as new arrivals or owing to corporate activity.

Most media coverage reflects this, so there are, therefore, many companies that have to 'fight' for attention and can find their shares undervalued simply because they are not obtaining their share of attention. In addition, there are companies listed on AIM, the Alternative Investment Market, established in 1995 to help nurture smaller, younger businesses. They too can have difficulty in securing much interest. So, although all quoted companies benefit from PR, by varying degrees, and continually need it, those that go relatively unnoticed for a protracted period may benefit substantially if they manage to overcome this handicap and then find themselves 're-rated' by the market.

Does a company need to be listed on the Stock Exchange first for PR to be of any real value to it?

PR can be of value from day one and certainly does not depend upon 'going public' first. This applies to all areas of PR, including corporate affairs. Very many small and medium-size enterprises (SMEs), and micro businesses with just a handful of employees, have greatly benefited from early adoption of PR, in 'selling' both their organizations and their products and services.

How do investor relations differ from PR?

Investor relations refers to the management of the company's relationships with its past, present and potential investors. It is not a PR activity, but is usually handled by the company stockbrokers. Responsibility within the company may lie with finance or PR. 'FTSE 100' and other larger UK public companies tend to allocate investor relations to either the finance department, a dedicated investor relations department or to the PR department's corporate affairs specialty.

What is financial PR?

Financial PR describes the task of communicating with key opinion formers who influence investment decisions. In practice, these people are, for the most part, investment analysts and financial journalists. For larger companies this can be a routine daily commitment, with plenty of two-way exchanges, for smaller ones more of an uphill struggle to be known. Incidentally, financial PR and investor relations are often referred to as being one and the same, which can be confusing.

Can PR help cyclical stocks?

Cyclical stocks are the shares in companies whose businesses follow cyclical economic patterns that result in successively better and poorer profitability, rather like a wave effect. This is seen, for example, in house building. The share prices tend to follow the pattern or discount it, that is, anticipate and allow for it in advance. PR can help to explain the nature of these businesses and thereby create better understanding and goodwill where otherwise there might be ample scope for misunderstanding.

What is a company visit?

This describes visits by individual guests, sometimes in small groups, to meet with company management and discuss its affairs. They provide an opportunity for senior managers to meet investors, analysts, customers, journalists, major buyers, opinion leaders and other key people on a one-to-one basis. It is usual for guests to be drawn from one such category alone. Hospitality is customary, usually lunch for those who have travelled any distance to attend, and it is commonplace for guests to also see around the company's operations. This may range from a short walk through a factory to a road or flying tour of installations or sites.

What is a facility visit?

This refers to the community relations practice of providing opportunities for organized groups of visitors to view company operations accompanied by a guide, who may be a PR person, a dedicated tour guide or a retired employee (who often make the best guides). Tours are scheduled and are usually limited to certain days of the week, mornings or afternoons, times of the year, and often they are followed by an opportunity to purchase products from a factory shop or the distribution of free samples. Large manufacturers such as Cadbury, the Birmingham chocolate manufacturer, pioneered the practice. It is a powerful way of communicating effectively with minimal disturbance to production. A 'facility' describes a factory, or plant, although in practice, group visits are also suitable for service organizations that have visually interesting stories to tell.

What are the main areas where other departments would or should consult with the PR function?

There are five main circumstances in which a unit manager might want to talk with the PR people:

- to obtain advice from an expert about a communication problem;
- for help in communicating externally, say with a supplier;
- to facilitate or mediate internal communication between units;
- to bring news and views from outside;
- to undertake marketing communications.

Can PR compensate for any weaknesses in other activities?

PR is about creating the most favourable conditions possible in which to operate. Goodwill and understanding, positive image and strong reputation can all provide some credit when the going gets tough, long enough, hopefully, to address the problems. Sometimes the admission of weaknesses, coupled with explanation of what is being done to correct them, can actually gain credit, but this is not likely to be sustainable indefinitely. It has been said that a good reputation takes 25 years to create and five minutes to lose; this is an exaggeration, but only just.

How does PR relate to the legal function?

The company secretary and solicitor (lawyers) most often require PR input in connection with contractual and litigation matters. These tend to revolve around personnel issues, for example, employment contract negotiations and terms plus tribunal and court proceedings relating to allegations of workplace discrimination and unfair dismissal. Occasionally, perhaps resulting from a crisis, there arise claims relating to allegedly illegal trading practices or compensation for faulty products and services or industrial injuries.

The relationship can be an uneasy one at times, because any PR-generated message that includes or refers to contractual matters has to be agreed with the legal department, to ensure the golden rule of consistency in all communications, and lawyers are trained to say as little as possible. Further, a key feature of successful communication is use of plain language, which can meet with some resistance over the interpretation of legal jargon that might be used later to the company's disadvantage.

Often these differences are made most apparent when there is a crisis, with PR wanting to communicate and the lawyers preferring to say nothing or, at worst (in their view), the barest minimum. The lawyers also routinely advise PR on the content of many materials, such as corporate brochures, the editorial elements of annual reports and accounts and any items that might have contractual implications, such as recruitment brochures, explanatory product use literature and workplace safety and procedures information.

The relationship has all the potential for being exceptionally constructive or downright destructive, so it greatly helps if the PR person has a legal background and the lawyer has an understanding of PR. This is not impossible. The two occupations are remarkably similar in a number of respects, but the inclination of the lawyer to say 'no comment' can speak volumes and do damage to reputation, sometimes almost as fast as it takes to say it.

Similarly, lawyers' preference for 'playing for time' can distort image, often unfairly, whereas the PR person values quick response when circumstances appear to require it. Also, lawyers can sometimes inadvertently do damage, from the PR perspective, simply by doing their job to the best of their abilities. This can occur, for instance, where they are vigorously defending a large organization against a handful of consumers who are suing for alleged trading malpractices and this gives rise to perceptions of bullying and unfairness.

Are departments likely to adopt different attitudes towards PR?

Every occupation and discipline within the organization may adopt its own perceptions and attitudes towards PR, based on its own worldview. Not only do accountants, lawyers, HR people and marketers have their differences; production people, engineers, designers, planners, researchers and facilities managers all tend to adopt their own approach to PR, interpreting their needs in the context of their own work and responsibilities.

Isn't PR just another self-serving function that looks to grow by attaching to other areas already handled perfectly well?

The PR department works with and between other units, to help them optimize their performance and try to iron out the consequences of frequent rivalry, sometimes amounting to hostility, arising out of struggles for resources and power. This is where PR can push towards its excellence ideal, maybe along the way having to mediate and try to reconcile differences, acting as the 'glue' of the organization.

The need for harmonious collaboration is probably never clearer than in the relationship of marketing with PR, but throughout the organization, PR has to take the greatest care to make sure that there are no mixed messages reaching the different types of employee. This is because how exactly every single employee in turn communicates with the external publics is very important. It is remarkable how much any organization can benefit from all of its people adopting positive attitudes when they are dealing with customers, suppliers, 'locals', investors, 'big wigs' and so on. And what damage can be done when they send out negative messages about the organization.

So no, PR is not driven by some empire-building imperative, or certainly should not be. Any impression it gives of this is likely to be the consequence of its 'busybody' involvement across the whole organization, up and down its spinal cord, out along its arteries and veins. There are very few organizations where the employees do not constitute in themselves a strategic public that should be communicated with within an integrated PR framework, as with other publics.

What are common failings in employee communications?

Firstly, the communication is weighted towards management views, priorities, perceptions and interests, with insufficient attention given to the views and so on of non-management people. In other words, the weight of flow is downwards and not upwards, and there is insufficient attempt made to create a two-way dialogue.

Secondly, communication is not 'something PR does' in isolation. It has to be a combined effort, with contributions by different units, coordinated but flexible enough to handle a variety of requirements. Sometimes communication requirements arise that call for input from a specific department because it alone has the relevant expertise.

Is there a standard, one-size-fits-all way of handling employee communications?

If only there were, but no, it all depends upon the size, nature and maturity of the organization. What works well here is very unlikely to work well there, and trying to adopt and adapt from elsewhere is seldom satisfactory. Corporate culture is a strong determinant of what works, and practices often develop in response to specific internal problems and how they were resolved.

Over and above considerations of culture, developing a strategy depends on the stage that the organization has reached in its development, what change influences are weighing in on it and what is required to reach the next stage. Then what is needed of employees, both collectively and by groups, can be decided and plotted, from awareness, through understanding and support to involvement and commitment. Often it is said that 'everyone is committed', but it may be that not everyone necessarily *need* be at any given point in time; some may reach differing stages by differing timescales. All of which argues for customized approaches and not 'one-size-fits-all' easy solutions.

How does PR relate to Personnel, or HRM?

In many cases, the answer appears to be, with difficulty. HR people mostly claim all communication with all employees to be strictly for them, and are often quite hostile to the idea of the PR people having anything to do with it. Historically, though, PR became the established function for *routine* communications, and this gave birth to the house journal that has in turn spawned several more channels of communication, such as the notice board 'newspaper' and the intranet bulletin.

HRM also contests PR over responsibility for community relations, how the organization communicates with its neighbours, on the grounds that this is an extension of employee relations. As a result, HRM may prefer to issue its own press statements on staff issues, although PR is often consulted when the news is about redundancies or other bad news. Other areas where HRM and PR activities might overlap include suggestion schemes, internal attitude surveys and any initiatives or meetings involving employees. HRM and PR both advise management, from their respective standpoints, about the management of change and the communication of organizational development.

Isn't all internal communication best left to Personnel?

Communication is a fundamental component of sound human relationships. Since PR is the specialist communications function, it seems logical that PR should continue to assist in facilitating the optimum benefit to be derived from human resources. Such support embraces use of communications media for providing the overarching communication framework and undertaking occasional projects, such as surveys and recruitment campaigns that are non-contractual and unrelated to an individual employee. As to internal communication more generally, again the role of PR is to assist where appropriate, using its primary skill set. Presumably HRM concentrates meanwhile on meeting its responsibilities to, for example, personnel administration and training.

How can the grapevine be controlled, or at least anchored in the real world?

Trying to control any grapevine is impossible, and anyone who thinks it can be done is missing the point. The grapevine exists to fill a vacuum, so the more that people get to hear reliably about what goes on and are progressively involved the less they need, or want, an alternative way of finding out. Of course, it is in human nature to enjoy informal speculation and diversion, but most people much prefer not to have to rely on this for all their information, or even for just the important bits. So the best form of control must surely be to render the grapevine superfluous for all intents and purposes.

Should the intranet now be our communication channel internally?

No, the intranet is but one of a number of internal channels of communication, and, like the others, it is better suited for some message requirements and less so for others. The intranet has to be judged by its ability to improve the quality and effectiveness of communication. In short, if we don't want to read our e-mail, we don't, except under protest. The novelty of electronic messages is not a sustainable excitement that induces waves of absorbed attention, and the temptation to daily bombard colleagues with multiple messages has to be resisted. This approach is not sensible.

The technology may imply that the training priority lies in its use, whereas how to communicate through it with optimum efficiency might be much more pertinent. Nor is this the only major area for consideration:

- The intranet empowers people and therefore militates against the type of organization that is based on hierarchical controls.
- It strengthens links between people who are physically dispersed.
- Its immediacy necessitates constant updating and quality content.
- Information has to be readily accessible, timely and actionable.

How do structure and culture interrelate?

Culture embraces the collective values, beliefs and norms that influence or decide attitudes, behaviours, social mores and expectations. Culture is complex and evolves slowly. It is not necessarily rational and is subject to much turbulence, as subcultures and countercultures form and reform, giving rise to tensions that lead to change. Sometimes a culture survives for generations; in any event, the introduction of new values and approaches takes time.

Structure is concerned with systems, rules, relationships and individual responsibilities. Clearly stated corporate vision and mission does not remove differences among various factions, groups and individuals who harbour interests that, in their view, transcend corporate aims and objectives. Employees decode messages to fit them within the culture and by reference to their own agendas. The culture influences willingness to engage in dialogue or preference for remaining silent, levels of harmony and attrition, degrees of loyalty and commitment and frequency of dissident factional and group priorities.

To what extent can employee participation benefit management?

Much depends upon what is meant by 'participation'. PR seeks dialogue, leading to involvement and commitment. High levels of support create very positive internal climates that are beneficial to management, but what can be achieved realistically has to take account of the need to overcome any established patterns of rejection that condemn its messages as being just so much 'spam', or corporate communications 'rubbish'. This may be the result of inadequate or poor previous communication or simply the product of a less deferential, more doubting age.

What contribution can PR make in developing corporate style?

PR is always looking for feedback and if it can persuade people within the organization to respond who usually prefer to say nothing and 'keep their heads down' it is engaging in dialogue that will provide intelligence for developing the culture, or style. It can also provide insights from outside that are helpful in this, because image and reputation are, to varying degrees, the product of culture. By these means it can assist to a better understanding of what decides and sustains the present culture, its consequences and likely evolution.

How do we know if we are making the most of our PR function?

The PR function's operation within the organization may be measured and evaluated in many practical ways, similarly to its performance elsewhere. 'Making the most', however, implies much more than this. It raises further questions, such as:

- How often have departments called on PR for support?
- Is senior management involving the PR people before decisions are taken, or only afterwards?
- Does PR get involved in communications between departments?

- Are we seeing PR more as a management function or a technical service?
- Could we be using PR more in our 'futures' thinking?

Answers to these and similar questions should be fairly indicative of whether the PR is being used to its optimum capability and, if not, why not.

eight

a stake in the **future**

- Why do we need to communicate with stakeholders?
- Might we ever have an ethical duty to communicate with them?
- Is the general public a stakeholder?
- Why should we have to consider our corporate social responsibilities?
- How can CSR provide any real return?
- What types of CSR activities are run by small businesses?
- What is the scale of this CSR activity?
- How can we discharge social responsibilities effectively and efficiently?
- Is CCI anything to do with communities?
- Why should we be concerned about the locals?
- Aren't community relations just a nice bolt-on for big companies with PR money to burn?
- Is it for the individual business to make the first move?
- What do investors think of CSR?
- What is socially responsible investing?
- What are the ethical implications of CSR for charities?
- How large is the charity sector?
- What is cause-related marketing?
- How driven are consumers by ethical issues?
- What do consumers dislike most?
- What is 'greenwashing'?

- Why might anyone be really bothered about pressure groups?
- Do any of these groups talk with companies sensibly?
- Can demonstrators damage more than reputation?
- Isn't emotion a large part of all this?

Outside the organization there are many differing stakeholders with whom to communicate, in particular cause-related and pressure groups, local communities and opinion leaders. Questions are asked here about the role of PR in fostering and maintaining positive relations with external interests, particularly with regard to financial performance, environmental policies and business ethics. A number enquire about corporate social responsibility (CSR) and corporate community involvement (CCI), the realities of dialogue and implications for future operations and the creation of a profile that increases shareholder value.

Why do we need to communicate with stakeholders?

A convincing argument came from an unlikely source, the Royal Society of Arts (RSA), which set up its Tomorrow's Company Inquiry that reported in 1994. This identified six 'forces for change', including 'the death of deference' among employees, customers and communities and companies' growing need to maintain public confidence in their operations and business conduct.

The Inquiry, which was conducted by senior managers drawn from 25 UK 'top' companies, argued that public confidence provided companies with 'a licence to operate', in other words, the stakeholders needed to be 'on side' in order to optimize performance. This concept has met with widespread approval.

Might we ever have an ethical duty to communicate with them?

Certainly, whenever the organization's operations affect stakeholders, or may do so, in such a manner as to raise an ethical duty to communicate. For example, if it is thought that food products have been tampered with, it does not matter whether only a tiny fraction are contaminated, or that there is a risk but no hard evidence, everyone has to know, and fast. It does not matter that only a few of the people told are, or could be, consumers of the food, or are routine customers. If everyone is potentially at risk everyone has to be told via the mass media and by whatever other channels are available.

Nor is this duty confined to crises. There are plenty of times when an organization knows 'in its heart' that it should be advising, telling, forewarning about some activity it is, or will be, engaging in, some detail relating to its products and services, some plan or proposal that warrants consultation and agreement. It may know precisely which public or publics to address, or it may have to tell everyone because being more precise is impractical. If 'being concerned about reputation' means anything, it surely must involve being prepared to take some 'hard-nosed' ethical communication decisions now and again.

Is the general public a stakeholder?

Since stakeholders are people who have a direct or indirect stake, or interest, in the organization, whether or not they know it, there will be times when, presumably, everyone in the entire population qualifies as a stakeholder, but such occasions are likely to be rare. For example, if the country was under attack by an outside power or it was proposed that our country should merge with another, it could be argued that everyone, including the newborn child, was a stakeholder.

For most practical purposes, however, it is necessary to divide the overall population into identifiable stakeholder groups. These, though, tend to be broad categories and therefore lacking sufficient focus for PR purposes. The publics are to be found in among the stakeholders. Some are active, others are passive; the key stimulant for publics identifying themselves is their perceived realization that the organization is doing something that involves them. PR that addresses the public at large might develop relationships with stakeholders, but this is likely to be haphazard and very expensive. Unfortunately, such broad brushstroke approaches can result in not much communication with anyone.

Why should we have to consider our corporate social responsibilities?

This is not about dropping coins in a collecting bucket; CSR can be seriously good for you. Companies that are active in this area argue that CSR makes sense to them in the enhanced quality of relationships with their publics that they derive from it. They see it as part of their corporate strategy. Business in the Community, whose member companies make 'a public commitment to continually improve [their] impact on society', claims that there are substantial company benefits covering competition, performance and recruitment, as well the creation of enduring 'healthy communities'.

> According to the UK government, quoting a report by Business in the Community's Business Impact Task Force in November 2000, in 1999 a survey of 25,000 people in 23 countries on six continents revealed that perceptions of companies around the world are more strongly linked to 'corporate citizenship' (56 per cent) than to either brand quality (40 per cent) or business management (34 per cent).

How can CSR provide any real return?

There is no guaranteed return, but plenty of evidence that CSR policies assist materially in creating favourable operating conditions. Both social and economic benefits are credited to their source, with resultant perceptions of an organization that is doing something for others and 'putting back a bit in exchange for taking out so much'. The image and the reputation are adjusted accordingly. Perceptions develop of an organization that is part of the fabric of the community and as one that has a sense of social purpose and leadership. This in turn brings benefits in three particular areas:

- enhanced features of the corporate brand;
- greater customer goodwill and loyalty;
- improved workforce commitment and morale.

The PR function finds CSR programmes to be valuable in securing feedback that identifies and helps to clarify concerns and issues. This combination of mutual benefit seems to be a powerful mechanism for encouraging people to want quality relationships, to respond and contribute, to offer 'tips' and opinions, even to will the organization's success in its operations. There is a kind of mutual adoption, so that beneficiaries, particularly those that live nearby, seem to gravitate towards the idea of adopting the company, while the company comes to think in terms of adopting them, or, more correctly, their particular interest. This form of bonding transcends commerce but provides a strong impetus to it.

Did Tesco's computers for schools programme have no connection whatever with that company's surge into market leadership, as the UK's largest food supermarket retailer holding nearly one-fifth of its market, and continued dramatic market share growth? That is a large company, but what of the many much smaller organizations that are running smaller-scale projects with comparable results?

What types of CSR activities are run by small businesses?

Business in the Community, in its annual report for 2001, offered two examples to demonstrate that this is not 'just for the big boys'. The first was a firm of solicitors (lawyers) in Cardiff, where activities include some 70 staffers each spending one hour a week reading to socially deprived school children. The second was a Bristol retailer, that gives about 60 used white goods per month, that have been traded for replacements, to a charity that recycles furniture, selling through its own shop a wide variety of reconditioned products at discounted prices to low-income customers.

Examples of what is being done by smaller organizations are legion. The main point about this is that it does not need to be expensive. Even when both funds and time are short there are multitudes of ways in which gaps can be filled and a real difference can be achieved in the local community. This is not new, but a modern interpretation of what the leading historic livery companies began in medieval times.

Employees value CSR, according to the Business in the Community report quoted by the UK government. Researchers MORI had consistently found throughout the 1990s that the vast majority of people favoured employers that they perceived to be supporters of 'society and the community'. Furthermore, management consultants Bain & Co found companies with the highest employee retention also had the highest customer retention.

What is the scale of this CSR activity?

In the United Kingdom, the 'big boys' spend 0.42 per cent of their pretax profits, which currently translates into £499 million (2000–2001). This includes not only cash but also time and gifts in kind. The percentage has held for 10 years; what has changed is the great surge of activity by other UK companies during this period.

How can we discharge social responsibilities effectively and efficiently?

The starting point is provided by the corporate strategy and objectives. Well-meaning philanthropy is laudable, but CSR should be anchored to commercial reality. There has to be a policy that firmly states what kinds of project are to be undertaken or supported, because they satisfy certain specific agreed criteria. The days when the pet charity of the chairperson's spouse scooped the jackpot are, hopefully, over.

Then there has to be a commitment to doing it 'properly'. This is particularly important, because often CSR projects flounder or fail to reach their full potential for lack of adequate support from within the organization. The stumbling block so often seems to be inadequate recognition of how much time needs to be committed, to make sure there are adequate facilities, training and management of projects. This applies whatever the scale of the proposed activity, from a substantial in-house programme to a modest level of support for an existing external project.

The PR responsibility here is in both providing the infrastructure that supports the programmes and also in guiding the company towards arriving at a balanced view of the competing interests presented by various stakeholders. It can be difficult to achieve this, steered by that nebulous concept beloved of politicians, the 'public interest', which is often susceptible to multiple interpretations. Many companies resolve to proceed with caution when first embarking on CSR, often opting for various forms of association with established projects and developing their commitment gradually.

Is CCI anything to do with communities?

'Corporate community involvement' is about community relations, implying a depth commitment to becoming 'part of the local scene', but after that its exact scope becomes a bit hazy. There is talk of 'investment in society', 'making a real difference to people's lives' and other such grandiloquent pomposity, but it appears to be an umbrella term for describing a variety of activities, from open days for the locals to special events and 'volunteering' staff for local tasks such as decorating old people's homes. It is also used to include some distinctly routine activities, such as press relations with the Town Hall scribe who produces the council's magazine and buying advertising in the local free newspaper.

The scientific part of this is the dissection of the community into its critical parts, rather like creating a stakeholder map on a broader canvas. So, for example, the company is likely to think first of its employees and their families, then their friends and relatives. The opinion formers and leaders, activists and office holders, who in effect run the community, always feature high on any list, and these may be further divided, depending upon perceptions of their relative power and influence. Then there are the various groups, social organizations and media. The science also includes knowing what success would look like in respect of each such public.

Why should we be concerned about the locals?

Because they are concerned about you, and it seems that their expectations of you are rising. Questioned about their attitudes towards companies, 74 per cent of the public at large agreed that 'Industry and commerce do not pay enough attention to the communities in which they operate' and only 2 per cent agreed that 'Companies should maximize their financial performance regardless of society and environment'. Half the sample thought that companies should give equal attention to social and environmental needs as to financial performance, and another 16 per cent favoured a 'major contribution to society and environment regardless of cost'.

Aren't community relations just a nice bolt-on for big companies with PR money to burn?

It certainly looked that way when Business in the Community was established in 1982. Over the years, however, more companies have joined this campaigning organization and after 20 years it had 696 members, of which just over half were regional, as opposed to national. Although the membership includes many familiar names, the growing interest of smaller businesses is also reflected in its membership.

Business in the Community is gaining a pan-European dimension, through the activities of companies and partners such as CSR Europe. British embassies have been used to promote community investment events and a major CSR European conference is planned for 2004.

Is it for the individual business to make the first move?

Yes, acting in accordance with a clear policy. There is seldom a shortage of approaches to aid inspiration. The alternative can be chaotic. Lack of a policy and organization has led many a business into disorderly commitments that are expensive, not necessarily much to do with company strategy and objectives and very poor value.

> A classic example of lack of policy is provided by the large professional practice, where every partner feels obliged to champion, or at least agree to, every approach that he or she receives personally, arguing or assuming that 'it must be good for business' in some way or other. The result can amount to millions of pounds spent annually on a widely fragmented basis.

What do investors think of CSR?

It holds interest for quite a lot of them. Nearly two out of five investors and industry leaders are said to consider that companies give insufficient attention to social responsibility. This is a combined figure, so it may be that investors are less concerned than is suggested here, but even then the figure is impressive. And the same survey reports that two out of every three financial journalists agree. Also, on average about one in every two politicians agree, but this varies according to their political allegiance.

When, in 2001, Business in the Community asked City of London sell-side analysts about the importance of environmental factors, 33 per cent agreed that they were 'quite or very important' in their evaluation of companies. This compared with 20 per cent in 1994. On social issues the same response was even higher, at 34 per cent, up from only 12 per cent in 1994.

What is socially responsible investing?

Socially responsible investing (SRI), in its strictest interpretation, describes investing only in companies that meet certain standards of ethical, environmental and social responsibility. A few fund managers now specialize in this. However, SRI is also used to describe the growing tendency of fund managers more generally to 'engage' with companies in order to exert pressure to improve policies and practices in this area. This acknowledges a growing sense that companies have social obligations beyond maximizing shareholder value. This pressure carries with it the threat of reduced share prices for companies that are identified as being 'guilty of serious wrong-doing'.

What are the ethical implications of CSR for charities?

There has to be a balance between self-interest and 'doing good' that, firstly, stands up to scrutiny on both sides and, secondly, managers can live with. Coupled with motive is the degree of commitment. Helping people is 'not just for Christmas' and a company that commits warmly to a project only to abandon it before it has run its course is not only probably hurting the people it is trying to help but also injuring its image and reputation as well. This is really a matter of resisting opportunistically taking on more than can be sensibly entertained, just because the chance has arisen and/or a competitor is to be denied.

Many charities and groups allege that would-be supporters are only interested in what they perceive to be the most attractive or prominent potential schemes. They say that chief executives want opportunities to wear dinner suits, that anything connected with children always wins out, that humble environmental improvements lack sufficient 'visibility', and so on. There is a grain of truth in this. Not unconnected to this is the vulnerability to exploitation of some groups. How honourable is the motive? There is widespread criticism, for instance, of some companies that are thought to 'target' rather than 'help', an area of concern to many. Presumably where such allegations are substantiated the company in question is needlessly doing itself damage.

Many projects are not intended as substitution for state provided social services, but some may begin to look like it. This can be the subject of much debate, because corporate social responsibility is not state social responsibility. It is highly unlikely that any company would ever want to take on the role of government in funding services, and any hint of this might raise many objections.

> The matter of associations is very sensitive. For instance, McDonalds has financed purpose-built hostels at hospitals, which are available for overnight use by the parents of seriously ill children. This laudable scheme has not met with any objections, probably because it adds to, rather than substitutes for, existing provision. The company, however, has experienced widespread criticism for its schools programmes.

How large is the charity sector?

It employs 563,000 people, or 2 per cent of the UK workforce and accounted for £5.4 billion of GDP in 2001. Total income was £15.6 billion per annum, of which the general public donated 34.7 per cent and government contracts and grants accounted for another 29 per cent. Business provided £325 million, or 4.9 per cent, to which must be added non-cash contributions.

What is cause-related marketing?

As the mention of marketing suggests, cause-related marketing (CRM) describes mutually beneficial commercial agreements made between businesses and charities. In reality, it is about companies trying to benefit from the overwhelmingly popular consumer appeal of products that are linked with 'good causes'.

Cause-related marketing is based on a virtuous circle. The vast majority of consumers say they want companies to support good causes, a substantial majority of charities have sought to use this to raise funds and the great majority of companies say they want to spend on supporting good causes. The 'catch' is that the deals have to make commercial sense. Time was when many charities appeared to think that they were doing the companies favours, but they are now more understanding and reconciled to the need for agreed 'win–win' strategies.

The key to success here is the willingness of consumers, or any customers, to 'put their money where their mouths are' and pay up. Support for good causes is not always as strong as consumers suggest in surveys.

> Camelot, the UK National Lottery organizer, labours long and hard to emphasize that gamblers are 'backing good causes' but the vast majority of its 'punters' resoundingly tell it that they do not care about good causes but about winning.

How driven are consumers by ethical issues?

They like to say so, but are they? According to a MORI survey, reported in *The Guardian* (25 November 2002), getting on for half of all consumers, 44 per cent, maintain that there is an 'ethical dimension' to their purchasing decisions, but observations in the High Streets and 'sheds' gives little indication of this, and in any event when asked by a researcher most of us will readily agree with virtue rather than sin.

> When the Cooperative Bank asked about 'green groceries' no less than 88 per cent of those questioned claimed to be ethical shoppers who took environment and social considerations into account (*The Observer,* 1 October 2002). However, when the bank asked in more depth about actions in the supermarket, only 23 per cent of the sample could recall any specific action to substantiate their claims. Furthermore, over three-quarters put brand name, value for money and customer services above ethical considerations, and about 60 per cent claimed that they had insufficient information to make an ethical judgement.

So the actual degree to which ethics influence markets is in some doubt. What is certain is that CSR does earn greater customer goodwill and loyalty and enhances perceptions of corporate brands, provided that it is communicated.

What do consumers dislike most?

It is said that there has been some boycotting of the products of companies that have been found to exploit foreign child labour and/or engage in, connive at, or simply tolerate sub-standard employment practices abroad. This raises moral contradictions, since people heavily demand price-competitive products, many of which in consequence have to be made overseas by cheap labour in poorer societies. There is much talk about environmental practices, which is commonly identified as being a particular concern of young people, but in research they are found to be far more interested in fashion and convenience than are other people.

The Ethical Trading Initiative (ETI) is an association formed by retailers such Sainsbury, a large UK food supermarket chain, trade unions and international charities such as Christian Aid and Oxfam. The ETI seeks to improve the conditions of workers in developing countries that supply its members, by implementing a Base Code, which is founded upon the International Labour Organization's conventions on labour standards. Each company in ETI membership is required to either implement the Base Code, or a similar code of its own devising, and to open its supply chain to independent monitoring. Benefits identified by Sainsbury include greater efficiency, risk management and staff retention and mitigation of disruptions caused by economic and social insecurity, shrinking markets and the depletion of raw materials owing to neglect of social and environmental issues.

What is 'greenwashing'?

This is a term coined to describe how companies seek to satisfy environmental concerns. It is not flattering, and covers a wide range of alleged deception and 'corporate fight back' against cause-related and pressure groups.

Why might anyone be really bothered about pressure groups?

Organizations might be bothered because pressure groups can damage, even destroy, reputations, and there are ever more of them. Indeed, organizing a pressure group to protest about something appears to have become something of a lifestyle for some people. When the grievances are real the protests are committed and usually succeed in securing change.

Do any of these groups talk with companies sensibly?

Although acts of violence are often used to further causes, many are pursued by reasoned argument. This is contrary to the impression given by the media, because they are only interested in 'action' that they can call news. A demonstration in the street lends itself to this; a discussion in an office does not. Demonstrations are a great way to get on television, whereas reasoned discussion, presentations of facts and sensible negotiation do not whip up public support so readily.

Sometimes the demonstrations appear to be a necessary ritual for groups, as a prelude to dialogue; the intention all along is to do some talking with the aim of achieving change, but first a little public 'dusting up' of the target is thought necessary. This seems to be something that companies have to recognize and not allow to get in the way of trying to establish constructive communication, if only to inject hard facts and lessen the emotion.

Can demonstrators damage more than reputation?

Some groups, such as the anti-vivisectionists, have inflicted more directly attributable commercial damage. For instance, their demonstrations resulted in a collapse in orders and loss of support by most of its investors for Huntingdon Life Sciences, which went into receivership, from which it emerged through a five-year refinancing by a US investment group in January 2001. Additionally, the company incurred higher professional and PR costs in mounting a defence.

Isn't emotion a large part of all this?

Many groups use emotional rhetoric in hope of raising public support, and their targets might be excused for becoming emotional too, particularly at the more scurrilous and inaccurate accusations. However, managers have to eliminate emotion from their kit. Sometimes there are much well-publicized public displays of emotion for causes that are not truly heartfelt, and the weaker ones wither for lack of conviction, often remarkably soon. Companies have to assess whether there is scope to ignore their detractors or venture to attempt a meaningful dialogue.

Individuals acting alone can be emotional in their own way, getting 'wound up' over what they perceive as injustices. People are now more prepared to complain and some try to punish, or, so to speak, hit back, by denigrating the organization among their families, friends and acquaintances. They see the brand as a 'trust mark' that the organization has to earn, but often suspect that it is no more than a superficial badge. About one in three consumers reckon that they have been cheated and as many try to negotiate prices in shops. Emotions seem to run particularly high over financial services and food standards.

nine

among the **climate-makers**

- What are lobbyists?
- What are public affairs, and how do they differ from political PR and government PR?
- How do public affairs relate to PR?
- Why is lobbying part of PR?
- What do lobbyists do?
- Why don't lobbyists want to be called just that, lobbyists?
- Why are lobbyists so anxious not to be part of PR?
- How can lobbying help if you are not an insider?
- Why should we be bothered to monitor proposed legislation and regulations when we have our trade association to do that?
- Is there any way of making sure lobbying works?
- Is there lobbying in Scotland and Wales?
- Is the lobbying similar to what happens in London?
- Is lobbying really only for business organizations?
- Is it worth hiring an MP to advise the organization?
- Would we be best advised to rely on our local MEP to unravel what happens in Brussels and Strasbourg?
- Is it worth even trying to lobby local authorities?
- What is the difference between PR and politics?
- Is propaganda strictly for the politicians?
- What are 'spin doctors'?
- What do special advisers do and what are their credentials?

- Can PR 'sell' ideas as well as products and services?
- What are focus groups?
- What is 'The Lobby'?

The climate-makers here are the rulers, those politicians, civil servants and bureaucrats who influence and determine so much of the context of everyone's life and times. Here we look at how PR communicates with the rulers and administrators on behalf of interested organizations, groups and individuals and at how PR is used by government, the civil service and political parties.

This is where PR is most often discussed in the media, where it is frequently depicted as being part of the political dark arts. Questions here relate to lobbying, propaganda, how PR functions in relation to the development of public policy at national and regional level within the United Kingdom and its role in researching EU developments and communications with civil servants in Brussels. Topics include the relationship of lobbyists to mainstream PR practice, the employment of politicians as consultants and the Lobby system of government media briefings.

What are lobbyists?

Lobbyists make representations to politicians and civil servants, more often the latter, in order to influence the content and timing of legislation and regulations from which they, or those on whose behalf they act, will benefit. This is done privately, often one to one, by lobbyists who may be directly employed by the interests they represent or act as consultants on a specific matter. It is a specialist branch of PR and there are dedicated lobbying firms, whose revenues have leapt in recent years. Commercial organizations, trade associations, charities and pressure groups make heavy use of lobbying.

What are public affairs, and how do they differ from political PR and government PR?

Lobbyists favour calling what they do 'public affairs'; some deny any connection with PR:

- Public affairs is variously described, but what it boils down to is relations with government, statutory bodies, government agencies and various semi-official organizations that wield clout in the political economy.

- 'Political PR' describes the PR activities of the political parties, aimed at depicting their philosophies, policies, opinions, credentials and personalities, in or out of power, in the best possible light. This is not, supposedly, to be confused with 'government PR', although in recent years the two have become intertwined owing to fundamental changes in practice following the introduction of 'special advisers'.
- Government PR is supposedly about providing public information, enunciating public policy and giving the government's views on current affairs. It is provided in the United Kingdom by the government information service, responsibility for policy resting with the most senior minister (politician) in each department. It also includes PR in the context of local authorities – where it is often referred to as 'local government PR' – and elsewhere, at EU and regional levels.

How do public affairs relate to PR?

Public affairs revolve around issues of government, typically trying to win favourable treatment or avoid unfavourable consequences, particularly in relation to markets for products and services. It is the lobbying part of PR.

There are some high-minded explanations of public affairs offered by some PR people, who appear to see it as being an integral part of a pluralistic democracy, the means by which every citizen may find a platform for self-expression without the mediation, or intervention, of the media. They depict an idealized contemporary vision of the public forum in some ancient city state. The reality is, however, of a very contested space, in which there is much hustling for share of shout by people who are usually PR professionals, extra skilled at getting through doors.

It certainly does have some connection with democracy, and when it provokes the Prime Minister to write about 'the tyranny of pressure groups' to generate pressure through public opinion to influence public policy, it must surely be a worthwhile public service. Lobbying entails PR-driven communication, in which one side seeks to change the views and actions of the other. This is certainly not 'tyranny', except perhaps to those who seek to routinely use one-way messages as the means to advance their own interests and resent having to engage in two-way dialogue that might result in their having to change their own positions.

Why is lobbying part of PR?

Lobbying is communications-based and about persuasion and negotiation. However, it is no longer entirely about advocacy, from whence it sprang. Much of the lobbyist's efforts are now directed at media relations, to ensure that the case is brought before the relevant politicians and civil servants in their preferred media. Companies that employ lobbyists are increasingly looking for advice rather than action, counsel that can be used in formulating strategy. There are four very good reasons for this change:

- Many of those organizations that employ lobbyists have developed sophisticated in-house public affairs teams, capable of presenting their own cases.
- The UK government is exceptionally sensitive to media comment, far more so than its predecessors. What appears in the mass media therefore can be every bit as influential as anything said by a lobbyist direct.
- Lately, power has been diffused in the United Kingdom, with the creation of regional mini-governments, similarly to many federalist states elsewhere, and through the growing influence of the European Union on domestic politics. Now it is intended to offer regional government to those that want it in England too. The lobbyists follow power, so the specialists are opening offices in cities where hitherto they would not, and there is a corresponding erosion of the value of lobbying centrally.
- Local residents have become very adept at organizing themselves around an issue and campaigning effectively. This is often to the disadvantage of an organization whose managers otherwise might have supposed that lobbying was their 'prerogative' and not connected with community relations.

These four reasons are present, to a greater or lesser extent, in many other countries, particularly where governments 'rule by spin' and/or there is a multiplicity of government power bases and/or there is rising pluralism among increasingly better-educated and knowledgeable populations.

Whoever is doing the lobbying, a careful balance of PR skills is required, in order to develop coalitions of shared interests that can create environments of opinion supportive of the cause and to which politicians are drawn, so that the sought after decisions are easier for them to make and to justify, in their own minds as well as on public policy grounds. Frequently, ministers acknowledge 'givens' that are in reality only recently created by influential lobbying, not only directly (say to their civil servants), but through stakeholders and publics, which have been persuaded to support and advocate the cause in hand. The basic principles of lobbying remain, but this is now integrated into a broader range of corporate affairs activities.

What do lobbyists do?

In essence, they closely monitor public policy developments, identify the policy-makers and decision-takers to approach about a matter that is of concern to their organization or client and secure access and/or make representations, with supporting information. Thereafter they keep contact with those people they have lobbied and apply whatever pressure they may devise to secure the outcome that they seek.

Lobbyists aim to present their campaigns as well-briefed argument of simple-to-grasp concepts and propositions. As always, lobbying depends upon sound advance intelligence, skilful timing and understanding the pressure points, the driving factors and vulnerabilities that can influence the development of public policy.

Why don't lobbyists want to be called just that, lobbyists?

In short, they have an image problem. Lobbyists have been widely regarded as spivs who bend the ears of friendly or amenable politicians behind closed doors and pester the life out of civil servants cowering in offices down long corridors. They claim this is increasingly unjustified, which of course is not a denial, and that the nature of their work is far more diverse than advocacy alone. They are expected to provide more background in-depth research, more strategic advice and more effort to place stories prominently in the national press.

However, the problem really is that they are thought of in the same breath as the politicians, and only 18 per cent of UK adults consider that politicians are trustworthy; research elsewhere indicates that this level of cynicism is not unusual. To overcome these image problems the lobbyists have created for themselves a code of conduct, but it is merely voluntary and does not require disclosure of business interests.

Why are lobbyists so anxious not to be part of PR?

The physical presentation of a case to someone of influence as a means to advance an interest has tended to be seen historically as having more in common with legal advocacy than with the media relations-based PR trade. They were anxious to assert a separate identity and a distinct professional status that befitted their walks down the corridors of power, their encounters with rulers and their discreet, private and confidential representations. The label 'public affairs' also sounds different and better than plain PR.

How can lobbying help if you are not an insider?

Outsiders presumably need all the help they can obtain in presenting their case. Members of Parliament and their assistants continue to welcome what they see as ideas and interests that 'bubble up' from pressure groups and local communities, which is understandable, since invariably they are not unconnected with securing re-election. Some prefer to hear direct from companies and other types of organization, instead of through lobbying specialists. However, lobbyists understand the system and have the appropriate skills that an outsider without public affairs training or experience probably lacks. Trade associations extensively employ lobbyists on behalf of their members, be they insiders or outsiders. Charities, benefiting from their emotional appeal, find that lobbying direct can be more effective, and this is often particularly so for the smaller outsiders: they report finding both politicians and civil servants obligingly receptive to hearing their cases, and many charities provide model examples of effective lobbying.

Why should we be bothered to monitor proposed legislation and regulations when we have our trade association to do that?

Trade associations vary in their levels of competence at political monitoring. Time was when a lawyer might have been employed as a 'parliamentary agent' to keep an eye on declared pending legislation, but modern conditions suggest the need for a deeper level of research and sensitivity to upcoming issues and trends. Some industries are noticeably more adept at this, and have established themselves as influential lobbies, whereas others are noticeably less well served.

Apart from understanding the system, trade associations have to avoid being lured into a false sense of security that can arise when change appears to be slow and protracted, because the pace can quicken dramatically if the policy-makers and decision-takers perceive the necessity. So each trade association has to be judged on its merits by its members. Many companies are perfectly happy to rely on their associations, some others prefer to paddle their own canoe or form collaborations with others independently of an association.

Is there any way of making sure lobbying works?

There are no guarantees, however well it is done. The chances of success might be increased though by giving attention to the further edges of the spectrum and not concentrating solely on the 'big hitters'. For instance, local, as distinct from national, politicians, can be instrumental in moulding public opinion and in dealing with issues and concerns long before they become of interest to policy-makers. In this way, the lobbyists may swim upstream closer to the sources that eventually flow into the great confluence of national politics.

Is there lobbying in Scotland and Wales?

Yes, the lobbyists have opened their offices in Edinburgh and Cardiff in response to the creation of the new devolved forms of regional government that have been created there recently.

Is the lobbying similar to what happens in London?

The approach of the Scottish Executive, or government, to PR is cautious. All government departments and agencies are required to undertake annual audits of PR expenditure. These include declarations of all contracts and, most relevant to lobbying, contacts. Its Parliamentary Standards Committee reported in February 2002 on a proposal to register all lobbyists, in order for them to be permitted to contact legislators and provide information and advice to clients. Offences would carry sentences of substantial fines and imprisonment. If this comes about it is expected to substantially inhibit lobbying in Edinburgh.

Is lobbying really only for business organizations?

Lobbying is for everyone, and is not some arcane activity that is prohibitively expensive for all but the few. Some MPs appear to prefer giving their time to hearing from the less 'professional' lobbyists. The political parties have groups and committees that concentrate on particular interests and there are a number of similar cross-party groups, all of which are usually glad to hear from informed outsiders. Probably their amenability reflects the vast range of interests covered.

Is it worth hiring an MP to advise the organization?

Members of Parliament adopt their own special interests, aiming to become particularly knowledgeable on specific areas of public policy and/or industries, sectors and so on. Among those who entered politics later in life, the choice is often influenced by their previous career experience. Acknowledged expertise wins membership of parliamentary select committees, of which there are now over 30, and resulting opportunities for media coverage and foreign trips. It can secure ministerial jobs or 'shadow' spokesperson status.

An MP with relevant specialist knowledge could be particularly helpful, but it has to be remembered that they are required to declare their interests, specifically any consultancies and directorships. Activities such as raising parliamentary questions for answer by the government and entering Early Day Motions for debate might be more appropriately undertaken instead by the 'local' MP, that is to say, the one who sits for the constituency in which the organization is headquartered or located.

Would we be best advised to rely on our local MEP to unravel what happens in Brussels and Strasbourg?

Yes, the 'local' MEP (their constituencies are vast) is a potentially very useful person indeed, and maybe not sufficiently recognized as such. The opportunities to participate in the decision-making processes are many, but usually action is taken too late; the complexities make lobbying a veritable minefield for all but the initiated. MEPs, therefore, can be very helpful, because they are familiar, or should be, with the procedures and can generate answers to questions placed with the Council of Ministers and with the Commission, or civil service. The EU parliament is gradually acquiring more power and influence and MEPs are gaining in status, to amend legislation, secure information and obtain documentation. They can act as the focus for widening lobby contacts and seeking particular expertise.

Is it worth even trying to lobby local authorities?

Most authorities are committed to fighting for their share and more of whatever economic development opportunities may be around. They have their plans and designate sites for development. They appoint officers with specific duties to attract incoming investment. So the door is open to all organizations that might bear potential good news.

The central reality about lobbying local authorities is that power is concentrated in few hands, either senior officers, or bureaucrats, or senior politicians, usually the chairs of key committees, according to the preferences of each body. Lately the national government concept of 'cabinet responsibility' has been introduced, but usually a few politicians and officers take decisions, ultimately, together. These people manage significant budgets and exercise substantial influence.

What is the difference between PR and politics?

Not a lot, it seems, and the remaining differences appear to be diminishing. The politician R A Butler famously remarked that politics 'is the art of the possible', to which the economist J K Galbraith responded 'Politics is not the art of the possible. It consists in choosing between the disastrous and the unpalatable.' PR, it might be argued, is the art of the possible *and* involves having to make 'real world' judgements. At their epicentres, of course, both are about communication.

There is much else in similar vein that has been said about politics over the years. Politics is, supposedly, the mechanism for resolving peacefully the conflicting interests that arise in life. In order to achieve this, modern politicians heavily rely on PR to handle what has been described as their 'inescapable promotional dynamic'. This the less cynical might interpret more prosaically as their need for promotion.

The politician's need to be known is never more clearly demonstrated than in the effect that mass media exposure can have on the individual's career fortunes. The type of media chosen can be critical. Local newspapers are needed for the weekly awareness drip dripping, but there is no beating the television interview, which, however short, can be worth more than 1,000 well-weighed words in a national newspaper.

> This hungry urge to televisual promotion is leading politicians into new ventures. For example, among UK politicians, Michael Portillo conducts a documentary inquiry into his Spanish ancestors, Mo Mowlem presents a hagiography of Winston Churchill and Charles Kennedy compères a comic 'current affairs' quiz show. Politicians around the world are similarly demonstrating their urge to present themselves on TV in new formats.

This level of exposure is the means to grasping fame, usually with an eye to gaining or retaining power. A strong personal presence in the mass media is considered vital.

> In the United Kingdom, Labour Party members in Carlisle told television viewers that they were choosing Tony Blair for their party leader because 'he will look good on television'. Liberal Democrat members selected Charles Kennedy for their leader because he was already well known for his non-political television appearances. Conservative members make public their endless despair at not having a charismatic leader comparable to Margaret Thatcher. Much the same occurs in many other countries.

At the constituency level, leadership of a political party transforms a modest majority into overwhelming support. Typically, in the United Kingdom, this goes from routinely obtaining around 40 per cent of the votes cast to receiving 65 per cent or more. Being Prime Minister or some other senior figure pushes the local majority even higher, because the local MP is then perceived to be as important as any show biz celebrity.

Is propaganda strictly for the politicians?

Propaganda is about telling, not listening, nor hearing. Politicians appear to adore propaganda, and those among them that are its greatest advocates are more often than not the noisiest at protesting the need for 'public debate'.

Perhaps encouraged by the politicians, there are plenty of other people around who rather prefer this form of communication to taking the trouble to foster dialogue, particularly if that might expose them to the risk of having to adjust their positions to meet the views of those they seek to persuade. Further, any one-way communication, such as talking up the attractions of a pop music concert, technically constitutes propaganda, since all that is wanted by way of feedback is compliance, such as 'bums on seats'.

The key ingredients of propaganda are the easy use of deceit, distortion of truth, careful withholding of material evidence, calculated deception, assertion of opinion as fact, ready use of command and plenty of self-congratulation. This may sound all too familiar. So no, sadly propaganda is not strictly for the politicians.

What are 'spin doctors'?

The media coined this description for those who are employed by government to 'control the news agenda', that is to say, decide what the UK government says about what from day to day and how it says it, and 'manipulate the media', so that government messages are communicated to readers, viewers and listeners consistent with its requirements, which always necessitate a favourable interpretation.

There is nothing much that is new about this, except that 'New' Labour has taken it to extremes hitherto unseen in the United Kingdom, arguing that it is entitled to continually campaign throughout each term in office as well as in the approach to and during elections. This entails proactive creation and management of 'news' 24 hours a day, 365 days a year, regardless of objections on grounds of democracy or just plain pleading to be let off for a moment. This intense media manipulation by the ruling party is, of course, to varying degrees commonplace around the world, including the United States, where virtually all the media have uncritically accepted the Republican agenda since the 2001 terrorist attacks.

The term seems to have come from the expression 'to put a spin on' a matter to describe the practice of best possible interpretation. Because PR is persuasive and always positive, the journalists have come to use the term spin doctors to describe PR people generally, so repeatedly on air and in print that it has slipped into common usage.

Government news is frequently attributed to anonymous informants. Complaining in *The Guardian* (16 December 2002) that 'our leaders' weapons of mass assertion deny us access to the truth', that newspaper's former editor, Peter Preston, cited the Associated Press item of 18 November 2002 that 'US intelligence has concluded that an audiotape of Osama bin Laden is real and was recently recorded', according to 'one US official' speaking anonymously. This, he had been advised by Douglas Turner, editor of the *Buffalo News*, conformed with AP's guidebook for reporters, which says one anonymous source is enough. 'Why', he asked, 'do the briefers want to stay anonymous? For the best and the worst of reasons: confusion, protection, advantage, manipulation. They serve a media growth industry, adding correspondents and experts by the minute; all of them reliant – to some extent – on sources we can't see and whose motives we can't judge'.

What do special advisers do and what are their credentials?

When the description 'special adviser' first emerged in the media, the name seemed to imply that here were people particularly knowledgeable on abstruse subjects that government ministers needed to know about if they were to perform their public offices. Gradually it emerged that most of them appeared to be specialist only in that the political party in power hitherto employed them, very probably as a researcher or press officer.

The impression has been given that being a special adviser is a camp follower's sinecure, which comes somewhere in the career progression between being a junior party employee and embarking on a lucrative career as an MP sitting in parliament well into old age representing a safe constituency. The government in the early and mid-1990s was said to have about 30 of these people, and the current government reportedly has 80, so the trend is towards more, rather than less.

As to what special advisers do, that seems to be largely about political PR on behalf of whichever party is in power. They work inside ministries, close to civil servants whose job is government PR, where they appear to be primarily concerned with trying to vet and influence all output to the media, with a particular view to promoting favourable images of government ministers and their wives. They are, according to the parliamentary Public Administration Select Committee of MPs, 'unmanageable and unaccountable', being employed by the taxpayer but not members of the civil service.

Special advisers are said by the committee to perform a valuable function but it reported that 'the boundaries between their work and those of career civil servants do not appear to be well understood'. Some are experts, while others are overtly political. They engage at a high level in the business of government. For instance, special advisers have run mixed teams of advisers and civil servants in the Downing Street Policy Unit. However, the abiding impression is of meddlers, political 'fixers' who are working deep within government, wielding power without much accountability.

> Serious damage was done to the occupational status of special adviser by Jo Moore's 'error of judgement' when on 11 September 2001 she e-mailed colleagues, one hour after the first aircraft had flown into the World Trade Center in New York, advising 'Media handling. It's now a very good day to get out anything we want to bury. Councillors' expenses?' A former Labour Party press officer, Jo Moore kept her job, for a while, apparently because her chief error was in getting caught. Subsequently she was again embarrassed and had to go, together with the civil servant employed as the communications director in the same ministry, the Department for Transport, Local Government and the Regions. The top civil servant moved to another ministry, the senior minister 'was resigned' and the whole ministry was dismantled after less than a year.

The Jo Moore scandal served to strengthen the impression that special advisers are really PR people with strong political loyalties, who are placed by the ruling party within the government apparatus in order to oversee government communications, with a view to making sure they are not impartial but highly supportive of the prevailing political will. This conclusion is strengthened by the recollection that all career civil servants traditionally 'doing a turn' at disseminating government information were gradually replaced by professional PR people and journalists brought in from outside. The proximity of the special advisers to the government's PR apparatus has led the media to include them in the description 'spin doctors'.

Can PR 'sell' ideas as well as products and services?

Yes, very much so. For instance, the US government now has a minister 'for public diplomacy and public affairs'. After a career dedicated to creating and building commercial brands, the Undersecretary of State is now 'selling' the United States, its values and foreign policy. The idea is 'to distil the values and virtues of American democracy', so that people will adjust their perceptions of the United States towards recognition of its noble ideals and away from its commercial culture.

PR can 'sell' ideas from the worthy to the unworthy, but persuasion may depend upon rather more reasoned argument and greater proof of facts than 'selling' commercially.

> At the former home in Virginia of the first US president, George Washington, the museum managers are trying to 'sell' the idea he was 'the most robust man of action you can imagine', but first they have to make a case that overcomes some well-established and unhelpful historic facts. However, sometimes such facts can help, not hinder. For instance, Mexican President Vicente Fox, a former multinational company executive, won power in 2000 by being 'sold' as a 'straight-talking cowboy', whose 'straight talking' appealed to voters tired of the 71-year reign of his predecessors.

What are focus groups?

Focus groups consist of about seven to 10 people, chosen from a public under scrutiny, usually recruited by telephone, maybe using a list of random digit phone numbers or people who previously expressed an interest in taking part in focus group research. Questions are asked in order to qualify each person as meeting the criteria for inclusion. The researcher 'moderates' the gathering, initiating discussion, using stimuli such as pictures to focus attention on an idea, topic, message and so on, and nudging participants back onto the subject matter when they stray from it.

The discussion is relatively free form and can provide rich nuggets of information from which intelligence may be gleaned. The skill of the moderator lies in:

- first putting participants at their ease;
- building their confidence in the value of the exercise; and
- then moving the discussion gradually from the broad, exploratory questions to focusing enquiries on the relevant research topics.

This leads into use of tasks, as a means to let participants more readily project their thoughts and feelings. The whole group then evaluates the results. When all appears to be said and done the moderator invites final thoughts, to give participants the chance to offer more, which they might have been holding back on, so possibly releasing further information.

Political parties, like retailers, public service providers and leading consumer products manufacturers, are using focus group research extensively, because it can be the source of much valuable detailed information about attitudes and perceptions. Its heavy use by politicians has resulted, say critics, in an intense 'talk back', by which politicians substitute 'telling people what they want to hear' for offering them policies to be enacted in exchange for being elected. A popular example used in support of this contention was the re-election of US President Bill Clinton in 1996.

What is 'The Lobby'?

The Lobby is a system by which journalists are accredited by the UK parliamentary civil service to report on parliament and politics. About four or five reporters from every leading newspaper, together with people from the main broadcast news organizations, are accorded access not available to other journalists. The system has existed for some 120 years and is named after the place within the Palace of Westminster (the UK parliament building, often referred to as the house of The Mother of Parliaments) where reporters would talk privately with ministers 'off the record'.

Over the years, Lobby members have become accustomed to attending informal briefings given by a Prime Minister's Press Secretary, in addition to obtaining information from individual ministries and private conversations. These briefings evolved into two daily sessions, attributed to 'authoritative sources'. Gradually the attribution has changed, to become 'Prime Minister's official spokesperson'.

The system appears in process of gradual dismantling. For the past three years, edited summaries of these briefings have been made available on a Downing Street Web site and recently the sessions have been reduced to one a day, the second being thrown open to all journalists. It is said that lobby journalists seldom rely on their private briefings for more than 'minor input', but then they would say that, wouldn't they?

Some Lobby journalists suspect that the admission of the world's media to the daily morning briefing is a ruse by government to reduce the number of searching questions by British reporters who are better informed about or more interested in UK issues. For instance, on hearing of the change, according to *The Times* (3 May

2002), one asked 'Do today's changes mean that Arabs and Czechoslovaks will interrupt our questions?' Czechoslovakia has, of course, ceased to exist. But then other tough questions had included 'Does the Prime Minister dye his hair?', 'Has the Prime Minister got a tattoo on his bottom?' and 'Where did the Prime Minister buy the shirt he was wearing at the Commonwealth Heads of Government Meeting?'

ten

what does **success** look like?

- Is effectiveness the sure sign of success in PR?
- What is really meant by effectiveness in doing PR?
- How do we relate PR's contribution to the bottom line?
- How in practice is PR evaluated?
- How can we be sure that any money we spend on PR will give us a worthwhile return?
- Don't PR people always make wild promises about what they can achieve?
- What is really meant by PR 'coping with turbulent times'?
- Why not just add up the press coverage and see how much it would have cost to buy as advertising space?
- What's the most common error in evaluating PR programmes?
- Do PR people have a preferred method of measuring their results?
- Are column centimetres an effective measure of success?
- Isn't some coverage better than none?
- Can a one-column single paragraph have the same impact as a whole page article?
- Is there some law of diminishing returns with media relations to look out for?
- How do you measure goodwill?
- How do you measure the immeasurable?
- What is the difference between attitudes and perceptions?
- Then what is the difference between beliefs and attitudes?
- What are demographics and psychographics?

- How much do different lifestyles matter?
- When can PR influence behaviours in the short term?
- How much of our PR budget should we allocate to measurement and evaluation?
- We can't afford formal evaluation. Is there any value in informal, subjective evaluation?
- What might we miss if we skip measurement and evaluation?
- When's the best time to start planning measurement and evaluation?
- What are audits in this context and do we need them?
- Are there any hidden advantages of evaluation that we should be aware of and use?
- Can we do a bit, see how we've done, and do more as and when, measuring carefully as we go?
- Isn't maintaining a high profile all that's needed?
- Is there some 'silver bullet' formula?

Now we consider what is probably the single most important topic of all, particularly for anyone contemplating embarking upon PR expenditure for the first time: how is PR to be measured and evaluated? It is widely asserted that PR activity is not measurable, so what methods are available and when might they be used? What measures are likely to be most relevant across a wide range of companies and organizations of different sizes and structures? And how might the individual best determine success? Questions here explore establishing financial criteria, considering how to trace other benefits to revenue outcomes and determining the non-financial contributions of PR and their value to efficiency and effectiveness.

Is effectiveness the sure sign of success in PR?

All depends upon what is meant by 'success'. Securing desired outcomes indeed suggests that effectiveness is the acid test, but what of the more balanced two-way dialogue, between relative equals in terms of their ability to change each other, the types of communication exchange that may even lead to negotiation and substantial compromises? Here the signs of success might also include the achievement of meaningful discussion, genuine engagement, observance of ethical standards and win–win outcomes that all sides can live with.

True, most communications never go this far, but, however relatively deep or shallow the nature of the communication, there are certain practical considerations that must surely apply. For instance, budgets are made to be kept, all messages should be absolutely consistent and changes are meant to stick, not promptly unravel. These key aspects might equally qualify as sure signs of success.

What is really meant by effectiveness in doing PR?

Effectiveness has two meanings, what is do-able and what is beneficial. All messages have a succession of stages to pass through from launch to reaching final destination and each succeeding stage gives the message greater impact. The simplest interpretations of this suggest that there are two or three such stages, such as awareness, understanding and acceptance. When there is willing acceptance the consequence is changed attitudes, leading in turn to changed behaviour. It has been likened to a domino effect.

The only snag with this is that it is far too simplistic. It cannot be assumed with safety that each stage will deliver the required level of impact in relation to each receiver. Far from it, with each successive stage the odds against are likely to lengthen. In reality, there are probably many more such stages that the message has to pass through before fulfilment. The more modest objectives are met sooner, via fewer stages, while the most ambitious, those relating to large-scale social, cultural, political and/or economic change, take longer and involve many more stages. The timescale difference is likely to be in months, or weeks, on the one hand, and in years on the other.

All programmes must be actionable and set against specific objectives; in that sense they are effective. However, for them to be effective also in the beneficial sense they must have a material effect on relationships to which the communication relates that is measured in terms of either change or maintenance. The skill is in deciding which stage the message has to reach in order to achieve the optimum balance, in effectiveness and efficiency, between merely being do-able and also being beneficial, in the context of the precise objectives for the programme.

How do we relate PR's contribution to the bottom line?

PR's principal contribution lies in two areas: management intelligence, that provides the means to build and sustain corporate reputation, which in consequence gains in value and materially assists the organization in meeting its objectives; and creation of the optimum conditions for the organization within the environment in which it operates, so that it may pursue all its purposes advantageously and expeditiously for its long-term effectiveness.

This is not to say that PR results in directly attributable revenues. However, it can have a startling impact, not by achieving sales, because that job lies elsewhere, but by creating the conditions that *favour* sales. It can be the means to achieving many successes that do not appear, at face value, to be attributable, but are in reality the beneficiaries of the PR effort. It can have a major impact on achieving higher productivity and cost efficiencies, by fostering a corporate culture that creates an appropriate beneficial environment.

How in practice is PR evaluated?

Quantitative criteria are heavily used to assess results against communication objectives. Numerous measurement methods have been developed, many based upon content analysis, notably in press coverage, where predetermined values are assigned to items of coverage and traced back to form value judgements about particular activities. This is complemented by the use of statistical data to indicate what types of people, in what quantities, had 'opportunities' to see or hear a message.

Formal 'before and after' surveys are used to measure changes, most often in attitudes and perceptions, and ongoing studies trace movement in levels of awareness and understanding. Research methods used also include focus groups and pre-testing. Data measures include levels of enquiries, sales leads, complaints and expressions of support. Comparative measurements are made using differing results for similar or identical events, where one had PR support and another did not. Cost benefit analysis is applied.

However, some results are not susceptible to measurement in any conventional sense. Many results are qualitative, rather than quantitative, and their assessment is based largely on knowing what works in the light of past efforts. For example, the intermediary in the supply chain may be making a better job of explaining to his or her customers, parents may be demonstrating greater willingness to be active supporters, job applicants may be coming forward with higher qualifications, donors may be demonstrating more interest in what they are helping to support, local communities may be taking more interest in what is being done around them, and so on.

What this boils down to is that, while PR can be largely measured by using conventional evaluation techniques, which abound, quite a lot of results do not necessitate sophisticated approaches, because the results speak for themselves, and some results bring tangible benefits but are not readily measurable. PR should be subjected to as rigorous evaluation as any other activity, but it has distinct characteristics that have to be taken into full account when deciding how best to measure and assess results against communication objectives.

How can we be sure that any money we spend on PR will give us a worthwhile return?

Much depends upon what is considered to be worthwhile. There are no guarantees of success, but PR is as capable of being properly and fully planned and thoroughly implemented in a timely manner as other knowledge- and skill-based occupations and activities.

A limited form of guarantee may be available, incidentally, from some consultancies. For example, one is offering 'minimum guaranteed coverage', to provide its clients with publication of 'two out of three key messages' within six months. The conditions attached to this are that the consultants must write the text and agree with the choice of media in which the said messages are to appear.

This has been described, on the one hand, as a stunt, counterproductive and a threat to the trade's integrity and, on the other, as demonstrating greater accountability and no different to lawyers' 'no win, no fee' offers. In practice, consultants routinely expect to do the writing, select the appropriate media and deliver at least as much coverage as this guarantee promises. If their clients want to do the writing and select the media, presumably they are capable of securing the coverage as well and have no need of a consultant's services.

Don't PR people always make wild promises about what they can achieve?

Unrealistic optimism about communication outcomes is not confined to PR people, but can seize senior and other managers too. PR people are incurably optimistic about their work, it seems, or if they are not they are accomplished at concealing it. Like sales people, every morning brings fresh opportunities, new ground to break and targets to exceed. It may be that they overestimate what is possible because they lack sufficient control over the use of techniques, particularly where intermediaries are involved, or the environment in which they are operating, which can be subjected to sudden turbulence.

The more ambitious the PR outcomes sought, generally the greater the time necessary for their achievement. Impatience can overlook that. You would not expect significant, widespread effects to be obtained in other functions without plenty of sustained effort, so why expect them with PR? If 'early wins' are so important, the objectives should be within the realms of what may be realistically expected sooner, rather than later. For instance, understandings, attitudes and perceptions change before beliefs and behaviours. And if the results do not turn out as well as expected nevertheless they offer time in hand in which to review and adjust as appropriate.

What is really meant by PR 'coping with turbulent times'?

Organizations of all kinds, not only companies but also, for example, hospitals and universities, have become politicized of late, as demands have grown for them to further justify their impact on society as a whole. In addition to meeting their primary responsibilities, organizations have acquired, or had thrust upon them, broader social purposes.

They find themselves repeatedly challenged by a variety of constituencies or publics, to demonstrate that they are 'socially responsible'. Constraints, which represent problems to be dealt with, had been familiar enough to managers, but now they operate in more turbulent times. Rejection of corporate values and opposition to organizational plans and aspects of operations have become ever-present pressures, with the potential to veto, impede and prevent managers' intentions meeting fulfilment.

Given these multiple corporate purposes, PR aims to engage with all the various publics, none of which necessarily need be friendly and any of which may be hostile. Confrontational factions that are intent upon advancing their individual agendas and beliefs routinely challenge the organizational desire for consensus. These single-minded groups exert disruptive power, often, sadly, as an end in itself.

PR therefore seeks 'a licence to operate' based upon a willingness of the 'big battalions' that represent consensus to acknowledge corporate acceptance of these growing social purposes, or duties. These licences do not come cheap; they have to be earned. Hence all the interest in communicating qualities of corporate social responsibility, and in the RSA 'Tomorrow's Company Inquiry' concept of 'inclusivity', which values reciprocal relationships with key stakeholders.

Why not just add up the press coverage and see how much it would have cost to buy as advertising space?

This is an old and largely discredited approach, simply because advertising and editorial carry differing levels of credibility. Just think of the last time you read a newspaper by reference to the advertisements that appeared in it, and only glimpsed the editorial in between. On the contrary, you bought the newspaper to read the editorial, and it may be that you gave so little time to the advertisements that you did not actually 'see' some of them. This is why the advertisements and the editorial are so often artfully intertwined across the pages, to make it more difficult to neglect those areas that have been paid for by the advertisers. Successive surveys over many years have indicated that the credibility of editorial far exceeds that of advertising.

So effectiveness cannot be measured by simply looking at the 'advertising value equivalent' (AVE) of the physical amount of editorial achieved. It may give a general impression of how much the editorial would have cost if it had been charged at equivalent advertising rates, and that might make the editorial seem like a bargain, but that is about all it would achieve. After all, the editorial space was probably never up for sale or going to be purchased. And even if the advertising was capable of providing the same results as the editorial, who knows how much would be needed?

The fundamental differences between advertising and PR serve to emphasize the point, and using AVE as some sort of measure of editorial worth has to also take account of another fundamental weakness: the decline in the pulling power of advertising. This has resulted in a pronounced trend among marketers to spend less of their budgets on media advertising and more on PR, direct marketing and sales promotion. This is despite falling charges for advertising and greater bargaining power among advertisers.

What's the most common error in evaluating PR programmes?

In this life it is seductively easy to be a 'busy fool' and most people like to think that their efforts deserve to be fairly recorded, summarized, tabulated and, preferably, admired. But no amount of energetic activity necessarily equates to effectiveness and efficiency, and PR work can be prone to this misunderstanding. It matters not how many messages are dispatched, if none of them are received. PR people in the United States are called 'flaks', to describe the indiscriminate bombarding of the media with press releases. It is a widespread practice, doubtless driven by equal quantities of enthusiasm and despair.

This frequent confusion of one measure – output – with another – impact, illustrates the most common error: mixing up what is being measured. It happens elsewhere; for instance:

- Participation at an exhibition may be valued by the numbers of people visiting the stand, when actionable enquiries would be a truer measure of how well those opportunities were being handled.
- The percentage of welcome responses to a radio phone-in may be cited as evidence of support, without proper allowance for the self-selection of the respondents.
- Heavy coverage in a trade newspaper may be taken as indicating success in press relations, when coverage among media serving customers would be more relevant than talking mainly to competitors.

Do PR people have a preferred method of measuring their results?

They do seem to love poring over their press cuttings, perhaps because they spend so much time in obtaining them. This is despite the very wide range of PR work, because communication lies at its heart and the mass media account for a very substantial part of communication.

Are column centimetres an effective measure of success?

'Column inches', as they used to be known before metrication in the United Kingdom, were elevated to an art form by many PR people, those who had managed to convince themselves and everyone else that the virility of their efforts lay in the *quantity* of resulting media coverage. Great was the time taken to measure these column inches, and to prove that every year there had been more than the year before.

In all this endeavour, however, little or no account was taken of content *quality*. It matters not, for example, that a whole page appears in the local free newspaper if what is needed is a couple of paragraphs on the relevant page of a national newspaper. It is agreeable to receive much attention through association, say by inviting a celebrity to open the new plant, but is that passing brief mention of the company really worth very much? These, and other such considerations, so often seemed to be swept aside in the chase for cuttings, those precious items that could be circulated triumphantly, displayed on notice boards, pasted lovingly into special cuttings books, even used to paper the walls.

> Some organizations spent very happily on pursuing column inches. At Rentokil (woodworm and pest control), a company then in the PR vanguard, executives flew the length and breadth of the United Kingdom to photograph properties, gather information about them and the work being done to them, fly back, write articles, process photographs and later delight in seeing the results appear in obscure local newspapers where the properties were situated. What a happy jet-lagged life, all for gathering the column inches.

Metrication did not dampen this ardour, so what did? The realization began to dawn that, as securing coverage became easier thanks to the 'PR-ization of the media', coverage alone was no longer an acceptable goal in itself. After all, some coverage might be counterproductive, hostile, superfluous, inaccurate or contain serious omissions. Some might be 'in the wrong place' or appear 'at the wrong time'.

In short, measuring coverage was *indicative* as regards levels of impact and so forth, but it was insufficient in itself. Coverage had to be related to satisfaction of very specific overriding PR objectives. There is where it rests. Press coverage is a valuable form of measurement, but it can be deeply misleading if merely taken at face value.

Isn't some coverage better than none?

Some rather than none does not always hold good. There are some times in life when no coverage is sought or needed. Nor, incidentally, is all coverage good coverage just because there is usually none, or it is a novelty.

Can a one-column single paragraph have the same impact as a whole page article?

Without doubt a single paragraph can be equally valuable, if the message is accurate, succinct and before the receivers for whom it is intended. The whole page article may look more impressive, but it does not follow that the target audience is the same or in some way better, or that the text does equal or greater justice to the message. It may be lost in a fog of words or the writer may have mangled or disparaged it. Indeed, if you did not write the article, it is a fair bet that a one-paragraph summary of what you *did* write is likely to be more effective. This is the quality versus quantity equation again.

Is there some law of diminishing returns with media relations to look out for?

There is certainly a nasty and widespread practice among journalists that has to be most definitely guarded against. They enthusiastically adopt people and organizations, going over the top in giving them high public profiles, and then just as assiduously start to 'knock' them, with the obvious intention of destroying what they have been largely responsible for just creating. It can be a surprisingly fast journey, up the hill of fame and down the other side again.

As malicious sport this may rank quite high with those who indulge in it. Fortunately, from an organizational perspective, it tends to affect mainly celebrities in general, politicians, sports performers, entertainers, writers, musicians and artists, but it has been extended of late to affect senior managers in all walks of life and their organizations. The absurd hype of the dot.com period, with its crazed promotion of 'new economy' companies and disparagement of 'traditional' ones, followed by its relentless dismissal of 'all that' as if the media had played no part, served to emphasize the risk. 'What goes up has to come down' is a saying well worth remembering here. So when media relations begin to look like they are yielding incredible results it is as well to bear in mind that they may be just that, incredible.

In an editorial leading article, *The Guardian* (10 September 2002) commented on the way in which this had worked for Zadie Smith, a young British novelist: 'She is young, black, witty, beautiful, charming and, by all accounts, remarkably modest about her success. All in all, long overdue for a kicking, wouldn't you say? Bored of lionizing an astonishing new talent, newspaper executives yawn, flip a coin and order up the opposite'. The paper went on to detail how this is done, adding that 'meanwhile she is clearing off to Harvard. And who can blame her?' Before quitting for the United States, Smith gave only radio interviews to promote her second novel and said that she might not bother to write another one.

How do you measure goodwill?

The feedback can be qualitative and quantitative. For instance, it may be measured by the number of people who volunteer to help, or act considerately to facilitate what might otherwise be more difficult or impractical. Surveys and focus groups may be used to track movements. Often, though, goodwill goes unstated, providing a purposeful or congenial environment, which should not be taken for granted.

How do you measure the immeasurable?

What is incapable of measurement obviously cannot be measured. The value of results that are self-evident have to be judged on their merits in the specific circumstances, using experience and comparables. It is understandable that this may irritate those who prefer management by objectives based on precise measurement, but ample compensation occurs should PR deliver its less measurable results in obvious and undeniable abundance, as it is capable of doing. Sometimes recognition is grudging, however, because it might detract from another's achievement, as where, for example, sales people may deny the contribution of PR in first 'softening up' their market to create optimum conditions in which they may then achieve sales.

What is the difference between attitudes and perceptions?

An attitude is a response predisposition, a mental state of readiness that is used by a person to provide a certain response to specific stimuli. It is what happens each time the same thing occurs, but it may be a fleeting thought and not an action that can be observed. What makes attitudes very interesting is that they are a mechanism for allocating common stimuli to our 'seen that, done that box', where we know what we think about this and that, so we don't have to bother again and can move on to investigating more novel or interesting stimuli. Attitudes take up secure positions in that box and may be seldom taken out for review.

A perception is an intuitive recognition, using the senses and intellect, of some quality, characteristic, truth and so on. Image is an object of perception that exists purely in the mind. It is formed by reference to what else is known, or thought to be, other points of reference. For instance, a company may have an image of being socially aware and concerned because its identity and behaviours fit what is expected of such an organization by reference to those that are known already to have those qualities. We use our perceptions to develop attitudes, so as perceptions change, so too may attitudes, and in turn behaviour.

Then what is the difference between beliefs and attitudes?

Beliefs are based on what are thought to be the attributes of an object. They are ideas based upon the available information about it. But what people believe about the qualities and nature of, say, an organization is not necessarily consistent with what they think of it, their evaluation, or attitude, towards it. For instance, a company may tell the world that it is socially aware and concerned, but some people may not rate those qualities in a company, may even think them inappropriate. We use our beliefs to develop attitudes, but beliefs are much harder to change than are attitudes; not for nothing are beliefs also referred to as values.

What are demographics and psychographics?

Demographics are the statistics of life, relating to age, sex, health, income, education, death and so on, used in demography, the study of humanity. They are the 'vital statistics' that tell us about people, but they are fairly bald facts that, without elaboration, are highly unlikely to be of themselves sufficiently informative for PR purposes.

The flesh can be put on these demographic bare bones with psychographics, which describe psychological and 'lifestyle' characteristics. For instance, identification of a cluster of '40-something' professionals resident in a district may not be of much use, but when the positions held by those people are traced, in their jobs, their professional associations, the local community and so on, overt positions of influence will be identified that in turn may form the basis of recognizing at least one relevant public.

How much do different lifestyles matter?

Lifestyles are an important factor. Analysis goes beyond the psychological characteristics, to segment people according to their perceived needs and degree of extroversion and introversion. It all began in the mid-1980s in California, with the proprietary VALS (Values and

Lifestyles) system. This assigned people to one of nine categories, using indicative, and sometimes tortuous, names: achievers, belongers, emulators, experientials, I-am-Me's, integrateds, socially conscious, survivors and sustainers.

Similar systems have been developed since, including a second VALS version that offered eight segments: achievers, actualizers, believers, experiencers, fulfilleds, makers, strivers and strugglers. These systems are used in PR, particularly in MPR, but they may not be adequate always, because a person's behaviour may be contrary to what might be expected of someone allocated to a given category, and in PR it is the level and type of activism that is of primary interest.

> Data mapping by Experian has divided the UK population into 31 categories within seven broad headings. 'Asset-rich families', for instance, comprise 18.6 per cent of the population and include six categories: capital gainers, professional heights, wealth from the land, cusp of retirement, upscale middleagers and ready for retirement. The remaining broad definitions are: money worth managing (3.1 per cent), grey lifestyles (19.9 per cent), benefits borderline (15 per cent), small-time borrowing (22.9 per cent), equity accumulation (15.2 per cent) and parental dependency (5.6 per cent). The consultancy told the *Financial Times* (6 October 2001) that 'describing data in map form makes it easier for people to understand the different sectors they are marketing their products to'.

When can PR influence behaviours in the short term?

Changing behaviours usually takes time. However, if the public is precisely focused and the behaviour change required is uncomplicated, by which we probably mean downright simple, it may be possible within a short time frame, given skill and a positive attitude within the public. The size of the public is relevant, and the identification of 'early adopters' who will make the change and be seen by the others to endorse it is valuable, because they can act as opinion formers to accelerate the process.

How much of our PR budget should we allocate to measurement and evaluation?

Given that some outcomes are measurable by conventional means, others are self-evident and some are immeasurable, what is prudent by way of allocation must vary depending upon the exact circumstances. Many PR people spend surprisingly little, probably no more than two to three per cent of their total budgets. However, when research is undertaken using, say focus groups, cost rise accordingly, and five to 10 per cent is more likely. Some argue for 10 per cent on principle, but this may be impractical on cost grounds. Nonetheless, skimping on this impairs efficiency and effectiveness.

The cost of measurement and evaluation has been the subject of perennial controversy. Consultants frequently accuse their clients of being unwilling or unprepared to fund it, while many of their clients appear to be not much convinced of its necessity. When the need arises in-house, however, it seems to be routine and fully funded. Shrewd consultants tend to avoid clients that refuse them appropriate funding for this purpose, because they reason that without proper measurement they risk their efforts being underrated and undervalued.

We can't afford formal evaluation. Is there any value in informal, subjective evaluation?

Almost any measure is better than none. For instance, often results can be measured using numbers, as where, say, membership has grown, donations have increased or enquiries have occurred. There are plenty of down to earth, economical ways of doing this. Similarly, results that defy measurement nevertheless may be assessed in a worthwhile way, as where directly attributable effects that relate to purposes can be observed.

What might we miss if we skip measurement and evaluation?

Probably the single most obvious consequence would be the lack of the ready means to keep an effective check on progress, so that running adjustments, reordering and so on could be undertaken in a considered and timely manner:

- Without measurement and evaluation there would be no structured approach to recording and comparing the number and nature of sales leads or literature requests.
- Without monitoring of awareness levels, attitudes, perceptions, lifestyle patterns, beliefs and so on, much valuable potential intelligence would be missed.

- So would be opportunities to achieve greater effectiveness and efficiencies through the early anticipation and understanding of effects, redeployment of resources and cross-fertilization of information to the advantage of differing units.
- And the scope for using current experience to plan future activity would be greatly hampered.

When's the best time to start planning measurement and evaluation?

It is said that if you don't know where you are going any road will take you there, and this certainly applies with PR. At the very beginning, corporate and communications objectives are required that can be quantifiably measured along the way. Measurement and evaluation have to be considered and fully allowed for at the planning stage. Agreed that some outcomes may not be quantifiable as precisely as others, and there may be some that defy quantification, but nonetheless they will be evaluated against the objectives, to guide progress and assess effectiveness.

What are audits in this context and do we need them?

The term 'audit' is used to describe the work of surveying, assessing, analysing and so on, implying the same level of scrutiny as would be expected of a financial audit. Yes, they are needed, from time to time. They are conducted in relation to communications, between the organization and its publics, and to PR, examining policy, performance and resources. Audits are also commonly undertaken in relation to: corporate social responsibility, risk, crisis, investment, behaviour, visual identity, management, employment and failure.

Are there any hidden advantages of evaluation that we should be aware of and use?

Analysis of the content of media coverage tells much about the current state of reputation and how it is changing, since it seldom remains static, for better or for worse. It is idle to suppose that any organization's reputation can long survive 'bad press' unimpaired, and beyond a certain point – research suggests about 20 per cent – the volume of unfavourable to favourable reportage and comment begins to inflict damage. So it is advisable to continuously monitor and analyse, even when 'the statistics look favourable', because in the media perception *is* reality.

That last point deserves emphasis. Journalists convince themselves that they are usually the first to know when an organization is heading into being labelled 'troubled'. The 'rot' is said to begin on the PR side, with slow, inadequate and/or especially defensive responses. This may be because journalists usually have primary contact with the PR function. It is human nature to suppose the worst and the ratio of favourable to unfavourable reportage can change quickly and unexpectedly.

Equitable Life Assurance clearly supposed that it could survive media controversy with a neat legal victory over the validity of the guaranteed returns that it had used to attract investors. It would be interesting to know what if any failure auditing was undertaken, because seemingly the company was unprepared for the ultimate court judgement going against it.

Then matters began to unravel fast, as they can have a way of doing. The financial accounts were found to be inaccurate, the senior managers quit, the new managers sued the auditors and £850 million had to be set aside to settle mis-selling claims. This saga has done huge damage not only to Equitable Life's reputation but also to the whole UK savings industry, and the damage continues. Could the warning signs in the media have been heeded sooner and acted upon?

Can we do a bit, see how we've done, and do more as and when, measuring carefully as we go?

PR is not like tap water, to be turned on and off as and when needed. It is a continuous process, whether comprised of one or more concurrent or successive programmes, even as effects are being measured and evaluated. If you do a little and then give up for a while, it is highly probable that whatever has been achieved by the effort will be dissipated and you will be starting from scratch again later, with all that implies.

Isn't maintaining a high profile all that's needed?

High visibility is not an end in itself, but a means to an end, based on measurable communications objectives. PR programmes are effects-orientated, not simply platforms for exhibitionism, a point that not a few celebrities might benefit from reflecting upon. Of course criticism about this can come easy, and not only from journalists. For instance, accountants can claim that 'the wages of spin are death' when they think managers should spend less time on PR, and more on, well, finance, maybe. The reality is that every organization needs its public face, or faces, and knowing when to say nothing as well as when to speak up is all part of PR. What is an appropriate level of 'top show' activity in support of marketing will depend upon the marketing requirement.

Is there some 'silver bullet' formula?

If only there was: as yet there is no single agreed method for measuring overall effectiveness. Instead, PR people measure differing levels of impact in a variety of ways. Nor is there yet one simple, easily understood and applied way of assessing image, identity and reputation together, both within and without the organization.

eleven

tools of the trade

- What is a public relations machine?
- How might this differ from an in-house department?
- Are all press releases sent by e-mail these days?
- Do you have to do a chase up call after each release?
- How does PR cope with the gossip and worse on the Internet?
- What PR opportunities have been created by the Internet?
- Who needs PR to design a brochure or Web site?
- Are speakers' panels worth the time and effort?
- What is product placement?
- What are infomercials?
- Why still write a letter to an editor?
- Do journalists secretly crave attention?
- What are their popular complaints about PR?
- Is news really entertainment?
- Why hire photographers when we all have cameras?
- Why run PR surveys when we already do extensive marketing research?
- When might advertising be part of PR?
- Can press coverage directly affect share price?
- Do City of London analysts believe what they read about a company?
- Is there a lot of 'red tape' with financial PR?
- What is the Friday Night Drop?
- What's the difference between financial PR and financial services marketing?
- What are investomers?

- Is non-financial reporting of any value to PR?
- What has PR got to do with sponsorship?
- Why might an organization consider sponsorship?
- What can be sponsored?
- What should be the key criteria in selecting a platform for sponsorship?
- Are there any real differences between sponsoring arts or sports?
- What does it cost to make sponsorship pay?
- What do viewers feel about TV sponsorship?
- How could a sponsored book make any difference to how people see us?

So what do PR people actually *do*? What are the tools of their trade? How do they use them to secure their objectives? What may account for apparent periods of hyperactivity and interludes of inactivity, for quiet spells of methodical calculation and bursts of swift and possibly rather loud reaction; or may not?

This chapter provides an overview of typical practice considerations. Questions are asked about various aspects of sponsorship and of media relations, including handling of financial information. Topics also include using the Internet, commissioning photography and undertaking opinion research. Explanations are sought of infomercials and product placement, of advertising as part of PR and about the continuing relevance of writing letters to editors or seeking public speaking opportunities.

What is a public relations machine?

This is a jokey description of the PR function, implying some sort of all-powerful fantasy juggernaut with *1984* implications, capable of irresistible mass mind-bending. It could be interpreted, alternatively, as a back-handed compliment, depicting a wonderfully well-designed, -built and -maintained vehicle for carrying messages. Probably only those who use it know what is meant exactly.

How might this differ from an in-house department?

It seems likely that a PR 'machine' might be an in-house department or a consultancy; there appears to be scarce authenticated sourcing on this one. Presumably either way the people who work the machine are highly accomplished and skilled at what they do.

Are all press releases sent by e-mail these days?

No, the majority of releases still arrive by the 'snail mail' post, and the next most popular method is transmission by facsimile. Accordingly, e-mail usage for contacting journalists is low by comparison. There are good practical reasons for this, not least that journalists tend on the whole to much prefer it, unless they are predisposed towards e-mail, as where they work on specialist IT publications and want to promote Internet use. Also, many object to receiving attachments, which PR people seem inordinately fond of sending, often in bulk. A growing number of publications refuse attachments as a matter of policy.

Do you have to do a chase up call after each release?

This really should not be routine practice, or even done at all, which may come as a relief. Newcomers to PR practice often suppose that all material should be 'chased', in hope of raising its prospects of success. 'Don't do it' is the advice. The experienced PR person produces the best statement possible, adds fully captioned and referenced illustrations where appropriate, offers names and numbers for follow up contact and makes sure the envelope is accurately addressed. After that he or she turns to some other purposeful employment. Pestering is not to be confused with persistence and journalists loathe being chased about statements, for understandable reasons.

How does PR cope with the gossip and worse on the Internet?

The Internet offers massive potential for communication between users. This is a healthy development, at least in theory, because it offers anyone who can 'get connected' (and probably around half of the UK population is), the opportunity to engage in unrestrained expression of opinions and prejudices, heated argument, learned discussion and so on. It is an all-pervasive electronic Speakers' Corner, filled with sound and fury.

All this concerns PR people. They fear that people may be

exchanging unkind remarks and hostile criticism about their organizations. In short, hard-earned and carefully maintained reputations may be placed in jeopardy. Perhaps it is the sheer anarchy of the medium that really worries them, for surely a deserved good reputation should be capable of surviving a bit of gossip, or even a coordinated verbal onslaught. However, some PR people are taking to monitoring as best they can, hoping to be able to rebut whatever they judge to be negative comment and, more positively, establishing more informative sites designed to counter speculation with fact.

Just how much of a threat the Internet represents to the PR trade is anyone's guess. It is certainly a boon to the disaffected and to organized groups, but when all is said and done it represents a dramatic new means to achieving two-way dialogue with publics, so why the paranoia? With the passing of time it is probable that all types of organizations will come to live with this free-for-all character of the Internet, except, presumably, those that have been well and truly exposed for being economical with the truth.

What PR opportunities have been created by the Internet?

Set against the negative concerns about protecting reputation from potential damage, there are the positive opportunities to promote and manage reputation. Here is a medium that is almost custom-built for PR, and as access grows, which undoubtedly it will, those opportunities will expand to global proportions. PR programmes are likely to extend well beyond site planning and development to, for example, regular Web chats with customers, online sponsorships, lobbying through campaigning sites and adding use of the Internet to crisis management plans.

Who needs PR to design a brochure or Web site?

Designers design with what they are given to work on, and they rely heavily on the quality of the brief they receive. Ask the average designer to write the brochure as well as design it and he or she is likely to point out that deciding on the content comes before the design service. Without PR input and direction most brochures fail, with it they are likely to succeed, because the brochure is a major PR tool that PR people are very familiar with and understand, whether they are categorized as corporate, product, educational, training, recruitment or anything else.

Whereas the brochure has been around for decades, the Internet is still in its infancy and many sites are woefully inadequate. There is plenty of potential for making a site attractive, interesting and/or useful, but it takes skill, time and imagination. Many designers are now skilled at working in this medium, but again they need direction, just as the sites have to do their jobs in terms of meeting PR objectives. They are used to build brands and generate feedback, and they are useful for complementing other media.

Are speakers' panels worth the time and effort?

Face-to-face presentations take some beating for achieving communication impact. Having a small team of ready-prepared speakers, who are trained and knowledgeable about presenting the organization's case, is a valuable PR asset. Audiences may vary from just one or two Very Important Persons (VIPs) to large public gatherings. The key point about this is finding the appropriate opportunities and not wasting the speakers' efforts through misdirection, perhaps out of some well-intentioned desire to maximize the number of appearances.

Running a speakers' panel needs to be properly organized. Speakers require adequate briefing in advance about who, what, where and, most importantly, *why*. They deserve encouragement, with demonstration of interest in how each presentation goes and feedback on any follow through obtained or received.

Just as appropriate opportunities have to be identified, inappropriate invitations need to be declined and relationships established through the programme should be developed further, in order to scoop up any further opportunities and other benefits. When this much time and effort is put into running them, speakers' panels can be well worthwhile.

What is product placement?

Anyone who has watched a James Bond film has been on the receiving end of product placement par excellence: just think of all those swanky motor cars, for instance. And what about those lavishly produced television dramas, in which the camera eye so often lingers long and lovingly on some object of desire, even when its connection with the plot may seem at best tenuous? Product placement is about just that, *placing* products. They are loaned for use in the expectation that they will be seen and that subconscious connections will be made between them and the circumstances in which they are viewed. Although film and theatre sets offer obvious opportunities for placement, products find their way into many non-fictional situations as well.

> A fleet of luxury Range Rover motor cars was made available for US singer Madonna's wedding in a romantic Scottish castle. The car is designed for use in rugged terrain and enjoys high status. It has a large and distinctive appearance. The product and the event therefore complemented each other.

Many, sometimes more humble, products find opportunities to be seen through careful placement, assisted by the fact that they come free; a film producer's or event organizer's budget can benefit substantially from obtaining loan of props or equipment without charge. However, while doubtless there is some value in product placement, whether for PR or marketing purposes, it remains an activity of uncertain worth. The products may never actually be used, or seen, or they may appear but fleetingly. They may appear in a favourable context or in circumstances that are distinctly unhelpful. From the PR perspective, product placement also raises questions about editorial integrity.

What are infomercials?

These are television advertisements that are presented in a programme format. In the early days of commercial television in the United Kingdom, similar programmes, in which a succession of products were presented in an editorial style, were banned. These 'advertising magazines' usually lasted 15 minutes, and of course all television then was 'terrestrial'. Their successors are more commonly of 30 minutes' duration, and tend to be in a chat show format using two presenters. In their latest incarnation, these programmes originated in the United States and they are now widespread on UK satellite and cable stations.

Presumably this time around they will not be banned, given the popularity of 'retail therapy', but infomercials also raise questions about editorial integrity. Are they protracted commercials, and seen as such, or programmes, accorded the respect reserved for the time that elapses between the commercials? If the former, might they represent a gross incursion into editorial space; if the latter, what is their production quality when compared with other informative content? From a PR perspective such questions matter; the context in which products appear in public is most important, and being seen on television does not alter that fundamental fact.

Why still write a letter to an editor?

The humble letter may seem a quaint channel of communication, but there are plenty of sound reasons for still writing letters to editors. A covering letter that attaches a news item can serve several purposes:

- It reminds the editor of who the sender is, and his or her reputation as a source of 'good stories' well researched and written. This can be an aid to the digestion of what follows.
- It is a neat way of making an enquiry or offering 'follow up', where seeing the item is necessary first before the receiver can respond.
- It can be the means of developing the contact further, by sketching possible future contact, availability of more or different material, forthcoming events, and so on.

Letters can also be used to raise editorial ideas suited to the editor's particular publication. These 'query letters' have to provide something new, which in practice usually means a creative use of available resources, provoke interest, be highly specific to the readers' interests, offer a choice of alternative treatments and establish both credentials and credibility. They are used to 'sell' ideas, in particular, for articles and reader competitions.

Both types of letter are sent 'not for publication', to distinguish them from those that are sent in the hope of appearing in the publication. These 'for publication' letters are an outstanding means of putting across an opinion, comment, fact or rebuttal in a part of the newspaper or magazine that has proven high readership. Most editors encourage letters and such letters generate awareness and understanding. The only problem is that they can be subjected to substantial editing, to fit the available space, so what needs to be said has to be expressed economically, to ensure that the message appears unaltered.

Do journalists secretly crave attention?

Many journalists appear to crave attention, and not always so secretly. On the whole they rather enjoy the attention they receive from PR people and they probably know, in their darkest moments, that they are quite glad to have them around, especially when they provide strong leads and stories. Many of them also seem to revel somewhat in the attentions of senior managers, politicians, celebrities and everyone else they encounter who wants something from them, but then that is surely only human. Displays of hostility towards the PR person can melt rapidly into sociable chat as soon as his or her principal appears on the scene, particularly if recognition is readily forthcoming, accompanied by remarks like 'I always read your stuff'.

What are their popular complaints about PR?

Journalists have a few well-worn clichés that they like to trot out routinely. These rotate around the central proposition that all PR people are inept, cannot write, never address envelopes properly, cannot remember names, are always late, have no news sense, deliberately withhold facts and are downright stupid. PR people, of course, know better.

Is news really entertainment?

Often news is presented in such a way as to entertain, or in some other way satisfy, the readers and viewers. This necessitates a degree of licence in accuracy and choice of facts, so as to obtain the most appeal. For instance, most national newspapers 'angle' their news and manufacture 'news' to meet the predispositions of their customers, with resultant distortions and misrepresentations. PR collusion or cooperation in this is most common with publicity for celebrities, but when it becomes more serious the maintenance of credibility and brand values may be put at risk. The prospect of a short-term gain in communicating a message should be weighed against the long-term potential knock on implications.

Why hire photographers when we all have cameras?

Many people own cameras, but few are expert in their use. There are some wonderful cameras available for consumer purchase these days, but when all is said and done about the technology, the central fact remains that photography is a creative art. That is why there are photographic exhibitions. That is why professional photographers often charge a lot for what can look like a little.

The creative power of photography can contribute significantly to PR programmes, both in quality and quantity, conveying messages for a broad range of applications. It can be embarrassing to compare professional and amateur efforts; access to a few 'shots' by an accomplished professional can be invaluable and always a great deal more reassuring than relying on a host of well-meant efforts by a gifted amateur.

Photographers specialize in their choice of subjects. For instance, some 'do news' and are expert at capturing that certain look, glance or gesture, in being 'in the right place at the right time'. Others specialize in fashion, theatre, industry, interiors, landscapes, sport and so on. PR people accordingly employ photographers that have the relevant experience, so that they understand and appreciate the framework of requirements, such as the speed required in producing news photos, buildings not looking like they are falling backwards and the dramatic urgency of sports action and excitement.

Photographers are also informed about the various PR applications. These include exhibition stands, where photographs are often enlarged many times and shown under harsh light, brochures, in which people portraits must flatter their subjects and news stories, where a fleeting detail encapsulates the message 'for all time'. Composition, texture, technical adjustments and quality control in printing and processing are all key elements in optimizing results.

Why run PR surveys when we already do extensive marketing research?

Surveys are very heavily used by PR people, probably more than any other research method. They want facts, not assumptions, and must establish a starting position from which to plan ahead, if attitudes, perceptions and behaviours are to be adjusted or changed. Marketing research is no substitute because organizations can choose their markets, whereas publics can choose their organizations.

There is also another explanation for the heavy use of surveys in PR. They are used extensively to generate news designed to serve a particular message. Much of these tidbits, which are constructed to attract headlines and 'soundbites', are carefully filleted of facts, so that only what is most memorable or impactful, and certainly not of value to a competitor, is used. It is an artful way of insinuating messages into the popular subconscious and daily gossip. Hence the frequency with which, for example, the Monday morning radio and television news is stuffed with 'survey findings' stories. Marketing research is no substitute for that either.

When might advertising be part of PR?

The main use of advertising as part of PR is to communicate a corporate message about the organization. Lately quite a lot of advertising has been done, for instance, to expound views about green issues, mainly along the lines of emphasizing dedication to environmentally safe and responsible practices. This corporate advertising is in support of corporate objectives and is not directly related to products or services.

Sometimes the right of the advertiser is used to put across a message that otherwise might not be conveyed editorially, to emphasize a point heavily that requires attention-grabbing techniques and/or to contact a public as fast as possible, say, for example, customers for product recall or investors in a takeover bid. Much advertising relates to matters financial, where, for example, public companies advertise summaries of their annual results and chairperson's statement. Companies sometimes use advertising to defend their actions against criticism, as where a pressure group has generated much hostile editorial comment.

Can press coverage directly affect share price?

Yes, the comments and tips published in the national press and consumer investment magazines are very influential in provoking the movement in share prices, whether by increasing or decreasing them. Many smaller public companies, in which there is minimal stock trading, can see substantial share price movement in response to occasional or relatively rare coverage. Publication of annual results also influences price movements.

Do City of London analysts believe what they read about a company?

Analysts are paid to be cynical, and, incidentally, some of them are ex-journalists. Of course they read as much as they can, it's a large part of the job, and financial PR brings to their attention the hard facts and figures they need, relating to performance and prospects, management and activities. They sift through all that they see, check and compare, visit and evaluate.

Many of them specialize in particular sectors and also use the trade media for gaining insights at an operational and cultural level, which may tell them rather more than national press reports, because content there is largely derived from corporate and marketing PR sources. In addition, some analysts have close links with trade magazines, to the extent of writing for them and supplying summary research data for publication. Many broadcast comments as experts on individual industries and sectors.

Is there a lot of 'red tape' with financial PR?

Yes, in the United Kingdom as elsewhere in the world's financial markets, there is a fair bit of red tape to be observed, particularly in relation to confidentiality and shareholder information. In addition to the Companies Acts, there are self-governance rules in the City's Takeover Code and, most pertinently for daily practice, the listing rules by which public companies must abide, which are contained in the Stock Exchange Yellow Book. This, incidentally, has turned purple since the Financial Services Authority (FSA) gained control from the Stock Exchange Council in April 2000.

The core of the work is based on the publication of the preliminary and interim results and the annual report and accounts and on the annual general meeting. Flotations, or initial placing offers (IPOs), mergers and acquisitions and hostile bids, all call for heavy PR involvement when they arise. Meanwhile there is an ongoing effort revolving around visits and meetings for analysts, private client brokers and financial journalists, to which are attached requirements on disclosure of information not already made public.

The Financial Services Authority gained sweeping new regulatory powers in December 2001, which include the imposition of unlimited fines on PR people who are held to be attempting to mislead the stock markets. A new offence of market abuse has been introduced, with the intention of eliminating the selective early release of price-sensitive information before it has been made generally available.

What is the Friday Night Drop?

This refers to the practice of selectively providing price-sensitive information to the UK national and regional Sunday newspapers on an exclusive basis, thereby ensuring substantial coverage in a major newspaper when the markets are closed for the weekend and before the information is supplied in the prescribed manner to them. It is a smart way of obtaining much greater share of shout than would be obtained amidst the mass of weekday announcements. It also benefits from the large, and leisured, Sunday readerships and from the way in which 'the Sundays' tend to lie around in the home for days afterwards.

The FSA has made clear that this practice is forbidden and it appears to have died out. If a company has to issue information over a weekend that it considers to be, or might be, 'market sensitive', it is required to tell at least two newspapers and to repeat the announcement as soon as possible on the following Monday morning through the official market news providers.

There have been repeated attempts in the past to prevent 'Sunday scoops' but to little avail, probably because a good story will out, and information is so widely shared among companies and their advisors that it has been virtually impractical to prove deliberate leaking. However, the FSA has powers to publicly fine companies.

What's the difference between financial PR and financial services marketing?

Financial PR concentrates on communicating with key opinion formers, mainly investment analysts, financial journalists and, to a lesser extent, private client brokers, who influence investment decisions. Financial services' marketing, on the other hand, describes the marketing of financial products by insurance companies, banks, accountants and others, both to intermediaries, such as independent financial advisers (IFAs), and to end users.

What are investomers?

This is derived from 'investor-customers' and implies that an investor's loyalty deserves to be encouraged by being rewarded, much as might be a customer's loyalty. Most public companies rely on dividend payments, their annual reports and accounts and maybe a modest discount on purchases of products and services. However, more generous shareholder loyalty schemes can substantially raise revenues, profits and shareholder retention. These schemes can be run economically on the Internet and companies in drink, travel and retailing have begun to develop advanced schemes. There is uncertainty, however, whether such schemes are a trend or a fad.

Is non-financial reporting of any value to PR?

The proposed Operating and Financial Review (OFR), by which larger companies are to be required by law to write about their corporate social responsibility (CSR) activities, their employee relations, environmental policies and so on in their annual report and accounts, is widely supported by senior managers. Research of companies in the FTSE 500 revealed 93 per cent support for the contention that non-financial reporting enhances a company's reputation.

PR people, as custodians of corporate reputation, argue that 'reputation reporting' is important because financial indicators alone are inadequate for reflecting true share value. For non-financial reporting to bear scrutiny, however, there needs to be objective measurement of these 'intangibles' comparable to what is required of financial reporting, not only since OFRs are to be audited but also, more generally, for the use of all organizations reporting on their reputation management.

What has PR got to do with sponsorship?

Quite a lot is the answer to this, ever since PR first began its involvement with sponsorship some three decades ago. Now sponsorship has grown into such a substantial activity that PR has been relinquishing some of its responsibilities for running it, to dedicated sponsorship functions and firms and to advertising people.

Why might an organization consider sponsorship?

Sponsorship is used very often to promote a name or brand or to position or reposition a brand. Sponsorship can also provide a variety of other benefits. These include:

- goodwill by association;
- media attention;
- market penetration;
- alternative advertising;
- hospitality platform;
- employee benefits; and
- strengthened identity.

An outstanding example of successful sponsorship was the Cornhill Insurance sponsorship of the international cricket Test Matches, which began when UK cricket's popularity was waning as football's was growing. The company was little known and not prominent among insurers, but its name exposure and its association with cricket changed all that. The sponsorship has ceased, to be replaced by others, and cricket has risen again in popularity, but mention Test Matches and still the name of Cornhill is readily recalled.

What can be sponsored?

Just about anything, within reason, can be sponsored, and often is. The more obvious examples are:

- sport;
- the performing arts;
- museums, art galleries and exhibitions;
- various types of shows and outdoor public events;
- expeditions and other exceptional athletic undertakings;
- festivals and similar linked events and activities;
- education and much more.

The list seems to be ever-growing; for instance, it now includes UK television programmes, for long prohibited from sponsorship, and there can be relatively few children who have not sought sponsorship for some personal event or endeavour, such as a 'fun run'. Charitable and community events are invariably sponsored. Organizations are seldom without plenty of choice in what they can sponsor.

What should be the key criteria in selecting a platform for sponsorship?

As always with any PR, it is necessary to trace the sponsorship right back to the corporate objectives, and ask how this or that specific proposal will materially meet, or help to meet, those objectives. Sadly, all too many sponsorships have failed to pass on this, having been chosen for lesser reasons.

In addition to this it has to be said that any sponsorship must address publics that are to be communicated with, not 'the general public' or some ill-defined stakeholder mass, and it should have some obvious relevance to the organization. This last is easier said than done, though, and sometimes the rule may be relaxed a little, for example, where a large bank sponsors an opera or concert performance.

> Sometimes the connection between the sponsor and the event may seem downright inappropriate, thereby seriously weakening the value of the sponsorship to the sponsor. For instance, the link between fitness and food is obvious, but when Mars chocolate bars were tied through sponsorship with the annual 26-mile London Marathon there was widespread criticism, since the product was perceived by many to be inconsistent with athleticism. The sponsor found it had to defend the product. No such criticisms were raised against its successor, low-fat Flora margarine.

Are there any real differences between sponsoring arts or sports?

Certainly there are differences, both in scale and purpose:

- Arts sponsorship is on a smaller scale and is fragmented.
- Sponsors are looking to achieve exposure, or attention, in order to benefit their corporate images.
- There are rich opportunities to do this at a local level, so arts sponsorship is widely used in community relations work.
- The related advertising potential is much less, so greater emphasis is placed on brand awareness.

By contrast:

- Sports sponsorship is on a larger scale and is more concentrated.
- Deals are done at generally much higher values.
- Corporate image is a factor here too, but the emphasis is more on heavy promotion of product brands, substantial use of advertising, significant media coverage and increased sales.

In other words, the arts sponsorship is more PR-orientated, while the sports sponsorship is more marketing-orientated.

What does it cost to make sponsorship pay?

It might be tempting to suppose that, once a sponsorship deal has been agreed, the sponsor has done enough spending, except for perhaps turning up on the day or organizing some related corporate hospitality. Tempting, but mistaken, because in order to optimize value out of sponsorship it is necessary to work the asset and, as a general rule, this may well amount to spending as much again, or more, as has been spent on the sponsorship itself. This is more likely with, for instance, the big sporting or leisure event but less so with the modest arts or education project, mainly because of the cost of advertising.

What do viewers feel about TV sponsorship?

The novelty has probably worn off, now that an increasing number of UK television programmes are being sponsored, and the brand-building value is uncertain. Research indicates that possibly one in two viewers associates sponsorship with inferior programme content. Maybe the general deterioration in UK television content lies behind this, with sponsors taking the blame because of their visibility.

> Sponsors' repeat messages can be tedious or downright clumsy, because of their context, and have to be chosen carefully. For example, the slogan 'If you can't beat us why not join us?' was used in the UK by Australian fund manager First State for its sponsorship of Australia v England cricket Test match edited highlights in 2002. The English had not beaten the Australians in an Ashes series since 1986, and the home team was the undisputed finest in the world, successive winners of the cricket World Cup and said to be the best for decades. The jokey slogan was widely resented and criticized as crass, possibly doing the sponsor more harm than good, particularly since the Australians won the series 4–1.

How could a sponsored book make any difference to how people see us?

It could make a great deal of difference and be a most useful brand-positioning tool. An organization usually sponsors a book in order to either become identified, or more strongly identified, with some particular market or interest that is relevant to its corporate and PR objectives, or strengthen expression of its existing corporate characteristics and/or associations. For instance, a honey producer might sponsor a book about natural food products, a garage about some aspect of travel, a PR firm about communications that made history.

These books have the potential to bring their sponsors' brands into some useful but hitherto unvisited territories such as food and drink shops, sports stadia and airports. However, just sponsoring, without regard to how it is likely to make readers regard the organization in the future, makes no sense, no matter how seemingly attractive the proposal. Just because the chairperson is into fly fishing or the CEO goes gliding does not validate books on those subjects when they have no connection, however contrived, with the organization or its publics.

Sponsored books should not be confused with so-called vanity publishing, where an organization commissions the production of a biography of itself. Titles tip off the potential reader, with the likes of *Our Exciting Times, A Romance in Steel* and *Begone Dull Care* (these are fictional but typical). Even those who write them may have difficulty at times in maintaining their interest, so it is perhaps understandable that subsequently readers may not be too riveted either. Basically, if the organization has a 'good yarn' to tell they can be very useful PR tools, but not much otherwise.

twelve

in the **beginning**

- How much should we budget for PR?
- Should we expect high expense accounts in the name of PR?
- Can PR be done on a shoestring?
- For a small business, how many hours a week is it realistically necessary to give to PR?
- How can busy people do PR when they barely have time for a sandwich at lunchtime?
- What types of objective should we set ourselves?
- Should PR be a designated responsibility for someone?
- Will we need a system for handling any incoming calls?
- Do journalists prefer to deal with a professional PR person, instead of a staffer who is acting spokesperson?
- Can PR be just as effective with anonymous spokespersons, or do quotes from a named manager go down better?
- Is the best PR done by people who first and foremost know your sector inside out?
- Just how important are the new electronic media to PR?
- Why do advertising people talk about copy but PR deals in editorial?
- What is an advertorial?
- How does this differ from an advertising feature?
- Why are ad agencies so wary of PR?
- Should we expect to buy advertising in order to get a mention?
- Can we ask to approve what goes in the papers before it appears?
- What is the publishing cycle?
- Do the media ever *rely* on their PR sources?

- Are there particular occasions when having no PR source means having no coverage?
- Why should any self-respecting journalist want to draw on a press release in preparing a report or article?
- Why are journalists so two-faced, very polite and interested when they meet you but never otherwise?
- Why do journalists ask so many questions but write so little?
- Why should I give so much time to the press only for nothing to appear afterwards?
- Isn't trade press coverage just talking to our competitors?
- How do we know that what we say will not be distorted to fit?
- Are press releases released or do they merely escape?
- What makes a good or bad press release?
- Are there any golden rules for writing press releases?
- What is media placement?
- What is an embargo?
- Should we ever use an embargo?
- What is the best time to contact a journalist?
- If we entertain the press what will they expect of us?
- What is a press pack?
- Will journalists respect our off the record comments?
- Can we decline to answer unwanted questions?
- How should we respond to a journalist who rings us with bad news about us and wants us to comment on it?
- How do we create news for the press?
- Should we tell the press our less-than-good news?
- How can we stop the press hearing bad news about us?
- Should we spend time on trying to write articles?
- Should we expect to be paid for any articles that appear in print?
- Are photos a necessary expense?
- How can a photograph be worth 1,000 words?
- What exactly is a news photo?
- If we want a photo how best can we obtain one?
- What if we want to photograph an event?
- How in practice should we supply a photo?
- Should we ever bother with TV and radio?
- What if TV wants an interview at short notice?
- Why should we drop everything to give a radio interview?

- How can radio interviewers know enough to ask worthwhile questions of us?
- What is a soundbite?
- Do we need training for radio interviews?
- What is a design brief?
- Should we expect a turnkey package from our printers?
- How can we improve on the written content of our brochures and leaflets?
- Should we do exhibitions?
- How special do special events have to be?
- Aren't internal newsletters a waste of time and money?

Now we are at the point of considering the practicalities of initiating and developing PR activity, whether by in-house staff or by outside consultants or other suppliers. This chapter looks at the practical considerations for the person who is responsible for PR, including:

- understanding the likely implications for him or her in terms of how much time and effort will be needed to supply the PR function with the information and resources it will need;
- establishing the criteria by which to judge the quality of specific PR activities;
- and deciding how to use limited resources to best effect in the small and micro company or charity.

Starting PR provokes many questions, particularly from:

- owner-managers of small organizations, for whom the available time and other resources for PR are limited;
- managers, whose main constraint is their unfamiliarity with the practicalities of PR, in any sector;
- voluntary PR officers, who wish to assess the exact applicability of PR to their particular type and size of organization;
- proponents of PR, who need practical understanding of what might be involved if they are to successfully argue for its introduction.

How much should we budget for PR?

An initial budget could be constructed by reference to turnover, where it is likely to be from around 2 to 10 per cent, maybe more. A similar approach might be taken, using revenue, profit or some other meaningful financial measure instead. Alternatively, where PR is substantially in support of marketing, it may be appropriate to set an initial budget that is a percentage, say 20 per cent, of the total promotion budget, itself probably about half of the marketing allocation. The big variable to look out for here is the amount of mass media advertising expenditure, because it can swell the total promotion spend and thereby reduce the PR percentage allocation.

But what if funds are very limited, there is little if any promotion done, or the PR is to be less about marketing and more 'corporate'? There are two further possibilities. The first is to set a budget by reference to what it is thought that competitors, or other similar organizations, are spending. This may be difficult to arrive at, but it offers the possibility of matching others or setting a figure that takes realistic account of the understood differences.

Alternatively, traditional activity costing may be the answer, building the budget against estimated costs for specified activities plus 10 per cent contingency allowance. Cost-benefit analysis is applied, to calculate potential return against proposed expenditure, even where there is no quantifiable commercial consequence. Where predicted outcomes are the means to achieving, or progressing towards fulfilment of, *further* objectives, non-fiduciary values that sensibly reflect those benefits may be assigned to them and also to communicating with each public in relation to those outcomes, in order to calculate their probability.

In arriving at decisions about budgets it is necessary to be sure about the PR objectives, because whatever budget is set must be realistic for the fulfilment of those objectives.

Should we expect high expense accounts in the name of PR?

Not as a matter of routine, because incidental expenditure is related to the scale of overall expenditure and to the exact purpose and nature of each programme. Plenty of PR is performed without recourse to heavy travel, entertainment or similar costs.

Can PR be done on a shoestring?

Impressive results can be achieved for less expenditure, as well as for more. However, beware false economies, which can destroy the best-laid plans. People are likely to be the largest single cost, and small amounts of time from an experienced PR person is very much better than open-ended effort by a novice.

Be wary of bolt-on PR services from a supplier looking to 'close the circle' against competition; such offers are almost always poor value, particularly if they are thrown in as extras. And do not believe anyone who says that PR is cheap, because it can comprise combinations of low-cost techniques; the thinking, research, objective and strategy setting, planning, costing and so on all play their part in determining the quality of results.

For a small business, how many hours a week is it realistically necessary to give to PR?

On average, half a day is a sensible, absolute, minimum. This needs to be in 'prime time', however, not in fragmented moments at the end of the day, only when every other last job has been done. When the effort starts to gather momentum more time will be needed, say, the equivalent of a day a week initially. Flexibility is important; tasks occur scattered through the working week, and sometimes at weekends too.

How can busy people do PR when they barely have time for a sandwich at lunchtime?

Is this a plea to be let off, or a genuine shortage of time? Time management is everyone's problem, but where there is a will doubtless there is a way. A lot of PR work is desk-bound: how about doing some of it while eating those sandwiches?

What types of objective should we set ourselves?

Setting objectives is based on current and anticipated issues. Objectives can be long-term or short-term, when they are anchored on specified short-term plans of up to three years' duration. In PR practice, quantifiable objectives are usually set for 12 months ahead. Sometimes they cover 18 months or two years, but often the annual time frame is preferred for its greater flexibility. More general mid-term (three to five years) and long-term (five to ten years) aims and, possibly, as yet unquantified objectives, may provide an overall direction.

Should PR be a designated responsibility for someone?

Yes indeed; even in professional partnerships and in voluntary bodies there needs to be someone who has the specific responsibility. Preferably, this person should be a trained PR person; otherwise, at least he or she should have the appropriate temperament and commitment, sufficient to develop a job specification and obtain some training.

Will we need a system for handling any incoming calls?

Absolutely; the very last eventuality you want is for incoming enquiries to be drifting around the organization, looking to land somewhere. Whoever is involved in taking calls eventually, initially they *must* be routed to the PR function.

> Tesco learnt the lesson about handling incoming calls the hard way. In the 1970s, any director who happened to be around fielded calls and in consequence the press made merry, so great were the contradictions, well meant though they were.

Do journalists prefer to deal with a professional PR person, instead of a staffer who is acting spokesperson?

Journalists allege that PR people are skilled at 'getting in the way of a story', by which they mean, skilled at preventing them from 'digging the dirt'. Many prefer to contact non-PR managers when they can, in the hope that such people will be better informed and more forthcoming, or indiscreet. However, company spokespersons may be inclined to use jargon or 'officialese' and be far too involved in their subjects for the journalists' liking.

An accomplished PR person is a better bet for journalists most times, because he or she can assemble the relevant facts and background information, distil the jargon and any complexities, answer questions and produce someone who already knows what the enquiry is about and has prepared a clear, succinct response that does not take hours to unravel. The PR person, in other words, does much of the journalists' initial work for them. This assists, not impedes, their 'getting the story'; it provides an efficient basis to further enquiry, should that be needed or desired.

Can PR be just as effective with anonymous spokespersons, or do quotes from a named manager go down better?

For all practical purposes it is always better to have a spokesperson that is identified by name and title. That is why very often a named chairperson, chief executive, managing director, finance director or chief operating officer is credited with remarks contained within press releases or company statements.

Is the best PR done by people who first and foremost know your sector inside out?

There are distinct benefits, which explains why so often PR people specialize in particular sectors and move around within them. They arrive complete with relevant knowledge, understanding and contacts. Accordingly their learning curve is much reduced and they become productive quicker. However, and of course there has to be some, there are downsides. It is easy to become settled in ways of thinking through over-familiarity and find the creative juices are dried out. PR skills are transferable and readily travel between sectors, bringing valuable potential for cross-fertilization of experience.

Just how important are the new electronic media to PR?

They are very important because of the opportunities presented by the Internet to communicate direct, not through the mediation of third parties such as journalists, and to customize or 'narrowcast' a message to meet the specific needs of the receivers, in direct contrast to the 'broadcasting' media.

The single greatest advantage of the Internet is that it permits one-to-one dialogue with people who individually may even constitute a whole public in their own right. In addition, immediate practical benefits include: online news, information and articles, both incoming and outgoing; newswire services; press conferences; e-mail and Web-based discussion groups; and intranet newsletters.

Why do advertising people talk about copy but PR deals in editorial?

'Copy' refers to the text within an advertisement and also to all material needed for print reproduction of an advertisement. 'Editorial' refers to non-advertising text that appears as reportage, comment and so on in the media. Matters get complicated when 'copy' is sometimes used more loosely, in referring to content generally, but there is always an implication of commercial purpose.

What is an advertorial?

Paid-for editorial, that is to say, an advertisement that is presented in an editorial format. It could take the form of:

- a flattering report;
- a reader competition;
- an offer of free samples;
- a 'photo spread' or event coverage;
- any other imitation of journalism.

There is usually a single theme. The idea is to borrow the credibility of genuine editorial and thereby increase the readers' interest. To make clear the difference, however, it should be prominently labelled as advertising.

Advertorials are effective in providing additional information about products and in encouraging product sampling. Readers gain added value from them provided that the products are relevant to their interests. There is ample scope for confusing the reader, however, and concerns arise about editorial integrity, but advertorials can work very well in women's interest magazines, where they are popular.

How does this differ from an advertising feature?

Here the editorial supports the advertising that usually surrounds it. They are commonly used, for example, when an organization wants coverage for its new premises: the editorial flatteringly reports on the organization, its new premises, prospects, employment ambitions and so on. All around are found advertisements from the suppliers for the project, such as the builders, specialist subcontractors, professional advisers and anyone else who can be roped in.

The editorial is written by a journalist from the newspaper and the advertisements should be, not always are, sold separately by ad sales people against a list provided by the organization. In theory, a decision to advertise is no guarantee of favourable editorial mention, but in practice, most advertisers usually end up with an agreeable mention; those that do not comfort themselves with the knowledge that nevertheless they demonstrated publicly their support for the organization in question.

Why are ad agencies so wary of PR?

It could be because PR is eating into advertising budgets, owing to the search for ever-greater targeting accuracy and cost-effectiveness. People generally have become a great deal more disbelieving and cynical, and they do not readily accept advertising messages. There have been 'turf wars' between advertising and PR for many years. The advertising people generally give a strong impression of regarding themselves to be superior to the PR people. There is much mutual wariness and insufficient trust and understanding. There are areas of common interest and potential agreement; they just need to be found, so that the work of each complements the other.

Should we expect to buy advertising in order to get a mention?

Being an established advertiser in a UK trade/technical publication certainly helps, but that is because the journalists' awareness is heightened by seeing your ads and you are plainly supporting 'your industry's publication'. Advertising is not a formal precondition to editorial coverage if what you have to say is rated a mention by the journalists. Otherwise, you may be expected to advertise in order to have a mention in a commercial directory or guide, such as hotel or tourist literature. It should be said, though, that practice differs around the world.

Can we ask to approve what goes in the papers before it appears?

Very rarely indeed, and then usually only because you are also buying space at the same time, or will be asked to do so, and the publication sells its 'editorial'. In the United Kingdom such titles do not have high reputations, and are really seen as being marginal. Appearing in them does little if anything to enhance anyone's reputation. Otherwise, the only time you *may* be invited to see what is going to appear beforehand is where the work is highly technical and/or complex and is destined for a specialist readership.

What is the publishing cycle?

The publishing cycle describes the frequency of publication, which in turn, importantly for PR, determines the news gathering cycle. So, for example, a weekly magazine has set times of each week by which certain tasks have to be completed by the journalists and by everyone else involved in its production and distribution. It is valuable to know the different stages of the cycle.

Do the media ever *rely* on their PR sources?

Journalists may complain about PR people but, however grudgingly, they know that the two trades are complementary. They are always working to deadlines, and they like to anticipate where they can find a reliable quote or some information on a particular issue or sector. Over the years, the PR people have demonstrated an increasing level of efficiency and credibility in helping to meet these needs.

Are there particular occasions when having no PR source means having no coverage?

Journalists still produce text unaided by PR people, in plenty. Sometimes a journalist will want a quick response, as he or she is working on 'a piece', and if no one is available to take the enquiry they will press on without trying a second time, usually working against an early deadline. Then the organization may miss out on a mention in the resulting report. Of course, that may not be necessarily a disappointment.

Why should any self-respecting journalist want to draw on a press release in preparing a report or article?

Press releases are a major source and if they are well written to journalistic standards, so much the better. The aim is to provide reliable, relevant material that is good enough to use with minimal alteration. Sometimes they fail such high standards but nonetheless provide the necessary substance to warrant being reworked, expanded upon or incorporated into something else. There is no shame in drawing on press releases for content and/or inspiration.

Why are journalists so two-faced, very polite and interested when they meet you but never otherwise?

For the chairperson or chief executive, say, who has just spent several hours being quizzed by a seemingly genuine inquisitor, it can be hard if the result is at some variance with what was actually said. Particularly if the outcome was hostile yet the encounter had all the appearance of being positive.

Maybe journalists appear 'two-faced' on such occasions because their purpose is misunderstood. They are employed to produce editorial that attracts readers, viewers and listeners. They operate in a highly competitive environment, where the margin between recognition of success and failure can be very narrow. When they are researching they deploy all the information extractive skills known, and later evaluate the results based on their loyalty to their employers and not, usually, to the people they write about.

Why do journalists ask so many questions but write so little?

Journalists are a bit like squirrels. They have to assemble masses of material against possible future need. From what they gather they later compose their offerings to the world, usually within a specified number of words. That, though, is not the end of the process. People called subeditors then intervene and may change the submissions, a process that can be deeply resented by the journalists, very understandably. The subeditors often reduce material to fit the space or time available, owing to various pressures; sometimes they rearrange it to adopt an entirely different emphasis, or 'angle'; sometimes they discard, or 'spike', it, so that it never goes any further. There are other reasons too, but that is largely why journalists appear to ask so many questions but write so little.

Why should I give so much time to the press only for nothing to appear afterwards?

In order to develop worthwhile media relations it is necessary to accept that sometimes, maybe quite often, your material or idea is not used, for any of a variety of reasons. Much of the time you will find that there are a number of loyal troopers who are usually interested and use what is on offer, and your media efforts are likely to be concentrated on them. There is also likely to be an outer ring of people who are positive, but less frequently contacted. So, for example, you may have a dozen or more technical and/or specialist media sources that together account for at least half of all coverage and a further similar number of general business, management, administration, import/export, council and other such titles or programmes that provide maybe one-third of the balance of coverage. That leaves the field wide open for gathering in the remaining 10 per cent or so via other outlets and it is among these that seeing results for efforts is most problematical.

Isn't trade press coverage just talking to our competitors?

Talking to competitors this way can be no bad practice. Yes, they cut and clip on you, just as you do on them, but what they learn from this largely depends upon you. It may be the means to demoralize, sow dissent, provide leadership, recruit talented deserters, attract approaches for merger or acquisition, inspire joint ventures and so on.

The main point about trade papers is that they also provide 'windows' on your world to a multitude of different types of reader who are looking in from outside. They may be investment analysts, potential customers, suppliers and recruits, corporate rating agencies and so on; the parochial character of these publications can be misleading.

How do we know that what we say will not be distorted to fit?

You don't, and if you suspect that there is a hidden agenda that the coverage has to serve you may decide not to say anything.

> When a television company wanted permission to film a well-known left-wing politician presenting a documentary inside her former, very status-ridden, private school it was sensibly refused. Nothing in her career had indicated anything but hostility to her alma mater, and no indication of content was being offered. Under the circumstances the school management was best advised to forgo coverage, which it did happily; it could live without it.

Sometimes, of course, distortions are simply inaccuracies arising out of insufficient facts, or ignorance of the genuine facts. But that does not justify the prevalent taste for sensationalism in the tabloid press, the red tops, which can be damaging and needs to be avoided if at all possible. Why so many genuine mistakes occur is a permanent wonder. *The Guardian* recognizes its frequent mistakes with a regular 'corrections and clarifications' section, in which it publishes corrections with readers' assistance.

Are press releases released or do they merely escape?

All releases should be properly planned, researched, written, processed, supervised, authorized, timed well and properly distributed; otherwise, why bother? If they give the impression of having escaped, presumably they emerge unintentionally, or worse, which is probably not amusing for those responsible.

What makes a good or bad press release?

A 'good' press release is one that communicates a message or messages with optimum efficiency and effectiveness. A 'bad' release is the opposite, probably sounds and reads like an advertisement and may invoke unwanted repercussions.

Are there any golden rules for writing press releases?

Yes: the whole content is summarized in the first paragraph, so that if necessary you do not need to read a word further in order to understand what it is all about. To achieve this magical effect, the paragraph must answer the following five, or six if possible, questions:

- Who did it/is doing it/will be doing it?
- What was happening/is happening/ will happen?
- Where did it happen/is it happening/will it happen?
- When did it happen/is it happening/will it happen?
- Why did it happen/is it happening/will it happen?
- How did it happen/is it happening/will it happen?

The remaining paragraphs expand on each of these components and are arranged in descending order of importance and/or interest, because the journalists and subeditors cut from the bottom up. The headline is a succinct encapsulation of the message, in as few words as possible, without humour, just plain factual.

What is media placement?

This is a grand-sounding description for persuading media to publish PR-generated material; a process that might be equally well described as 'selling', 'talking up' or plain generating interest followed by commitment.

What is an embargo?

An 'embargo' is a request, at the top of a press release, asking that the content should not be published before a stated date and time. This occurs usually when advance information is being provided, say on a report or speech, or in order to overcome differences in advance notice periods created by various deadlines, time zones or production schedules. The purpose is to assist the journalist in providing time to assimilate the material, decide what use is to be made of it and plan accordingly, probably by trying to obtain some extra dimension such as ancillary comment or reaction.

Should we ever use an embargo?

It should be used very sparingly, only when it obviously helps the media. Most journalists have an aversion to the embargo, which they see as potentially anti-competitive interference, so they need to be convinced that it is in their own interest to observe it. Otherwise it can be a great irritant and probably ignored. From the PR perspective the embargo can be very useful to avoid the kind of embarrassment that can occur when, for instance, a speech is published before it is given and the speaker then makes changes to it in order to take account of unexpected events that have occurred since it was written.

What is the best time to contact a journalist?

The only 'best' time to call a journalist is in anticipation of sending a press release, to check whether, or not, it is likely to be of interest. Such calls have to be short and to the point, with ready answers to questions. They are best made right at the beginning of the cycle, say mid-morning on the first news gathering day for a weekly publication, or in the early evening on the national press, when a peripatetic journalist is on stand-by at his or her desk for late breaking stories. Further calls are restricted to adding relevant information, not simply to talk about what went before.

If we entertain the press what will they expect of us?

Journalists expect to obtain more information, both generally and specifically, that they might otherwise miss. This may amount to specific new material that they can treat as news if they wish, and many think this to be a basic requirement. It may include useful background information, probably too long and/or complex for routine dissemination. It may be general impressions, from developing regular contact, seeing around, meeting more people within the organization and so on.

As to the nature of the hospitality, journalists who travel a distance expect lunch. Press conferences and similar multiple gatherings may be followed by buffet lunch, to permit circulation. Meetings over breakfast are popular with managers, but not much with journalists, particularly those whose working day is different, say mid-morning to mid-evening. PR people often meet journalists for drinks in the evening. Overseas trips involve travel, accommodation, all meals and entertainment.

What is a press pack?

A press pack is a collection of information compiled for use by a journalist. It may comprise a press release, fact sheets by way of background briefing, captioned photographs and relevant printed matter, such as a corporate brochure. It is usually contained within a folder, for convenience of handling. These packs are usually prepared in connection with an event such as an exhibition or annual general meeting. Some argue against inclusion of any printed material, because it is not like a press release or photo caption that can be used there and then, and against using folders, much less overprinted ones, because they cannot be tucked into a coat pocket.

Will journalists respect our off-the-record comments?

It is a very good rule to assume that no journalist will respect any so-called off the record comments. After all, why should he or she? It is 'on the record' comments that are wanted, even in an apparently informal situation.

Can we decline to answer unwanted questions?

Of course, but it is advisable to be polite and it helps if you offer an explanation. Sometimes the question may be unanswerable at that time but you can specify a future time when you will be able to respond. Trying to avoid by procrastination is inadvisable, because the politicians and bureaucrats have overworked that technique to death. It can worsen impressions, possibly quite unnecessarily, as where there is a perfectly reasonable wish to not answer but evasion makes it look like there is something to hide.

How should we respond to a journalist who rings us with bad news about us and wants us to comment on it?

Obviously this is a situation that all the PR communications procedures are designed to avoid, but it can happen, and when it does it has to be taken seriously. Try to obtain the detail, chapter and verse, and offer to respond as soon as possible. Do not be bounced into an immediate reaction, whatever tactics may be used. You are entitled to take at least some time to consider your response, during which you will be wanting to check facts, evaluate the 'bad news' and consider what scope there may be for taking the initiative back. Delay in replying can begin to look like evasion, so if necessary a holding call or two may be prudent. If a journalist is bent upon hostile intent in pursuit of an 'exclusive scoop', there is always the option, if the circumstances warrant it, of calling a press conference, so that everyone hears your answer.

How do we create news for the press?

The marketing mix offers a good source of inspiration: product; price; place; promotion; people; processes; physical evidence. To this may be added further inspirational 'P words', such as: packages; parallels; passions; patents; performance; personalities; practices; precedents; priorities; prime points; profits; puzzles.

These words that trip the memory can lead to interesting nuggets, from the predictable export order and annual results type of stories to the less common, such as introduction of new technologies or opening of new premises, and the unusual, maybe the result of happy coincidence or exceptional endeavour.

Should we tell the press our less-than-good news?

It would be mistaken to suppose that all PR is about communicating good news. Sadly, there are times when messages are about such matters as profits warnings, redundancies, recall of suspect products, accidents, reduced pensions, closures and so on. Organizations, supposing they survive, can emerge from bad news with credit, since honest, truthful communication is much preferred to silence, however well intentioned it may be, about matters that affect, or may affect, publics. Obviously 'less-than-good' is open to sensible interpretation; the acid test is whether non-disclosure is defensible.

How can we stop the press hearing bad news about us?

In the final analysis it is usually impossible, no matter how hard you try. Much better would be redoubled efforts at environmental scanning, trying to further improve the feedback systems and assiduously tracking issues, so that the earliest whispers are heard and contingency plans invoked. What are the most likely sources of such bad news? Here are some possibilities:

- Could they be, for instance, health and safety at work, industrial relations, redundancies or terms of employment?
- Could they be a downturn in markets, disappointing results or dodgy overseas investments?
- Or could the source be a lot nearer to home, just around the corner, in fact, maybe owing to environmental issues or poor relations with the locals?

- Or might there be problems with product quality, service delivery or consumer affairs more generally?

Should we spend time on trying to write articles?

Articles are a most excellent way of fostering awareness and understanding, particularly for organizations such as professional firms and public bodies that would not advertise much, if at all. A well-written and *relevant* article, in an engaging style and packed with hard information, experiences and anecdotes, is usually very welcome to any editor. It should not need editing, and even if it is 'subbed', it appears 'bylined' in the name of the writer and his or her organization. Many better quality trade, technical and professional magazines routinely publish such contributions and actively seek them.

Should we expect to be paid for any articles that appear in print?

Such articles are submitted without charge. Sometimes, though rarely, a payment appears, probably because the publication considers that as a matter of principle it should pay something, particularly if it formally commissioned the piece against your initial proposal.

Are photos a necessary expense?

They can make all the difference. Many editors ask about potential illustrations at the outset and the prospect of having the use of quality material, without charge, usually makes the difference between whether or not the article will appear. This is not just because editors are reluctant to spend on illustrating your article. There can be real problems for them in trying to source appropriate visuals; they may even end up having to commission a cartoonist if there are no appropriate photographs of the required quality to be found. So photographs are very much a necessary expense, and a powerful means to securing acceptance of articles for publication.

How can a photograph be worth 1,000 words?

Photographs can tell a story, convey a message, provide insight or reveal a passing look so effectively that to do so alternatively in text would take many words. They can bring to life an otherwise mundane subject, explain exactly what was happening or create a truly magic moment that 'leaps off the page'. Talk of 1,000 words is to emphasize the degree of impact, although it may be literally correct to say that indeed 1,000 words might be needed to fill the space taken by many press photographs, so large are they printed on the page in the print media of many countries.

What exactly is a news photo?

This is a photograph that, literally, tells news. In other words, it records a newsworthy event or occurrence, preferably with such effect that only a brief captioned explanation need accompany it.

News photographs have enduring value, as demonstrated in May 2002, when the world's first-ever news photographs, two images of the 1848 Paris uprising, sold at auction in London for £182,650 to the Musée d'Orsay in Paris. Taken by a photographer known only as Thibault, using the daguerreotype process of one-off images on silver plates, they were converted into engravings for publication. The lot included the engravings and a copy of the edition of the newspaper, *L'Illustration Journal Nouvel*, in which they appeared together with a report.

If we want a photo how best can we obtain one?

Engage a photographer who specializes in the type of photo you want. For instance, if you need to record an event find a news photographer to record it. Make sure you brief the photographer and be careful about how much discretion you allow, because some are inclined to interpret freely in accordance with their own preferences while others insist on being told exactly what is required and why. This applies particularly if the photographer is working without your presence, say on studio portraiture or product pack shots. As to locating photographers, they can be found in a variety of directories and many can be traced through enquiries of the press. Remember that copyright will reside with the photographer and this will need to be addressed at the outset; the photographer can be asked to agree to an assignment of copyright as a term of the commission.

What if we want to photograph an event?

Don't leave anything to chance, by, for example, expecting that one of the photographers from the press will have a suitable photograph that you will be able to purchase later. It is always as well to have your own hired photographer present, regardless of how many others there may be there. Plan as if the worst happened, and there were no others present.

> Try to create your own tableau that tells the story, for your photographer to record, whether or not this is an event you are organizing. For instance, demonstrators against 'loan sharks' in London's Parliament Square brought with them several inflatable plastic representations of 'sharks' for posing against, wearing swimmers' inflated life belts.

Often the relevant people of particular interest to you in an event can be posed separately afterwards, maybe recreating the event, such as cutting a ceremonial ribbon or digging a sod of turf.

How in practice should we supply a photo?

All photographs should be supplied in the format specified by the publication. For instance, many magazines require 35 mm or 6 cm (2.5 in) colour transparencies. For routine volume distribution it is usual to provide well-contrasted black and white (monochrome) gloss or semi-gloss prints, usually 15 × 10 cm (6 × 4 in) or sometimes 25 × 20 cm (10 × 8 in). Lightly attached captions should accompany all prints, so that when viewing the print the related text may be read by opening out the caption below (the caption should not be readable only by looking at the reverse). Transparencies should be dispatched in protective packaging and prints are placed in board-backed envelopes, their faces to the board. Under no circumstances should paper clips or pins be used.

Should we ever bother with TV and radio?

The short answer to this is: yes, but go carefully. Certainly, in the United Kingdom at least, there are very few appropriate programmes on national television, whether terrestrial, satellite or cable, and those are dominated by politics. However, there continue to be a number of opportunities on UK regional television and there is a welter of openings on radio, whether international, national, regional and local. This tends also to be the pattern in many other countries. The skill is in matching the audiences with publics, which is no mean feat. This involves not only trying to work out the audience profiles, or composition, by reference to content but also to time of day, what the broadcasters call 'time segments'.

In addition to thinking about live or pre-recorded interviews, PR people use video news releases. These are commissioned of specialists, who cover events to broadcast standard and then issue news reports on video, ready-made for inclusion in the next news broadcast. It works where these stories provide genuinely newsworthy material, such as some daring-do in a frozen Artic wasteland, that the broadcasters lacked the capacity, opportunity or funds to obtain for themselves.

More frequently, PR people also use syndicated radio tapes. These are the audio equivalent, again produced to broadcast standard and supplied ready for use. They usually contain interviews and were pioneered by publishers wanting airtime for their authors. Some incorporate sound effects and/or elements of drama. They can be used very conveniently in music-and-chat programmes around the clock and are popular with some radio stations, but their very flexibility makes them vulnerable to the possibility of being broadcast at the 'wrong times', such as in the middle of the night, when not a lot of people are listening and those that are may not be that attentive to what they hear.

What if TV wants an interview at short notice?

If such an opportunity comes your way it must be for good reason, so ask: why us and why now? Try also to find out all the salient facts that you will need, because if you do not seize the moment it is highly probable you will not have the chance again. For instance:

- Which programme; what transmission time; how long on air?
- Is the interview to be in a studio, at an outdoor location or on our premises?
- What is the subject to be discussed; what are the topics to be included?
- Does the interviewer have sufficient information to work on?
- Can we have a 'dry run' beforehand?

So there is quite a lot of quick thinking needed right away, before beaming with gratitude and saying that of course you would be delighted and how kind of them to think of you.

The biggest question of all then, of course, is how best to fulfil. In short, who is the most appropriate person that is available, willing, able to handle the heat and the hype of a studio set piece or make himself or herself heard in a noisy, busy public place? If the interview is on the organization's premises, that is wildly to be preferred; 'home turf' engagements start with a strong psychological advantage and a controllable environment.

Why should we drop everything to give a radio interview?

Many people pause to ask themselves that question, after they have just had a couple of hours 'hijacked' for two minutes on air that may not have been heard by many people anyway. It can seem like an act of faith, in particular, when the call comes to dash to a studio for an early morning or late evening deadline.

At such times ask not the worth of the individual effort but of the accumulative effect. Those 'interview junkies' who seem quite unable to stay off air are happy, figuratively speaking, to do somersaults for the broadcasters if it gives them and/or their organizations the PR benefit they seek. Frequent appearances can be very useful indeed, provided they are handled appropriately, and it can be surprising how often acquaintances and contacts will want you to know that they heard you on the radio.

How can radio interviewers know enough to ask worthwhile questions of us?

Interviewers prepare for interviews, or so it is said, and to do so they rely on whatever relevant facts, figures and background information their editor or producer has received in advance that have prompted the invitation to interview. They need this information in an easily assimilated form, as brief as possible, long enough in advance for them to have time to think about their questions. Offer to take questions beforehand. Usually the interviewer will run through the proposed questions privately in advance anyway, in order to learn the likely replies, but this does not preclude an 'unscheduled' question in the interview. This could be inspired by the prior run through. Be prepared for this. And be prepared also for the interviewer who asks why you are there, explaining that he or she has not had time to prepare at all, and who are you anyway? This happens too often, and can be 'hairy'.

What is a soundbite?

This is a tightly expressed summary of a key message, using all the words that may be spoken audibly and intelligibly within 9 seconds, or up to 15 seconds if the speaker is more fortunate. Often 'sound bites' comprise phrases rather than whole sentences. They may be spoken direct to camera and microphone or be buried within a speech, the intention being to insinuate their way into news broadcasts and to remain memorable. They were conceived by politicians and have been instrumental in both projecting key concepts and ideas and in enhancing image. Print journalists often refer to them long afterwards and they sneak their way into compilations of quotations and anthologies.

Do we need training for radio interviews?

Anyone can give an interesting, engaging radio interview. It just takes a reasonable degree of self-confidence, knowing well the scope of what is to be covered and adopting a style that is enjoyable to the listener, whatever the time of day or night. This calls for variable pitch of delivery and lively choice of language, without hesitation, deviation or, what politicians love, repetition. Remember that radio is entirely aural, so visual attractions don't exist to make up for audio deficiencies.

If all this sounds daunting some training may be a sensible move, particularly if there are a number of spokespeople being regularly or frequently interviewed. Then consistency can be established in both the style and content of delivery and the training may be obtained more economically because a whole group of colleagues learns as one.

> Surrey County Council, located just outside London, opted for training when it found that a number of its traffic engineers were being frequently interviewed about travel conditions on the main arterial roads through its territory, usually against the roar of passing vehicles and overhead planes coming and going from adjacent Heathrow.

What is a design brief?

This is the document that equips the designer with the means to deliver a design solution, whether that is for a visual identity to be applied across a wide range of applications or a simple refreshment of the stationery, and all projects between. The brief should cover:

- organizational background;
- market background;
- product background;
- existing materials;
- existing visual symbols and applications;
- objectives;
- budget;
- timing;
- evaluation.

It can include anything and everything else that may be relevant, so that the designer is immersed in the culture and can quickly master the brief. If the designer excels, at least some of this will be attributable to a quality brief; conversely, if disappointment follows, the explanation may well be traceable back to an inadequate or poor brief.

Should we expect a turnkey package from our printers?

Printers usually provide comprehensive service packages centred on printing, covers, binding, wrapping, storage and delivery. Many also provide design, similar to 'design and build' in construction, either in-house or via design associates. Editorial content is the customer's responsibility, although there may be a writing service available.

How can we improve on the written content of our brochures and leaflets?

There are writing services that will write text against a brief, similar to a design brief. These writers may specialize, for example in producing annual reports, corporate brochures or technical manuals, or offer a range of different styles across all applications, from substantial documents to promotional leaflets.

Should we do exhibitions?

Think hard first. There is seldom any shortage of choice, and it can be very difficult to choose. In any sector, certain commercial events will be fairly obvious 'must do's' because it appears that everyone else is there (although even that may not be a good enough reason), but there is usually considerable scope for making the wrong choice. Questions to be asked before deciding must include:

- How long has the event been going?
- What official support does it enjoy?
- Are there any supporting conferences?
- Are there any clashing events?
- Is it a trade, public or combined event?
- What is the reputation of the organizer?
- What have been the recent attendance figures?
- What other hard facts can the organizer provide?

In addition to deciding which exhibitions to appear at, there are three key components of organization:

- design, construction and fit-out of the stand, or design and fit-out of a standard preformed shell stand;
- management and control of the stand, during build up, duration and breakdown; and
- PR support before, during and afterwards.

How special do special events have to be?

'Special' is used in the sense of being non-routine, as where, for example, an organization decides to commemorate an anniversary with a dinner or some such occasion. So be assured, it does not imply that only the most amazing spectacles qualify, although many do tend to end in fireworks displays these days.

Aren't internal newsletters a waste of time and money?

They are not automatically a waste of time and money, but quite a few may give that impression. Newsletters, whether electronic or printed, need readers. It matters not that they can now be produced quickly on an intranet; the task is to integrate them into the culture to the extent that people readily go to them and try to take in what is there. The ground rules are fairly straightforward: monotonous management strictures, rules and regulations, false bonhomie and implied threats constitute an unedifying diet. A more balanced mixture of content, with substantial scope for everyone to contribute and a fair degree of give-and-take discussion, can make for a very useful and worthwhile investment.

thirteen

who does the **work?**

- Can we attract the right calibre of person on a part-time basis, at least initially?
- Is part-time employment in-house practical?
- For best results should this person be out of consultancy?
- Are people who have worked in-house better able to adapt quickly and become team players, even if part-time?
- Should we expect a part-timer to contribute extra by way of cross-referencing experience?
- Do PR individuals handle one-off short-term assignments?
- What are the advantages of such arrangements?
- Do PR people charge more for limited period projects?
- Should we expect a part-timer to be self-employed, or would we take him or her onto our payroll?
- Is it OK to 'hot desk' a part-timer, or should we assign space?
- Can a part-timer function effectively without support staff?
- How much likely support staff time would a part-timer on a limited period project contract require?
- What can be done to ensure confidentiality once the project is completed?
- When they are looking for their next projects, do PR people thrive on testimonials or rely on published evidence?
- Does the part-timer's greater independence of us encourage a more candid approach to advising us?
- What ratio of advice to action can we expect from a part-timer?
- Should we avoid part-timers who seem to be well-heeled casuals just looking for something to do?
- What is a PR self-starter?

- Since there are so many of them in the trade, are women better at PR?
- Do women returnees have the quality of contacts needed?
- How can we test claims made by applicants about their contacts?
- What are the typical job satisfactions that drive PR people?
- What are the key characteristics of an effective PR person?
- Do journalists make the best PR people?
- What is the ideal background for doing PR?
- Will employing a professional publicist guarantee media coverage for us?

Someone has to do the work, but who? The PR function has privileged status, access to confidential information and regular contact with senior managers, so matters of loyalty and commitment may be particularly sensitive. It is also ambassadorial, representing the organization at various levels within its external publics, where it reflects the corporate image and reputation.

Questions here explore the options, about developing the job description and person specification, examining the qualities best suited to PR practice and what may be most appropriate in differing types and size of organization. Several questions ask about employing part-timers, one-off assignments and limited period contracts. Questions also include enquiries about ideal backgrounds, suitability of journalists for the work, typical job satisfactions and how to verify claims made about contacts.

Can we attract the right calibre of person on a part-time basis, at least initially?

Hiring someone part-time should not be a reflection of a weak or casual commitment to PR but based on perceived level of need and available funding. Given the appropriate motivation, to make this appointment the start of something really worthwhile, there is every possibility that a suitable calibre of person will be found, who has sound reasons for being interested on a part-time basis.

Who might this person be? Possibly the recruit is already doing PR on a part-time basis for someone else. This is common, as where, for instance, a self-employed freelancer is pursuing the 'portfolio living' ideal, or has one or two regular part-time commitments and wants to fill the remaining time to secure a full week's work. Some such people combine a part-time job with spending the rest of the week on other, quite different, interests, which may have a connection, such as journalism or design, or may not, such as charity volunteering or working with a partner in his or her business.

The answer may lie in engaging an interim manager. These people tend to be senior people with specific skills who are hired to deliver on a particular project or piece of work within, typically, 3 to 12 months. They specialize in absorbing a brief very quickly and beginning to secure results early. An interim manager may cost more but in exchange provide greater experience and flexibility. It might be the best way to kick-start the PR effort and be very helpful in designing a job and person specification for recruitment towards the end of the interim's contract period.

Is part-time employment in-house practical?

Yes, provided, above all else, that other managers have confidence in the appointment and willingly cooperate when necessary, to be sure that the new function has the best chance to be effective. If the fact that it is a part-time post is allowed to colour their perceptions it may not be appropriate. In addition, the post must be properly established, with a budget, authority to act, support when needed and equipment. All the features of a full-time post must be there, including reporting procedures, performance monitoring and measures of cost-effectiveness.

It has to be recognized that the part-timer probably seeks part-time work in order to benefit from greater flexibility and, in any event, is likely to be more independent, in temperament and economically, than a full-timer. Care is needed to ensure that what may be a relatively routine post is not filled by someone who is too 'high powered' and probably passing time between full-time jobs, a point that applies also, of course, to recruiting someone who is full-time.

One further point worth remembering: there absolutely must be systems in place to handle absences, because PR work cannot be neatly limited to just when the part-timer is in. Fax and e-mail messages can await attention maybe, but what is to be done about the incoming telephone calls during the days when he or she is not employed to attend? How will non-scheduled occurrences be handled? How will the function be represented?

For best results should this person be out of consultancy?

No; on the contrary, the ideal candidate may be someone who has worked in-house previously for a similar organization. Then he or she would bring a ready understanding of the culture, know the structure of the sector and have a wide range of relevant contacts. A former consultant, though, is probably better attuned to working in a variety of environments and competent at readily engaging with relative strangers at all levels in the hierarchy. He or she is likely to be particularly time and cost aware, less inhibited about observing conventions and more accustomed to being tested for ideas and creativity.

Are people who have worked in-house better able to adapt quickly and become team players, even if part-time?

In respect of collaboration, strong interpersonal skills, understanding how to get the best out of people, knowing the pressure points, providing impetus and dynamic, and so on, differences in levels of aptitude and skills will be caused by factors other than simply whether previous employment has been in-house or in a consultancy. This is because PR people have to demonstrate very strong teamworking credentials wherever they are, whoever they are with, including not only colleagues but a wide range of people, such as suppliers, journalists and contractors.

Should we expect a part-timer to contribute extra by way of cross-referencing experience?

Cross-fertilization of experience is fine provided confidentiality is not compromised. A part-timer may well be able to offer some benefits here, based on current workload across a variety of differing circumstances.

Do PR individuals handle one-off short-term assignments?

It is very common for individuals offering PR freelance services to undertake one-off time-limited assignments, usually measured in weeks or months.

What are the advantages of such arrangements?

They provide plenty of flexibility without ongoing commitment. They are commonly used to expand staffing of a department during a busy time and when specific additional skills are required, or to undertake a discreet campaign or activity as a special project. Typical examples include research projects, public exhibitions, educational schemes and sponsorships. For smaller organizations, such assignments can be particularly useful for developing environmental scanning skills and techniques, testing research methods and generating suitable materials.

Do PR people charge more for limited period projects?

Sadly, these projects are usually premium-priced because they require concentrated effort and are short-lived. If you have several such projects in mind you may be able to negotiate a discount on volume, but be prepared for the possibility of opt-out penalties if later projects fail to materialize.

Should we expect a part-timer to be self-employed, or would we take him or her onto our payroll?

This is very much a matter for negotiation and the particular circumstances. Many part-timers are self-employed, and want it that way; many organizations prefer direct labour, unless they thereby incur heavier statutory responsibilities, owing to the increase in numbers employed.

Is it OK to 'hot desk' a part-timer, or should we assign space?

'Hot desking' refers to the practice of providing a desk or workstation that is occupied by a different person on different days of the week, so that it is not for the exclusive use of any one employee, with his or her personal possessions in, on and around it. Ready access to essential facilities is the key consideration. These obviously include all IT equipment, as and when needed, but there is also a requirement for secure physical storage and access to support services. That reflects the nature of PR work.

If everything needed is available right away and there does not have to be any sharing (two or more people using the same desk at the same time) or making do off the end of some meeting room table, hot desking could be a practical economy. It would not make sense, however, if time was being lost by someone having to wait for a desk to become available, having to track down lost materials or trying to reconstruct mislaid messages or fouled up systems, all because there was not a small but practical permanent arrangement made for that person.

Can a part-timer function effectively without support staff?

This really all depends on whether the extent to which the work is either, on the one hand, advisory or, on the other, technical. Some part-timers are engaged to solely advise, and obviously they can travel light. Most though are there 'to do a job', implying implementation, which in practice means that they most definitely need support. This is likely to be shared, unless there is plenty of practical help needed when the part-timer isn't there, which can happen. It does not make sense to have support time tied up during the PR person's duty days on doing jobs that could just as well be done in his or her absence, for example, packing and dispatching of product samples to journalists. A senior manager's PA/secretary might undertake some responsibilities: say, maintaining the photo library, booking venues, sending out literature and updating contact lists.

PR people are usually fairly flexible about doing the incidental chores provided they are kept within sensible proportions. Many understand the constraints of the small business environment and respond more readily to the exigencies of the moment than might someone whose only work experience has been in larger organizations. However, they cannot allow their quality time to be snatched away by inadequate support mechanisms, because they are judged by results, not on their procedural efficiencies.

How much likely support staff time would a part-timer on a limited period project contract require?

Most limited period projects are of a technical nature and require intensive effort, for which full-time support is needed. For example, the press officer for a public exhibition would probably need two full-time assistants, plus access to other support as needed.

What can be done to ensure confidentiality once the project is completed?

Confidentiality clauses are written to be kept, but can be difficult to enforce. As in any occupation where sensitive information is accessed, loose talking can injure career prospects, which is probably the best assurance available. However, care has to be taken not to mistake observance of confidentiality with restriction on trade.

When they are looking for their next projects, do PR people thrive on testimonials or rely on published evidence?

They are likely to use both, because PR work does not necessarily result in published evidence. Testimonials are useful, but usually circumspect and often given grudgingly. The most popular vehicle is the self-congratulatory case study, which names brands and proclaims achievement, closely followed by the evidence of media coverage, in press clippings and broadcast transcripts. Some offer for inspection a portfolio comprising a medley of open testimonials, clippings, photographs and other evidence of work done.

Does the part-timer's greater independence of us encourage a more candid approach to advising us?

In theory you should obtain greater candour, because he or she is cast more in the role of a consultant than that of an employee. In practice much depends upon the deliberative nature of the work, personal chemistry and levels of mutual commitment. Someone who has only ever had full-time employment before and knows that the immediate outlook constitutes only two days a week for the next seven months is unlikely to be much incentivized in the candour stakes. Someone else, who has an established record of self-employment and current full order book, with an open-ended contract to supply three days a week, may very well be prepared to be more forthcoming.

What ratio of advice to action can we expect from a part-timer?

How much time and budget is allocated to advice and to action depends upon individual needs and can be adjusted in the light of experience, either towards more advice or more action. A little more advice can help to reduce quite a lot more of the action needed, and an experienced PR person, whether part-time or full-time, will be able to provide quality advice, the provision of which involves relatively little operating costs.

Should we avoid part-timers who seem to be well-heeled casuals just looking for something to do?

Any impression of a shallow interest or commitment, for whatever reason, is likely to be a strong indication of possible problems to follow. Such is the pervasiveness of PR and its rapid growth, there do appear to be a few people who suppose that they can readily drift into PR employment, often with minimal skills and training but plenty of social contacts. However charming or seductive, these folk are best avoided, in this context.

What is a PR self-starter?

This popularly describes someone who gets on with it, the sort who can look at a cleared desk, a blank sheet of paper or a 30-page brief and plunge into action, without first needing detailed instruction, coaxing reassurance, bonding sessions or quiet contemplation. This is a person who is a seasoned performer, with the appropriate levels of knowledge, experience, skills and self-confidence to represent a good investment, the sort, in short, that PR firms are continually trying to pilfer from each other.

Since there are so many of them in the trade, are women better at PR?

So you have noticed that the great majority of people in PR are women? Some unkind explanations are offered for this, by some men, it has to be said. These rotate around supposed superior female persuasiveness, calculation and survival techniques. Certainly women have had to develop strong communication skills, for very good reason, and a gallant man might add that it is as well for both sexes that they did.

The explanation, though, is probably a good deal more mundane. The simple fact is that the vast majority of consumers are women and the greater part of PR work is in support of marketing, which is, yes, very largely about consumers. So what better than to have women communicating with women? On the whole they do it exceedingly well, and there are complete consultancies entirely comprised of women. Similarly, women dominate the more consumer-orientated media. This does not exclude men, however; it is a matter of 'horses for courses' and many consumer products and services interest women more than men.

Do women returnees have the quality of contacts needed?

That must surely depend upon where they are returning from, how long they were away and what they were doing before. Have they been gone months or years? Were they in PR before? Have they been doing something else that is relevant? Obviously someone who has taken five years out to raise children, care for an elderly relative or travel abroad is likely to have largely lost her contacts, because life moves on so quickly, but that does not necessarily mean that she could not use her skills at contact making to pick up again fairly quickly. Women in this position often say that it can be very tiring but they are determined to prove they can do it. It is observable that most do.

How can we test claims made by applicants about their contacts?

You can talk to a few journalists, to check whether they have had any experience of the applicant's work and what impressions they have gained.

What are the typical job satisfactions that drive PR people?

They are probably not much different from those of any other occupational group. They do derive, though, exceptional levels of satisfaction in achieving for other people. This is because they deliberately avoid the spotlight for almost all the time, working instead behind the scenes, in the back office, on behalf of others, and their success is therefore measured, usually, in other people's gains.

This may seem either remarkably self-effacing or highly calculating. It is established, nevertheless, that the PR person who comes forward, to the point of being centre stage, is thought to have transgressed, become 'part of the story' and thereby neutralized his or her effectiveness. This is so to the extent that it may well result in resignation or dismissal. Accordingly, the most prominence any PR person is likely to accept is introducing the people he or she represents and occasionally helping out if they are at a loss for words during an interview or public appearance.

It does seem, though, that this readily subservient posture is dependent upon degrees of success. PR people who see their employers or customers succeed disproportionately to their own reward, or to what they know privately about those people's abilities and competencies, can expect and may command proportionately greater reward for their efforts. Levels of remuneration in PR have risen dramatically in the past 20 years, but it can still be poorly paid when compared with the benefits that may directly accrue.

What are the key characteristics of an effective PR person?

Probably the one quality, above all else, that is most valued is creativity. The single core skill that is most required, however, is the ability to write. Where these two are strongly present there is scope for excellence. Creativity involves not just imagination but the ability to perceive and understand from outside the prevailing conventional thinking and to use often disparate bits and pieces in order to create added value. Writing skill involves not just production of a product press release but the ability to write, to order, in a wide range of styles for a variety of purposes and communication channels.

There are also some other, fairly predictable, abilities needed. Self-motivation stands high among these, because PR work can be a lonely path to tread at times. PR people also need, in generous quantity, to be articulate, intelligent, responsive, energetic and resilient. Maturity has its advantages too.

Do journalists make the best PR people?

On the whole, the answer has to be no. Journalists frequently cross over into PR, officially, supposing that it is entirely about tendentious journalism, so dead easy really. They are ignorant of much that matters most in PR, though. They know little about strategic planning, unless they made it out of journalism into media management first, suppose environmental scanning is not much different to accessing the newspaper's cuttings library and think impact evaluation amounts to opinion polling. They are unlikely to have had much training as such in attitudinal and behavioural studies.

Journalists also often lack those star qualities that make for PR success. They can be lacking in the necessary reserves of patience, for instance, and be a mite too arrogant or complacent for their own good. However, if they are engaged entirely on media relations, better still, working with the very people they have known for years, they take some beating. Their writing skills should be very advanced, and they understand well the perceptions and needs of 'the other'.

What is the ideal background for doing PR?

The ideal background is an occupation where well-developed two-way communication and dialogue is essential. That may bring to mind the law, as well it should, but in practice recruits come from a remarkably wide range of backgrounds. Apart from journalism, these include marketing, advertising, management consultancy, politics, engineering and medicine. A growing number are, of course, going straight into PR having graduated in PR or media studies.

Will employing a professional publicist guarantee media coverage for us?

People who specialize in publicity cannot guarantee media coverage, in the sense that this question implies, but they are exceptionally skilled at securing it and what they do is entirely about attracting attention for advantage. The bigger question is whether it is more appropriate to engage a publicist rather than a PR person with broader skills. It may well be, in the circumstances, particularly for a short assignment.

fourteen

the **consultancy** for us

- Is there a scheme to help distinguish between the consultancies?
- Are there good firms without the accreditation?
- Do you pay more for the people in the trade association?
- Are large firms likely to be more expensive?
- Are one-man or one-woman operators to be avoided?
- Would dealing with one or two owner-managers for all our requirements be advisable, or preferable?
- Are long-established firms preferable to the recent start-ups?
- Are all consultants in their 20s and early 30s?
- How much weight should we give to the experience and qualifications of the people who do the work on a daily basis?
- How important are the size and quality of the PR firm's premises?
- Would evidence of experience across a variety of sectors be an advantage to us?
- What quality and type of evidence of work done for others should we require?
- Should we favour a firm that already works for one of our respected competitors?
- Should we insist that they switch to us, recognizing that we may have to pay for this?
- Are we looking for a firm that has done a good job for one of our competitors in the past but doesn't work for them now?
- Are there circumstances in which employing a PR firm that has several clients in our sector might be beneficial to us?
- What obligations do the PR firms have to disclose to us any potential conflict of interest between their clients?

- Is there an established procedure we might use to select a firm?
- Do consultants initially come to see you or should we start by going to see them?
- Should we be looking at their trade papers first?
- Would journalists on our own trade papers be useful?
- When we have a shortlist what may we expect to happen next?
- Why should we pay for proposals?
- How do we make sure that we can assess the people and not just their sales teams?
- If a firm has young personnel making frequent career moves would we be better advised to hire project by project?
- Should we require evidence of a minimum number of hours worked each week on our behalf?
- In our brief should we be expecting tactics or an outline strategy as well?
- If after we have taken proposals they all seem to be much the same, what next?
- Should we use the experience to start again then?
- How do PR firms charge for their services?
- How do PR charges compare generally with advertising?
- What elements are likely to make up total cost in buying PR?
- How much of our time should we expect to allocate to PR once the consultants are on board?
- How can we be sure that our confidentialities will be kept?
- How can we rely on the consultants to demonstrate integrity handling our sensitive financial and commercial information?
- Should we operate a 'need to know' policy, telling the consultants only what they absolutely need to know?
- How do PR firms check out the veracity of what their clients tell them?
- Is there a common optimum length of time for the relationship to flourish and subside between the client and the provider?
- When or how might a PR firm outgrow us?
- Can we expect a consultancy to be eyes and ears for us?
- Should we be wary of any extras the consultants bring us?
- Do PR firms change tactics mid-stream if this is necessary?
- Could a change of tactics alter the contractual position?
- How do we get rid of a PR firm without damage to us?

Many organizations kick-start their PR by engaging a consultancy, on a retained annual basis or for a limited period, with the aim of learning what they can empirically and maintaining optimum cost flexibility until they consider the time is appropriate to establish an in-house department. Later they may employ one or more consultancies to advise on specialist areas in support of the internal function.

There are hundreds of consultancies in the United Kingdom from which to choose, and very many more elsewhere. A number claim to earn multimillion annual revenues, many to 'make a good living' for their owner-managers. Some are subsidiaries of multinationals, formed by amalgamation of PR firms or of differing marketing services companies. Others are members of international networks of independent PR firms. Most are national in their geographical reach, many are regional and some are local. There are those, mainly the larger ones, that offer a wide range of services across all sectors and there are the niche players, specializing either by areas of work and/or sectors, products and services.

How to choose the most appropriate provider from this welter of choice can be daunting, especially for managers with limited familiarity with the practicalities of employing this type of specialist supplier. In this chapter, developing a profile of the preferred consultancy is explored, whether it is to be retained annually or for a limited period, to initiate PR activity or to supplement the work of an in-house department.

Is there a scheme to help distinguish between the consultancies?

The symbol that denotes membership of the UK trade association might be thought of as an equivalent of the various logos and marks used around the world to denote that approved standards have been met, but how much reliance should be placed on this is uncertain. Further, although the association claims that its members' aggregate fee income accounts for three-quarters of all UK consultancy earnings, they number only about 135, which is a small proportion of the total number of consultancies.

Are there good firms without the accreditation?

If accreditation means membership of the trade association, the answer has to be yes. There are many excellent consultancies that prefer not to be in membership of the trade association, which is primarily a sales vehicle for its members. Among these non-members are many that serve niche markets for their services exceptionally well.

Do you pay more for the people in the trade association?

Most of the largest and many of the larger firms are in membership. Since they tend to charge more rather than less, which presumably provides a clue as to why they rose to their current size, it is probable that the little symbol spells extra cost. Fees range widely across the trade, but it is noticeable that many of the big PR spenders, such as government departments, appear to commission association members.

Are large firms likely to be more expensive?

The large PR firms have always tended to charge more, relying on their product surround and dedication to 'PR-ing' themselves. Many are publicly quoted. They hunt for and win multimillion pound fees, in a trade where the majority of fees paid are significantly lower. However, most of them like to handle one or two charities, declaredly for image purposes, presumably at discounted charges.

Are one-man or one-woman operators to be avoided?

The 'operator' description might be taken to imply that such people are imposters, which would be both inaccurate and mistaken. There are some remarkably able people who operate singly, or perhaps in pairs, often on an advisory basis only. They tend to be very knowledgeable about specific sectors and may be engaged as interim managers.

Would dealing with one or two owner-managers for all our requirements be advisable, or preferable?

Owner-managers, in any sector, are noted for their commitment to delivering quality service, and if there is one very solid reason above all others for preferring them it has to be this. Time and again clients complain that they do not receive comparable service from the employees of larger suppliers, not that it deters most of them from continuing to insist on buying from the larger consultancies, which itself may well be a cause of their problem.

Owner-managed PR firms can provide a sound access to cost-effective consultancy, maybe when the organization is first feeling its way with PR, or when highly skilled and demanding specialized inputs are required. Most consultancies affect to be disinterested in fees of less than £50,000 per annum, but in reality many projects are undertaken at lower figures, and the trade competes keenly on price as well as quality.

Are long-established firms preferable to the recent start-ups?

This is a young and youthful trade, in which any business that can trace its ancestry back 50 years is at risk of being called geriatric. Listening to these few, mostly with advertising origins, it might be supposed that extreme longevity is a hallmark in itself. It is not. Some of the most able and energetic people have started up recently and offer just the range of skills needed in many contemporary markets. The economic slump at the beginning of the 1990s did not deter many newcomers from setting up during the years that followed. This trade, more than most, mirrors current economic conditions closely, in its successive faster and slower expansionary phases, and start-ups usually consolidate quickly.

Are all consultants in their 20s and early 30s?

At times it may seem that way, and certainly the vast majority are under 40, by which stage many have graduated to management or moved off into second careers, rather like UK advertising people deciding to run restaurants in Spain. Presumably with time the average age will rise. It has often been remarked by PR people themselves that theirs is a younger person's occupation, but when the magical mid-life tripwire is sighted more than a few prefer to press on regardless.

> When the then 38-year-old publicist Matthew Freud, incidentally the great-grandson of Sigmund Freud, was reminded by his interviewer in the *Financial Times* (4 December 2001) that he had once said 'there's nothing sadder than a 40-year-old PR person', he replied 'When I said that, I assumed I'd be out by 30'.

How much weight should we give to the experience and qualifications of the people who do the work on a daily basis?

Many clients complain, often bitterly, that the people who get to do the work are much younger and less experienced than the people who 'sold' it to them. In other words, the consultancy they employed has a polished sales team that deceived them. A similar complaint is that these younger executives keep moving around between different employers, resulting in discontinuity of service and unnecessary learning-curve expense for the client, as each successor in turn grapples with the account (service contract). To hear these complaints one might be inclined to extend sympathy, but so often the complainants appear nevertheless to accept their lot, instead of moving their business to a consultancy where what they see at interview is what they get, more or less.

The fact is, experience and qualifications matter a lot, whether the people are in-house or in consultancy. PR is now taught at undergraduate level in well over a dozen universities, there is a choice of diplomas to be taken part-time and a multitude of training opportunities, including some in-house schemes. It seems difficult to conceive of any career being embarked upon now that would not necessitate obtaining formal qualification of some kind. The longest established industry trainer has been around for over 30 years.

How important are the size and quality of the PR firm's premises?

Premises are a component of corporate identity and a major influence on image, so the larger PR consultancies tend to attach great importance to the appearance, style and fit-out of their premises. In this they often compete with law firms, designers and others who want to seriously impress. In so far as the overwhelmingly status-drenched presentation can be taken as indicative of service standards, premises are of course an important consideration. Unfortunately, the one does not guarantee the other. And where the visitor senses that he or she is being led through what is effectively a theatre set, it can be interesting to test the reaction to asking to see the workroom. It may be refused, on grounds of 'confidentiality'.

Some consultants seem to revel in offering their clients a scruffily robust contrast to this. Should a client remark, for instance, on the bare floorboards, the response may be along the lines of 'if you would like us to carpet for your next visit we will happily do so if you would like to pay for it'. The clear implication is that every penny of the fee is going on service, and not being frittered away on posh premises, a rather artful way of selling supposed value for money.

Many consultants operate from small but perfectly formed offices that, while not glitzy, would do credit to any number of trades. Others carefully fit out their space to mimic the supposed tastes of their customers. So, for example, PR consultants who specialize in publishing may just happen to have offices that, to their clients, reassuringly look more like studies or libraries, real home-from-homes, so to speak. Just how much importance is attached to all this has to depend upon individual circumstances and tastes, remembering that offices may not be that indicative unless the working areas are seen and the numbers of staff, or at least their workstations, are counted.

An artful ruse is to imply much more space and people than is the case by judicious use of long corridors and closed doors. The aim appears to be a variation of peer group pressure, implying: 'Our being this large, surely you would not want to be left out by *not* being one of our clients?'

> One leading consultant rented space in an empty office block and routinely told visitors that the firm occupied the rest of the building. Unfortunately one would-be customer suspected otherwise and suddenly threw open a door as he passed on his way out, to reveal an obviously unused, unfurnished room.

Some consultancies place emphasis on the location of their premises appropriate to their desired image and identity. Thus you find IT specialists on landscaped science parks, property specialists in the smartest central streets, fashion specialists in recognized trade 'quarters', lobbyists almost next door to the parliament building, and so on. Modern communications make redundant the need for such physical proximity, but clients often gain reassurance from it.

Would evidence of experience across a variety of sectors be an advantage to us?

Undoubtedly the cross-fertilization of experience across sectors can be very helpful. Whether that would be an advantage must depend upon circumstances, because depth experience of your sector might be preferable if the PR consultant must have a sound knowledge and understanding of technical and/or complex processes. For instance, drug companies tend to favour people with medical qualifications, film makers need publicists who have relevant international marketing experience, food manufacturers incline to consultants that know the food laws and regulations and their industry.

The extent to which, in practice, experience can be transferred may seem limited, but it is surprising how often it holds the key to a creative solution. This is not about imitation so much as adaptation. So samples of programmes undertaken in entirely different contexts that might at first seem remote may be nevertheless valid.

What quality and type of evidence of work done for others should we require?

Many case studies are bland, with generalized results, sweeping claims and little detail. Presentations can be just as uninformative. The evidence needs to differentiate clearly what was achieved by the PR effort from what was the result of other factors. Although the consultancy has to respect confidentialities, it should be possible to be told the objectives and how the results were measured and evaluated. It is also appropriate to be given an indication of how the work was managed in practice. The degree of substantiation must vary depending upon the type of work, but it should be expected that physical evidence would be forthcoming to support the claims satisfactorily.

Should we favour a firm that already works for one of our respected competitors?

Many organizations, of all types, are drawn to engaging consultants who are already retained by a competitor, rival or fellow traveller. It can seem especially attractive when that 'other' is much respected, maybe a good bit bigger or better known. The temptation is to think in terms of 'crumbs falling from tables'. However, there can be drawbacks. Firstly, what about levels of confidentiality; is this an attempt to obtain intelligence without risk of imparting any? Then, what is the risk of being a 'me too', perceived by the consultancy as the lesser of the two? And what quality of creativity may be expected? In any event, the consultant will want to disclose to the 'other' and may well find that there is an objection raised, resulting in a commercial choice being necessary.

Should we insist that they switch to us, recognizing that we may have to pay for this?

If the contract is to be 'exclusive' presumably that will be reflected in the fee, and if the purpose is to secure a switch, the consultancy's existing contractual commitments will be a factor in both the timing and the expense. Persuading a consultant to transfer loyalties in this way may well prove to be a costly exercise, although project-based contracts may ease the complications.

In practice, most consultants work at any one time for only one client in each sector, usually under an annually renewable retained contract. This can represent a substantial risk of trade for them where the client accounts for a substantial proportion of earnings. Furthermore, all contracts have to be profitable. It may be that either or neither party plans to renew. Should the consultancy happen to be searching for a replacement at the time of the enquiry, the switch might be effected more economically.

Are we looking for a firm that has done a good job for one of our competitors in the past but doesn't work for them now?

That sounds like an ideal, but how long ago did they cease working for them, why did they part company and what has kept the consultancy busy since then? The answers to those questions may provide acceptable explanations and the people who did the work, which you admire, are still available to work on your account. Most consultancies that have a strong track record with a prominent player in a market, and subsequently lose the connection, are often hired by a rival soon afterwards.

Are there circumstances in which employing a PR firm that has several clients in our sector might be beneficial to us?

It does happen, probably more where a consultancy is engaged project by project rather than on annual retention. It has to be well known and strongly connected, and the various clients do not perceive themselves to be competitive on a scale that worries them in the PR context. For example, commercial property developers may compete for purchasers and tenants, to buy or occupy their buildings, but this has not inhibited many of them from hiring the same firm, presumably deriving comfort from their collective 'herd instinct'.

Again, for instance, fee-paying private schools share suppliers, as do many other sectors where there are established communication channels, such as well-attended annual conferences, for exchanging tips and recommendations. Similarly, a consultancy may work for several interests in the same field, but each one has its own distinctive position; maybe one is a trade association, two or three are manufacturers with complementary rather than competitive products and two or three more are elsewhere in the supply chain.

What obligations do the PR firms have to disclose to us any potential conflict of interest between their clients?

They have every obligation to disclose if they are in membership of the trade association, whose rules state clearly that a member may take fees, commissions and other valuable considerations from others only provided these are disclosed to the client and must not represent conflicting or competing interests without the express consent of 'clients concerned'. Similarly, individual members of the trade's institute undertake to declare conflicts of interest, or circumstances that may give rise to them, to clients and potential clients.

Both organizations aim to set a standard for the whole trade, but commercial reality is probably more influential with non-members. If a consultant does not disclose, a very real risk of trade has been created that he or she has to consider to be worthwhile. Most times it is unlikely to make commercial sense. Of course there may be some occasions when there is a genuine misapprehension about the potential for conflict, but in practice that is rare. Other PR trade bodies around the world broadly follow similar rules.

Is there an established procedure we might use to select a firm?

The best procedure is recommendation from a reliable source, but if you have to start from scratch there are some fairly predictable ways of going about it, starting with assembling a list of people that may be of interest. This can be done by reference to sector specialism, locality, international credentials, probable size, type of PR work required, reputation with journalists or other key contacts, and so on. The trade association offers its corporate members for selection, recommending that the list comprises no more than five or six names, although at this stage you should choose as many as you consider to be needed to have made a thorough search. The trade's institute has a similar service and other trade and professional bodies can be a good source of names that may be more directly relevant.

Do consultants initially come to see you or should we start by going to see them?

You could start by visiting each of them, but that takes time and you may end up not being that enamoured of any of them. Better to start by inviting them to come and see you, without obligation on either side. That way you can begin to filter straightaway and form a short-list, or go on looking, which will make more efficient use of your time. There is unlikely to be any resistance from the consultancies, because this way they gain a more informed impression about you before engaging in any significant expenditure with presentations and proposals.

Should we be looking at their trade papers first?

You certainly could, although bear in mind that these PR trade titles are also platforms par excellence for PR, probably unequalled by any other trade papers. The largest firms, which have people dedicated to their own PR, are likely to have a disproportionate share of the coverage in any randomly chosen issue. The news is largely concerned with marketing of big commercial brands and highly priced government campaigns. Items about individuals are exceptionally flattering.

Would journalists on our own trade papers be useful?

They may have their favourites that they wish to mention, and this can be helpful. Bear in mind, though, that they may not be disinterested when making those recommendations, since many are rewarded for their efforts if these subsequently result in contracts. Also, journalists may mention firms simply because they hear from them more often, which is not necessarily a reflection of their worth.

When we have a shortlist what may we expect to happen next?

Once you have a list of potential suppliers that you consider to qualify for your serious consideration the time has come to visit each of them by turn. This is the opportunity to see what they get up to, meet some of the staff, or at least have a sight of them, and look around the facilities. It is customary to give a credentials presentation, and these can become laboured, so it is as well to establish the programme beforehand to make sure that everyone understands at the outset how much time is available for this.

The looking around part of the visit can be a nerve-wracking experience for younger staff, and in consequence the atmosphere may be somewhat contrived. The more confident operations tend to present more bustle and less interest in the visitors, but do not necessarily expect noise and activity and be equally prepared for a quiet room of screen-riveted thinkers, more like a library or control room. Ask about how exactly accounts are managed and for terms of business. Look for resources in depth, such as a design studio, and test the quality of responses to your broad objectives.

From these visits you will be in a position to form a shortlist of three (the customary number) consultancies. Each should be told how many others are involved, invited to prepare competitive proposals and asked how much they will cost. Over the years, various attempts have been made by consultancies to voluntarily enforce blanket agreement to charge for proposals, with mixed results. Some prominent firms, for instance, have been known to solemnly swear that they will charge in future, only to break ranks and provide them without charge at the first opportunity.

So be prepared to pay a fee that fairly reflects the degree of effort and time expended, *and* be prepared to be let off paying anything. Do not allow the latter to detract from the former; more often than not the 'freebies' are assembled quickly and without much effort, 'off the shelf' concoctions of what has been done for clients and prospective clients previously. You may also encounter a firm that offers a hybrid solution: a free outline that is purely indicative, and a charge for anything more substantial.

Why should we pay for proposals?

PR proposals that are worth having are the result of substantial effort. They are competitive documents, generated from detailed briefing, which takes your time, with creative ideas and recommendations, which are explained fully in a presentation, that again takes your time. You are making a substantial time investment, and the consultancy is responding proportionately, or quite possibly more so. Bear in mind that if you do not pay for them you may become liable to an action under the law of confidence if you later use any of their content without engaging the firm that produced them.

How do we make sure that we can assess the people and not just their sales teams?

One answer is to buy from owner-managers, because they, usually, have a direct hand in delivery. Another is to ask to meet the very people who would be working on the account. This could be done during the visit or at the competitive presentation, which may be at either premises or at some independent venue such as a hotel. You can contractually specify the people, who barring illness or accident can be expected to be around for a project of a few months' duration, but with annual retentions this might be seen as an unreasonable and impractical requirement. Usually there is a service hierarchy, from director or partner down through group heads to senior executives to junior executives and support staff. Hopefully the senior people remain, so that the turnover of people at the lower levels still leaves the primary contacts in place.

If a firm has young personnel making frequent career moves would we be better advised to hire project by project?

It is unlikely that this would be a main consideration in deciding between commissioning a project and retaining for a year at a time, or longer. The nature of the service required must surely take precedence, for instance. However, finding that after a few months 80–90 per cent of the service is being provided by an entirely new set of faces is not amusing. Maybe this is another argument for preferring owner-managers.

Should we require evidence of a minimum number of hours worked each week on our behalf?

The nature of PR programmes does not readily lend itself to even work flows. On the contrary, there can be periods of intense activity and times of relative inactivity. Nor does time expended of itself indicate effective and efficient use of time. All consultants keep time records, or should, mostly for their own benefit, but doubtless these could be made available should you need to see them. If you are this concerned about service implementation activity levels maybe you should be thinking of hiring in-house instead, so that you can supervise the work and satisfy yourself that it is being performed conscientiously. Otherwise, best leave it to the consultancy to worry about how many hours are needed and when, to deliver the contracted service levels.

In our brief should we be expecting tactics or an outline strategy as well?

Both.

If after we have taken proposals they all seem to be much the same, what next?

It could be that there is some weakness in the way in which you assembled the original list. It might be worth looking again at this, to see if you made sufficient enquiries or widened your search far enough. For instance, perhaps you stuck with recommendations and names familiar to you from within your sector, and in consequence ended up with some fairly predictable and time-honoured approaches, when what you were hoping for was some really fresh thinking. That may have to come from outside, from people who are not working in your sector yet but have transferable thinking skills and been exposed to contrasting situations.

Alternatively, the problem may lie with the brief. Was it sufficiently detailed, to allow the proposers to give of their best? It can seem fine to take other people's knowledge and ideas in the form of proposals while giving as little away as possible to them, but this is not always conducive to quality outcomes. This is not some sort of guessing game or quiz show, to see how much they can conjure out of thin air. Or, by contrast, was the brief so detailed and definitive that it constrained the responses, or simply prescribed them, so that what came back was best calculated to be what you wanted to hear? Briefing can be 'tainted' by such factors, leading to disappointment with results. Maybe the brief needs to be thoroughly reworked.

Another explanation may lie in how you took the presentations. It could be that a few more questions might have made all the difference. These can range over not just the proposed programme and who will do what but to consultancy culture, practices, charging procedures, range of interests and so on. Some of these questions may have been answered already but need re-asking in a different format to double-check on understandings and prise out additional information that could differentiate.

So many presentations are won or lost not in the performances themselves but in the questions and answers that follow, when competencies can be demonstrated and the personal chemistry is more clearly identified. When all has been said and done, successful client–consultant relationships depend upon a degree of mutual respect and trust. If the chemistry appears to be lacking, or thin, at the outset there is every probability that there will not be a satisfactory, or better, level of collaboration later that will optimize results for both parties.

Should we use the experience to start again then?

You could do, but it would greatly extend your costs and the time factor, so it is probably not appropriate unless you are really convinced that none of the proposals were any good. Having said that, only you know how they compare with the scale of your requirement, and if they were a miserable disappointment it may well make sense to start again, with the benefit of the experience, and take your time to obtain the 'right' result. Alternatively, it might be time to go back over what has happened and do some fine-tuning, perhaps by asking more questions, revisiting or inviting further discussion. Or you could decide to hire in-house, albeit part-time at first, and reconsider consultancy later.

How do PR firms charge for their services?

Under retained contracts of one, two or three years duration, it is usual to pay monthly in advance a retainer that represents one-twelfth of the annual fee, together with reimbursement of disbursements incurred, such charges being in relation to specified routine necessary expenditures. In addition, any exceptional costs, agreed in writing beforehand, will be recovered. Sometimes the frequency of payments is bimonthly or quarterly.

Alternatively, a similar but lesser retainer may be paid monthly in advance, together with a charge for time expended during the previous month and disbursements incurred. This way there is ongoing consultancy but variable costs to reflect more pronounced differences in the amount of work being done at varying times during the contract period. There may be protracted periods during which only the retainer and minimal disbursements are payable. A third possibility is that only a retainer is paid, purely for counsel.

Arrangements for limited period projects vary too. A common practice is to pay one-third of an agreed fee at the outset, a further one-third at around the halfway stage and the balance on conclusion. Alternatively, a fee might be agreed for the project and then paid in equal instalments, monthly or otherwise, throughout the term. Some projects are half paid for in advance, with the balance on completion. Expenses incurred in the performance of the contracts are in any event reimbursed, by agreement.

How do PR charges compare generally with advertising?

Favourably, is the answer to that. Only generalizations are possible, because practice varies widely, but where PR is in support of marketing it is commonplace for the advertising budget allocation to be four times greater than that of PR. However, an increasing incidence of PR being used more and advertising less may erode the scale of the difference with time.

What elements are likely to make up total cost in buying PR?

The well-run PR consultancy aims to keep its labour costs to around 50 per cent of its gross income. This compares with 2001 figures of 56 per cent in advertising, 58 per cent in direct marketing and 61 per cent in design. In practice this means that executive time is charged at three, three-and-a-half or four times the annual gross salary of the executive. So half or more of the fee goes on salaries, which is to be expected in a labour-intensive service. The balance covers all the usual overheads plus profit, for these are businesses that aim to make profit.

The key factor for them is their cost of producing chargeable time against the rate of increase in the sales value of that time, and that cost is largely determined by wage inflation. The PR trade routinely claims to be under pressure and certainly it tends to be price competitive, with salaries comparatively modest, from top to bottom, when set against those for similar occupations. This, however, is not always readily apparent to its clients.

How much of our time should we expect to allocate to PR once the consultants are on board?

At first you may find that you need to give quite generous amounts of your time, assuming that the consultants intend to give of their best. With retained contracts, this level of input should subside as the return on effort begins to gather momentum, so that eventually between routine monthly contact meetings you may have only occasional involvement. Obviously if you are participating directly, say in interviews or conferences, your time commitment will reflect that.

Be prepared for having to give rather more time, proportionately, to one-off projects, particularly the more important or sensitive. Equally, try to make sure that the consultants feel that they have sufficient independence of action and delegated authority to do the job without feeling inhibited or the necessity to run back for approvals at every twist and turn. Once that kind of blanket inhibition sets in, most consultants are tempted to start abrogating responsibility and in consequence the client's time commitment begins to grow.

If you are engaging a consultant purely for counsel, advice but minimal action, at least by him or her, your time commitment increases proportionately to that of the consultant. Much of the time necessarily is taken in consultation, but then presumably this is no different to consulting, say, a lawyer.

How can we be sure that our confidentialities will be kept?

You cannot, and it is foolish to suppose that in our contemporary culture it is possible to rely entirely on ethical decencies. Both trade bodies, naturally, commit their members to respecting confidences. The consultants include their past clients in this and allow themselves the only let-out of where such information is in the public domain, in which case surely it ceases to be confidential in any usual understanding of the word, or there has been agreement to disclose or a court orders disclosure. As with conflicts of interest, probably the best guarantee of confidentialities being observed is commercial necessity. If a consultancy gains a name for being talkative about supposedly private matters it is doing itself no favours and is almost certainly embarking on a self-destructive decline.

How can we rely on the consultants to demonstrate integrity handling our sensitive financial and commercial information?

In much the same way that you would expect, quite rightly, anyone in-house to do so. For instance, financial PR people necessarily handle price-sensitive information, and they know that one premature leak would be extremely damaging to their business, so they take good care, just as might, say, a security printer. Indeed, a case might be made for saying that you are on a safer bet with consultants than with your own direct labour.

Should we operate a 'need to know' policy, telling the consultants only what they absolutely need to know?

That is nonsense. Why on earth would you want to hamper them by being parsimonious with the 'actuality'? If you withhold information, it has to be your decision as to what is or is not relevant. Why not give them all that they may reasonably need to know, and why not trust them to tell you what that might be?

If you decide to limit what you tell them you cannot reasonably complain later if the outcomes are not as you would have wished. And, frankly, seasoned consultants do not give their best when they suspect that they are not being adequately informed. Conversely, they tend to respond very positively to being taken into confidence.

Further, how can you expect them to give you the full benefit of their environmental scanning and feedback if they suspect that they are working in ignorance of important information from you? They do not appreciate being shown to their valuable media contacts to be uninformed or partly informed. Those contacts are their stock-in-trade and they do not need clients who in any way jeopardize their standing or relations with them. Journalists despise PR people who are misinformed or only partly informed, and rightly so.

How do PR firms check out the veracity of what their clients tell them?

They tend to rely on their own judgement and what they may learn by talking around. Sometimes actions speak louder than words, other times people with long memories can fill in great lacunas in the potted client versions of events. Journalists often find few greater pleasures in life than to disabuse a PR consultant about one of his or her clients, especially the newly acquired ones. It is a small world within marketing communications generally, public affairs generally, the media generally. Word travels in these 'chattering classes' and clients gather their own reputations there in consequence.

Is there a common optimum length of time for the relationship to flourish and subside between the client and the provider?

It is a fact of life, yet to be explained, that seven years does seem to bring on an itch for change, but that is probably as soundly based as any other superstition. Some relationships buck the trend and survive much longer, but these are often underwritten by close personal relationships, as well as business ones. In the purely commercial context it is likely that mutually beneficial relationships typically last four to five years. After that one or other side is usually looking for fresh solutions. The client is probably thinking of having more people in-house or a larger supplier, the consultancy is probably plain bored and wishing for some fresh challenges, preferably better paid.

When or how might a PR firm outgrow us?

This is a good question. It can happen that the supplier 'gets too big' for the purchaser, just as the client can decide that the consultancy is no longer appropriate on grounds of size and status. This business of the relative pace of growth of the two parties can be most interesting. Usually one side or the other outgrows the other, either through dramatic organic growth, which is fairly unlikely, or through acquisition or merger.

Much of this is, of course, in the mind. If a consultancy has given good service for a number of years why change it? Sometimes pressures come on to do so, as where, for instance a company has had excellent MPR service for, say, five years, then goes public and is told by its City advisers that it has to replace this firm with a financial PR specialist or a combination of that plus a large, prestige and, invariably more expensive, 'leading consultancy' nomination. Of course this happens in accountancy and law too, but with PR it is less likely to make sense.

Then again, executives on the client side usually want to feel comfortable with the consultancy. Typically, this is expressed in terms of matching large with large, small with small, and so on. The absurdity of this is that it is all about perceptions and vanity, little about getting best value and quality relationships. Such is life, but all those who demand change because the 'other' is seen as being inferior should bear in mind the old adage about meeting people on the way up and again on the way down.

The fact is that, probably more with PR than other occupations, a single person may well provide a quality of advice to a major organization that well exceeds that available from a large, big name supplier, and conversely, a small organization may well benefit greatly from the service of a much larger provider, supposing it can be afforded or is discounted for some charitable reason, which happens.

Can we expect a consultancy to be eyes and ears for us?

Environmental scanning is an integral part of PR work, so you would expect a consultancy to provide feedback in relation to the commission. Beyond that it depends upon the quality of the relationship. The stronger and more continuous the relationship the greater the probability that the consultant will come forward with valuable information or observations worth having in the wider scheme of things. PR consultants are strong networkers, and they are often in a position to effect introductions, 'know a man who can' or offer a few tips. But there is likely to be understandable reticence about coming forward beyond the call of duty where there is poor prospect of an ongoing relationship.

Should we be wary of any extras the consultants bring us?

If those extras amount to sales leads, trade gossip or customers' opinions, for example, you are likely to welcome them and they are provided within the fee. But if by 'extras' is meant additional services for extra payment, then presumably they would be discussed in principle first and agreed. It is common for additional one-off services to be undertaken supplementary to whatever is being supplied under a retained contract, as where, say, there is a corporate PR service being supplied already, the client embarks upon a stock market flotation and the consultancy is engaged additionally to handle financial PR.

Do PR firms change tactics mid-stream if this is necessary?

Tactics are kept under constant evaluation and, being by their nature relatively short term, they are subject to change, although more probably they may be adjusted or refined. It is unlikely that any tactic would be accorded totemic status that precluded any change.

Could a change of tactics alter the contractual position?

It might do, but it is improbable. The change would have to be on such a scale as to challenge the very purpose of the commission and presumably the objectives and strategy would be reconsidered first, before turning to the contract.

How do we get rid of a PR firm without damage to us?

A termination of the contract would have to observe the provisions within the contract and the statutory position if the contract was silent on this. A typical clause in an annual retention allows for at least three months' written notice on either side, to expire by the last day of the year covered by the contract. This has the effect of obliging both parties to act by the end of the eighth month of the current year of the contract if they are to avoid automatic renewal for a further year.

It is also usual to have a provision under which either side may assert a breach of the contract by the other by written notice and terminate without further notice in the event of there being no remedy within a specified time, usually 14 days or one month. This right to terminate can be exercised provided that it does not prejudice any rights that either side may have acquired prior to that time. Obviously the decision to exercise such a clause would have to be based on grounds that could be sustained if challenged in court.

In practice, most premature termination of contracts is negotiated, as where, for instance, the client side has been bought out or merged and its PR is to be handled elsewhere or differently in the future. This is the fate that usually befalls a PR consultancy that is engaged with a view to 'fattening for market' its client's image and reputation, because, for instance, the family owners plan to dispose of the business. Negotiation usually involves a settlement that recognizes the outstanding period of the severed contract and the value of the lost earnings to the consultancy, which will have liabilities generated by the contract, not least staff to be redeployed at short notice.

As to damage in a broader sense, an amicable settlement should ensure cooperation with any handover to a successor, which is always a delicate moment, for there is a current workload to be explained and discussed with competitors, and observance of confidentialities in the future. Any less than amicable disruption, as where, for example, the client goes into receivership owing money to the consultancy and other suppliers, is of course another matter.

There is a point here that some organizations would do well to remember. Treating the PR consultant badly is inadvisable, a particularly poor choice because he or she is actively working to maintain and strengthen goodwill, understanding and sound reputation on behalf of the client. This is paid-for work, but consultants are only human. If they develop a poor opinion of the client this is bound to affect how well they perform on its behalf because of the divergence, as they perceive it, between reality and fiction. If their services are abruptly terminated, without agreement and compensation and outside the terms of the contract, the scale of bad treatment is raised by several hundred per cent, and must leave the client unnecessarily vulnerable. Is it worth it?

fifteen

changing into **overdrive**

- Does the continuing effectiveness of PR depend on ever more effort by us?
- How do we calculate our optimum commitment to PR?
- Could we find at some point that we begin to experience diminishing returns for our efforts?
- When might we wish that our PR effort was not so successful?
- How might substantial ongoing PR help marketing in a practical way?
- How does ongoing PR help sales in a practical way?
- How much does PR succeed on the choice of tactics?
- Should we keep the tactics simple and concentrate on their content?
- Once started, is PR impossible to stop?
- Is publicity more suited to the occasional effort?
- How proactive do we need to be for an effective PR presence?
- How do we maintain momentum without increasing costs?
- Would we benefit in the longer run from having a combination of in-house and consultancy?
- Do companies eventually hire several consultancies to address different requirements?
- Does multiple sourcing lead to costly control and risk loss of direction?
- Are there areas where PR and marketing can share costs?
- In what ways should PR be contributing to future planning?
- Is PR ever likely to be a senior management function?
- What about PR's contribution internationally?
- How international is PR?

- What might be the consequences for organizations?
- What about the developing countries?
- How is PR likely to develop in the future?
- What is the likely significance of this for organizations?
- Will the media remain central to PR?
- Will Internet information remain free?
- Will broadcasting standards improve?
- Is there any real future for radio?
- Will press reporting come under the law?
- Is our use of language getting in the way of communication?
- Is McWorld a consequence of PR's international reach?

In this final chapter the questions look to the future, developing applications and emerging trends and issues. They reflect a familiarity with and confidence in the use of PR, which has become, or is in the process of becoming, part of the corporate culture. Questions here are about ongoing activities, areas where PR may contribute to addressing broader management issues and how the function may be best developed further. Quite a few questions ask about the underlying trends that affect practice, such as the likely future role of the media in PR, its regulation and standards, and about PR in a global context, and how that might relate to the organization in its future thinking.

Does the continuing effectiveness of PR depend on ever more effort by us?

When you start 'doing PR' you tend to think in terms of trying not to run until you can walk. This makes sense because there is a learning curve involved, whether you are doing the work yourself, employing people or hiring a consultant. With time the pace quickens, as early wins encourage greater effort and allocation of resources and as the effects of what has been done so far begin to exert their own pressures. There is encouragement derived from growing segmentation of publics from stakeholders, better understanding of the publics, gathering confidence in environmental scanning and more interest in PR among fellow managers, as they begin to see some results.

Much of the early effort, which appears to be almost entirely one way and giving so little back, begins to show signs of turning into a [illegible]xchange, with, for instance, journalists phoning in unprompted and customers making more frequent enquiries throughout the year. This process unfolds over time, and as the momentum gathers, the balance between effort and reward comes more into equilibrium. At some point the organization begins to gain from levels of awareness, understanding and goodwill that produce benefits disproportionately greater than the effort expended in obtaining them. What seems like an exhausting uphill struggle starts to become progressively more rewarding.

Publics start to demonstrate loyalty, a desire to communicate without prompting and identification with the organization's perceived values and ethos. Typically, the organization throws ever more energy into its PR effort and as it does so the feedback from its publics grows until the point is reached at which it needs relatively little outbound communication to stimulate substantial response and there is an increasing level of unprompted inbound communication to be answered.

> The airline companies, or 'carriers', are an example of unprompted communication. Particularly the more popular ones such as Virgin seem to provoke remarkable levels of customer response and desire to initiate communication. Passengers like to write little messages, chatting about their trips and offering a few tips about how things might be even better on their next flight. It may be that this is a reflection of deep anxieties associated with travel, that people who feel safer with this airline or that want to express their relief and feelings of comfort. It provides colossal feedback and raises costs in replying.

Clothes retailers can also provoke quite remarkable levels of two-way communication with their customers. When fashion changes catch out a favourite store, trade may slacken but customers have been known to surge forward with their explanations and recommendations, as if a friend needed comforting and guidance. Furthermore, they show every sign of willing early recovery, and having difficulty in staying away for long.

Nor does this apply solely to customers. Other publics also tend to provide growing levels of feedback over time, and for the organization there can come a point when it may be in danger of overdoing its PR, by fostering hyperactive communication, when the need of the moment, the 'more effort', might be for it to focus a little less on communication and a little more on research, planning and so on.

How do we calculate our optimum commitment to PR?

Put briefly, you calculate by reference to your recognized and anticipated communications needs and your continual monitoring and assessment of the environment. Corporate activities, such as mergers and acquisitions, will be a major factor in this. Senior managers who are involved in the PR effort may also include in their calculations the amount of their time that is being taken by it, compared with their other core activities. Prudent judgement is required as to what is appropriate under the current circumstances.

Allegations that senior managers are giving too much of their time to PR matters may be well founded in some, probably rather few, instances, but are largely invalidated by sweeping assertions that many directors embrace the art and act of spinning in a headlong pursuit of media coverage, taking more time on this than is allocated to all core activities. PR is not, apparently, a core activity and is dismissed as 'spinning', a popular term easily adopted to describe pretty much anything.

Accountants who make these claims may not be, of course, entirely without personal interest; perhaps the ascent in importance of any function other than their own needs to be interpreted by them as a challenge to be rubbished. But talk of PR activity being contrary to prudent management, some sort of substitute for the 'real thing' and, amazingly, leading to corporate death, smacks of insane ranting.

Could we find at some point that we begin to experience diminishing returns for our efforts?

Clearly, any PR programme will be redirected from time to time in response to fresh objectives, and all techniques of communication can begin to lose their potency over time. For example, a sports sponsorship may have run its course and no amount of extra effort will overcome that. Creativity can do much to extend and enhance effectiveness; creation of something new out of existing raw materials adds value.

When might we wish that our PR effort was not so successful?

Engaging with publics encourages their participation in dialogue. That has to be fully funded, because failing to respond, or respond adequately, to communications such as e-mails, letters and phone calls from people with whom you are supposedly in dialogue can inflict unnecessary damage. Just think of the times when you have been irritated, annoyed, angry perhaps, by the failure to reply of an organization that you thought you were involved with in some way. If people are to be encouraged to adopt some form of 'ownership' of a brand, membership of an organization, sharing of an ideal or mission, and so on, good faith has to be demonstrated.

Quality communications, therefore, raise their own costs as well as benefits. Furthermore, some people are beginning to display the responses that hitherto might have been confined to personal relationships. This is understandable. If they are being engaged in relationships with organizations that resemble friendships they are likely to invest them with all the intellectual and emotional elements of interpersonal relations.

If, for example, they consider that they have received shoddy treatment from 'a friend' they are likely to respond by withdrawing and maybe retaliating. A small but growing number of consumers are using the Internet to do just that, warning others and hoping to inflict retaliatory damage. Rather more tip off their friends and relatives. Bear in mind that shoddy treatment could constitute almost anything, from ignoring well-meant greetings to refusal to change a customer's incorrect name on the database or answer a private investor's enquiries to denial of liability for effluent pollution, and worse.

In addition to this growing volume of communication, PR programmes can generate increasing levels of unwelcome attention from hostile groups. All active publics affect an organization more than do passive ones. Among active publics there are varying levels of commitment to securing adjustments in corporate policies and actions, from benign approval of the status quo to demand for substantial change. The pressure groups and cause-related groups are among the most demanding and hyperactive elements of these publics, so much so that an individual group may warrant classification as a public in its own right.

Publics that are interested in issues tend to fall into three types. The first of these demonstrate interest on any and all issues that come to their attention. This means that they can be very voluble and any organization with a high profile may gain their attention and interest. This is not to suggest that they are necessarily difficult or demanding, but they are likely to raise serious and reasonable wide-ranging concerns.

Single-issue publics, by contrast, concentrate, as their name suggests, on a single issue, or perhaps a small group of closely related issues, that deeply concern them, but are of only passing interest to the great majority of people. These publics are vigorous campaigners, experienced PR users, who work tirelessly to gain their objectives, and often assume the mantle of some kind of permanent watchdog. Their members may display near-obsession with their cause.

The third type of pressure group also pursues single issues, but these groups, significantly, command widespread support, probably because they involve most people in some way. These 'hot' issues can generate much media attention, and demonstrations of active support. A typical example was the UK petrol protest in 2000, when farmers and road hauliers combined to create widespread discontent and disruption about the government's heavy fuel taxes.

There is a progressive pattern that occurs that assists in anticipating such problems. First the stakeholders are identified, then the publics among those stakeholders and then the issues that those publics raise. This assumes that publics form because they recognize a problem that affects them. Many publics, however, perceive not a problem but a relationship, with which they may be very happy, so the incidence of issues being raised differs between publics. Furthermore, an interpretation of what constitutes an issue may vary widely, from no more than, say, being able to return a product and get a refund on demand to heavy pollution and dangerous processes.

Issues management, therefore, is a laborious and skilled activity, which has come to stay and has to be fully funded. The relentless rise in commercial and social pluralism has brought to the fore the importance of this work, not only in anticipation of potential 'trouble' but also to identify possible opportunities, recognizing that corporate prominence and strong brands can attract supporters and detractors alike.

How might substantial ongoing PR help marketing in a practical way?

PR provides usable intelligence to inform marketing planning. It can provide a better return on investment than other marketing communications such as advertising, direct marketing and sales promotion, owing to its ability to explain complexities, its persuasive credibility and its low-cost techniques. It creates awareness, educates markets and is widely pervasive, reaching markets through multiple channels. It counters negative perceptions and can contribute significantly to brand positioning, development and maintenance.

How does ongoing PR help sales in a practical way?

MPR seeks to satisfy the uncertainties in the potential buyer's mind that will eliminate hesitation and strengthen commitment to purchase. It generates enquiries, sales leads, sampling, inspection and plain curiosity. It educates and informs ahead of a sales encounter.

How much does PR succeed on the choice of tactics?

Operational PR depends heavily for its success upon the choice of tactics and techniques used, so short-term tactical objectives are needed that are flexible and honed to the local and the specific. The need for overall objectives, strategy and planning is emphasized time and again, but within that framework the tactical decisions and actions are key determinants. They benefit from what has gone before, but if, for any reason, they are not working they should be reviewed, and not slavishly adhered to in obedience to an inflexible master plan.

Should we keep the tactics simple and concentrate on their content?

Some of the simplest tactics are the most effective, particularly where there is creativity in their construction and/or implementation. So often tactics succeed through novel interpretation, not owing to some blinding insight. There is, in practice, very seldom a genuine 'big idea'. Messages that are easy to absorb and understand are often the result of a simple tactic, but that is not to plead for simplicity in all PR tactics. It is also as well to be wary of being driven by impatience; some of the simplest solutions have required the greatest time and attention in their delivery.

Once started, is PR impossible to stop?

No, but ceasing has its consequences, sooner or later. The 'heritage factor' may enable you to cruise fairly effortlessly for a while, maybe months, during which time you continue to benefit from all your previous efforts, but it would be imprudent to rely on this indefinitely. PR is a continuing commitment that brings cumulative results. It is unwise and impractical to 'stop and start' sustained communication. This is an important point about PR, which is not always appreciated or understood.

Is publicity more suited to the occasional effort?

Publicity, in the sense of being some credible and relevant contrivance for drawing attention and creating awareness, is best undertaken at spaced intervals, within a larger PR programme. Yes, the celebrities, politicians and entertainers undertake successive publicity-seeking activities, but even then you can 'have too much of a good thing', as was once famously remarked of a new Beethoven symphony. If indeed publicity is an intervention in the routine of life, it must surely follow that there needs to be a reasonable amount of routine between its interruptions. Deciding about this, there is one acid test that seldom fails: if the cry goes up 'Not *that* again' or 'Not *them* again' you can be fairly sure that the publicity is at risk of losing its efficacy resulting from overdoses.

How proactive do we need to be for an effective PR presence?

This has to be a value judgement based on the specific circumstances relating to objectives, the range and number of publics and stakeholders, the numbers and types of competitors for share of shout, the availability of resources and the number and range of proposed activities. If that sounds like avoiding the question, here are five areas to question for gaining a general overview of how proactive you may need to be:

- 'Are we obtaining our fair share of shout?' If not, be honest: does it matter that much? Or is it a real problem that needs to be addressed?
- 'How confident are we about the quantity and quality of research information that is being gleaned from the environment?' There is always scope for more, to be sure. The bigger question may be: 'How much of this can we turn into usable intelligence?'
- 'Do our image and our reputation satisfy our needs? If not, can we be doing more to address this?' If the current situation appears to be fine, as it is understood, ask then: 'What plans do we have to sustain our image and our reputation?'
- 'How are we doing at meeting our customers' communications expectations? Should we get real about this, with more measures and deeper analysis? Or are we confident that the current levels of service quality here are appropriate and mutually satisfactory?'
- 'Can we fairly claim to be creative in what we are doing? Are we making best use of disparate, seemingly unconnected information and of our available resources, both knowledge and skills? Could we be coming up with fresh ways of looking at old communications challenges? Or do we think that we are already about as creative as we can be?'

How do we maintain momentum without increasing costs?

'Momentum' implies a growing level of commitment, and that usually necessitates extra expenditure. However, such is the nature of PR work, it may be possible to avoid this, at least for a while. For instance, generally speaking the larger the public to be addressed the greater the costs involved. Going to opinion formers instead of to the relevant public direct might be more effective and efficient. The momentum has been maintained, but the cost has been contained, or even reduced.

Similarly, collaborations can achieve more with less, because costs or labour may be shared, or messages are communicated more effectively or thoroughly through the 'other' such as a charity or institution. Concentration of effort where competition is weaker can yield higher results, maybe at less cost than challenging a stronger opponent. Timing a programme or campaign to benefit from another, probably much more heavily promoted, event or circumstance can generate more for less.

Would we benefit in the longer run from having a combination of in-house and consultancy?

In the longer run, yes, you probably would. Most larger organizations opt for an in-house department whose work is supplemented by occasional, or possibly retained, use of consultancies. That way the in-house team can develop its own specialist skills, based on what is needed routinely, and access missing skills where necessary. For example, some have public affairs competencies but use lobbyists for providing advice on specific issues, based on their particular experience and connections.

Do companies eventually hire several consultancies to address different requirements?

It is quite common to employ several consultancies, each dealing with a particular area. For instance, there may be one or two working on MPR projects while another is lobbying, another handling sponsorships and another engaged on a community relations programme. Sometimes several offices of a multinational consultancy, or several firms within an international network, may be engaged on related programmes. Then again, a consultancy may be retained on an annual basis while others are commissioned from time to time on limited term projects.

Does multiple sourcing lead to costly control and risk loss of direction?

Provided the internal function is adequately designed and staffed and there are robust reporting procedures, it is unlikely that administrative costs will become burdensome, and certainly there should not be any loss of direction as a consequence of multiple sourcing. Anxieties about remoteness, in that the consultancy staff members are removed from the organization's premises, are largely unfounded, given modern communications technologies. Of greater relevance may be the limitations placed on consultancy time in relation to the size of fees paid and the influence on consultancy performance of divided client loyalties.

Are there areas where PR and marketing can share costs?

Many PR costs are interrelated with costs that arise in other functions, notably marketing, because publics are often addressed through various communication channels used by different parts of the organization. With marketing's focus on customers there is bound to be an overlap between its activities and those of PR when the latter is also contacting customers, although not directly in support of marketing. This is to mutual advantage, because the customers perceive every contact to be from one source. Costs may be shared, say, on market research and print production.

In what ways should PR be contributing to future planning?

The PR function should be providing useful feedback from its environmental scanning, participating in the discussion of issues and sharing in the resultant decisions taken by the dominant coalition of managers. It should be identifying the communications policies necessary to give effect to corporate aims and business objectives, implementing and evaluating those policies and collaborating closely with senior managers in the conduct of the communications elements of their functional plans.

Is PR ever likely to be a senior management function?

This implies that PR is never represented in the boardroom. In practice, however, it began to appear in Britain's boardrooms in the 1960s, and by the 1970s some 30 publicly quoted companies had PR directors, either on their main or subsidiary boards. Since then there has developed a trend towards the appointment of PR directors, which seems likely to continue.

It is clear, however, that in most cases PR has yet to berth alongside finance, marketing and HRM at the top tables. This may be attributable to reluctance among other functions to acknowledge the value of PR. It may be PR's own poor general image and reputation. It cannot be for lack of examples of companies and a variety of other types of organization that have demonstrably benefited from PR representation at senior level.

What about PR's contribution internationally?

PR has global reach and is well advanced throughout the developed world. Organizations that operate internationally often engage consultancies in individual countries in order to benefit from local cultural understanding and contacts, recognizing that this is preferable to trying to handle PR from the centre. Global and multinational companies may have presence in sufficient depth to enable them to establish PR functions in each of their operating territories or markets, supervised and supported from the centre, or may fund regional distributors' PR efforts on their behalf.

Whatever the arrangements, the main consideration is the degree of local knowledge and know-how. Typically, for example, there may be, say, a dozen operating subsidiaries, each with its own PR function, enjoying a relatively substantial degree of autonomy and responsible for a region or market, and the central PR function at corporate headquarters is responsible for communications elsewhere in the world, in all other, minor, markets.

How international is PR?

Interest in PR is fast becoming universal. For example:

- It is said that there are 100,000 PR students under training in China.

- The Russian PR people at the trade's European federation pass a resolution against providing PR services to terrorist organizations.
- Argentinians denied access to their bank deposits demonstrate volubly before the news media.
- Palestinian Arabs make adept use of PR to promote their cause against Israel, which in turn displays US standards of media management skills.

All around the world the message is out: PR provides a range of low-cost techniques for communicating through the mass media. This 'universalization' of PR is of critical importance. It fosters adversarial democracy and competition that is not only about commerce but ideas, cultures, ideologies, resources and much, much more. This loud process deals in casual glimpses, fleeting impressions, partial disclosures, exploitive emoting and coarse symbolism. In consequence it nurtures understandings and resentments, agreements and rows, harmony and bitterness; it offers universal truths and selective truths, reasoned persuasion and bullying browbeating. It is humanity's new mechanism for talking with, or shouting at, next door or across the world.

What might be the consequences for organizations?

As the sound levels continue to rise, organizations across the world are obliged to concede that what might have been a discrete resource for commerce, diplomacy, politics, academia and science is turning into some kind of electronic babble of inconsequence. Worthwhile communication with publics cannot be left to the vagaries of over-simplistic message hurling. As this great tidal wave of PR messages washes around the globe each day and night, the PR manager has to redouble his or her efforts to keep feet on the ground, making sure to select the correct 'shout' to 'share' and continuing to balance quality against quantity in communications with publics.

What about the developing countries?

Global and multinational companies' PR in the developing countries tends to be primarily centred on education. There are tremendous obstacles, caused by widespread illiteracy, multiplicity of languages, extreme poverty and inadequate secondary schooling. However, conditions are improving and there is obvious desire in many countries to benefit from 'Western' imports, ranging from basic hygiene and dietary instruction to labour-saving consumer goods and personal care products, and a fuller knowledge of the world and its ways.

Owing to the climatic, economic and social conditions, much PR is undertaken by the public sector, with civil servants, many Western educated, engaged on establishing the primary infrastructure, such as universal education and health care. Their efforts are also largely educational. PR is seen as being an essential function within all the public services and the larger indigenous companies and trading organizations. Viewed as markets, these countries present communications problems that are far removed from the advanced mass markets of, say, south-east Asia, but there can be little doubting PR's growing role in their future progress.

How is PR likely to develop in the future?

The future in at least one important respect is already signposted. Historically, corporate and political interests, people who had the funds and the need, engaged in PR. In practice this meant, very largely, governments and business. As the mass media have grown rapidly in recent years the use of PR has burgeoned, so that now very few organizations of any type do not engage in PR activities designed to improve and sustain persuasive communications to their advantage. That increasingly includes even unincorporated local sports and social clubs, churches and just about any 'wannabe' celebrity. The techniques are low-cost and readily accessible, basic levels of technical competence may be readily acquired and a multiplicity of willing and waiting media are on hand to assist.

In short, it appears that everyone is doing it and that this is an unstoppable trend. Well, not quite, yet, but in the next decade, perhaps sooner, it is not too fanciful to suppose that PR is going to become a universal 'right' of every citizen, or subject, as a means of persuasive self-expression. 'Ordinary people' are already using PR instead of the law, to put their case, argue their corner, defend their interest, and they are doing this at a fraction of the cost that they might otherwise incur by employing lawyers. Maybe PR advice centres will begin to offer help to people who have limited resources or are in some way socially excluded or disadvantaged.

This implies a massive democratization process that is going to occur at the expense of the politicians, who talk about democracy while displaying almost manic obsession with determining what is, and what is not, the 'public interest' and in steering 'public opinion' to their purposes. They are fighting a rearguard action to dominate the media against the incursion, as they see it, of the so-called ordinary people. Whether they will demonstrate the ages-old British skill for adaptation and compromise remains to be seen, but the surge in pluralism is now a fact of life.

What is the likely significance of this for organizations?

Accessible, rational, unemotional and 'full' public debate is not a threat, far from it, and, as a social phenomenon, may very well prove to be a tremendous advance. Presently there is much talk by politicians and media about open dialogue involving people generally but it has to be on their, often rather insulting, terms. Indeed, the more they talk about it the less likely it may be to occur. People are not responding very favourably to what might appear to be important opportunities. There is deep cynicism and a widespread belief that actions speak louder than words, that invitations to debate are hollow pretence, sham gestures, empty rhetoric.

As politicians and their cohorts in the United Kingdom purport to worry about the missing 40 per cent of voters (in the 2001 UK General Election 40 per cent of voters didn't bother to vote), organizations may perceive a widespread and growing desire among consumers for quality communications that are worth having and rich scope for benefiting from this through their own efforts. Might the next few years offer not less but more demand for meaningful two-way dialogue between organizations and their publics? Could organizations adapt to this growing universality and pervasiveness of PR, offering greater outlets for the pent up frustrations of thwarted pluralism?

Will the media remain central to PR?

The growth in the media continues to be technology-driven, and presumably for so long as technology bowls along at its current pace the media will continue to burgeon. However, the rate of technology advance varies from time to time, and we are now overdue for a slowdown, based on experience over the last two centuries.

The net effect of this multiplicity of message outlets is dramatic fragmentation. For instance, it seems light years away since BBC radio routinely summoned managers to its studios to give expert opinion but denied them any mention of their organization's names. Now no mention means strictly no can do. PR managers have an enormous choice of mass media channels, plus all their own created media and of course the Internet. They can pick and choose, develop quality relationships directly, not through mediation, fine-tune in numerous combinations and generally achieve greater control than was possible until only recently.

Another consequence of technology advances has been the contraction of the labour intensity in the traditional news gathering process. Ever more media content is PR originated, because there are ever fewer journalists to filter and reject, interpret as they prefer and generally assert control. The media in their present guise are also likely to be losers to rising pluralism, as they strive to assert their selective and distinctive worldviews, through which their readers, viewers and listeners peer. In the United Kingdom, television and newspaper audiences are in steady and relentless decline.

So the probability is that the mass media will continue to play a pivotal role in PR over the coming decade, but that this will steadily fall away owing to fragmentation, growing alternatives, stronger pluralism and greater democratization of PR. It will mean that there will be ever-greater erosion of the remaining differences between PR and journalism, in its traditional sense, and ever more direct participation by readers, viewers and listeners in the media. The content will steadily change from one that is largely the product of relatively few, well-paid and privileged producers to a broader mix of contributions from multiple sources, including not only organizations but also private individuals and, basically, anyone who wants to use the media as a forum for discussion, display, pretence, exhibitionism and so on.

Will Internet information remain free?

That almost certainly will depend upon what types of information are being provided. For organizations the best current indications of what is likely to occur probably come from the traditional trade press, where venerable and young publications alike have prospered over the years from heavy advertising revenues. As these have 'softened' of late publishers have invested in creating 'advertising-led' sites carrying free information, hoping to 'monetize' their largesse through selling space in the form of banners, 'pop-ups' and so on. However, when the dot.com bubble burst, many such sites had to be closed or drastically reduced and 'free content' is widely considered to lack sufficient credibility, at least for business purposes.

The nub of the matter is value: what value is genuinely placed on the available information. It is a re-run of that old familiar problem, identifying what needs to be known from what is merely nice to know, which is an important consideration in all PR work. For managers all information has to be of real value to them in their work, and without that it becomes optional, even if it is free. If it passes that test then most managers expect to pay something for it, supposing that usually very little that is worth having is free.

So it is likely that useful information gained on the Internet is going to be paid for in the future, but just how remains uncertain. The probability is that many managers will opt for subscription-based schemes, whereby they gain access by first buying an annual subscription to the hard copy, traditional title and then buying an annual entitlement to come and go at the corresponding site for one year.

It sounds a neat solution for the existing committed reader, the person who probably reads most of the paper or magazine each issue, but what of the occasional reader, such as those many managers who look through briefly or only read what is drawn to their attention? What also of the environment scanner, the researcher, the student, the market commentator, the financial analyst, the librarian and so on, all those people for whom trade publications are valuable sources but not thorough or regular reads? How they may be charged for visiting sites in a similar fashion is likely to be one of the major determinants of how payment for information will evolve.

Nor will the convenience and practicality of payment schemes, from an organizational perspective, be a guarantee that the information is worth having or that there are any material benefits to going to the site instead of looking at the printed word. Publishers are likely, therefore, to provide additional features not possible in hard copy. For example, instead of simply reproducing the current issue after a decent interval has elapsed, they may take to offering summaries of news 'as it breaks' between issues. The value of such immediacy is likely to be variable, depending upon the individual visitor's exact circumstances. Nevertheless, up-to-date intelligence usually finds a ready market.

So the probability is that, eventually, much information will be charged for, based on its proven value to managers, but that some will not, either because it is not that valued or it is offered by way of a tempting sample of what is available at a price. What is on offer at these sites will have to be strong enough to be worth paying for, and there may be considerable reluctance to migrate from a free to a paid-for source borne of familiarity with readily available free content.

Will broadcasting standards improve?

The question implies that in the United Kingdom they have sunk, which appears to be generally agreed, and that they need to be improved, which does not appear to be generally agreed. British television and radio used to be held in the highest regard around the world, and still benefits to some extent from that heritage factor. For instance, in the Iraqi military campaign BBC radio news again became one of three preferred popular sources of information internationally, and about 150 million people around the world hear its long-running entertainment, *Just a Minute*, each week.

UK regulation of television, radio and telecommunications is now to be undertaken by a new 'super-regulator', the Office of Communications, or Ofcom, which replaces a cluster of bodies covering different sectors. This new regulator is to oversee television and radio content standards as well as everything else, from telephone numbers to takeovers.

These are exceptionally turbulent times for UK broadcasters and much is being made of the efficacy of new codes, including local content codes for radio, and a reduction in the number of radio stations permitted to operate within localities. The diminution of radio broadcast standards has coincided with burgeoning commercial radio, now provided by about 70 companies through 240 local licences, and a consequent reduction in the influence of publicly owned broadcasting. So the restriction to just two commercial stations per locality may well bring about greater variety and quality of output, which would have helpful consequences for PR people.

However, there is to be greater, not lesser, concentration of ownership of commercial radio, despite the misgivings of the outgoing Radio Authority. Foreign ownership is expected, particularly from one owner who famously remarked at a Radio Academy conference to the effect that 'radio is an advertising medium, there to sell hamburgers'. Foreign ownership of television is also likely, subject to a three-year sector review, which presumably will be benign, owing to the probable impracticality of then bringing ownership back into UK hands and reassembling displaced programme-making teams.

Television content may well, therefore, continue its current drift. The delivery of services and 'strands' are to be judged by Ofcom across the whole of television, leaving plentiful scope for granting exemptions and making allowances to one channel against another. To counter this, the 'public service' remit now includes not only information, education and entertainment but also social issues, science, international affairs and programmes for children and for young people.

The regulatory framework is in three tiers: advertising and editorial; production quotas; and public service review and reporting. Complaints from viewers and listeners, which are counted in their thousands, will be referred to the broadcasters and telecommunications companies, rather than handled as before by the regulators, who will be involved solely in dispute resolution. Allowing the people who are the source of the complaint to be judge and jury in their own cause may dilute the benefits of regulation, as with the press and financial services in the United Kingdom. Obviously, from a PR perspective, broadcasting has to take fuller account of burgeoning social pluralism and thereby it may offer more, rather than less, communication opportunities in the coming years.

Is there any real future for radio?

Digital radio points to a very promising future for a medium that still commands vast audiences throughout the world. The invention of the clockwork radio, a brilliantly inspired example of intermediate technology, has boosted radio consumption in the developing countries and challenged the domination of battery-powered transistors in hand-held portable radio markets.

Digital radio has been slow to take off, but it promises a surge of new interest, for it eliminates, truthfully for the first time, the irritating interference that can hinder reception, and it provides automatic tuning and a leap in sound quality comparable to what happened when compact disks (CDs) supplanted long-playing records (LPs). These new audio advances are going to draw audiences, which cannot be bad for PR purposes, but there is more.

Ancillary services already include the ability to scroll through a list of all the available stations where the radio is presently located. This will be developed, so that the chosen station's daily programme schedule highlights will be accessible, like reading an online listings magazine. And when a programme has been chosen, more details about it will be accessed, or it can be set for recording or storing, the kind of convenience now taken for granted with television.

This scale of advance is expected to restore radio to some of its former glory as a major medium, yet there is a further dimension. Radio is going to get together with mobile, or cell, telephones, rather as photography married radio to produce television. Radio and mobile telephony are complementary. Text, pictures and video will be sent from one mobile to many, simultaneously, using digital radio's data channel. This 'broadband broadcast outpath' offers opportunities for mobiles comparable to that of the new radio, in addition to existing mobile uses. For instance, photos of the happy wedding scene could be phoned to relatives and friends far and wide, say as bride and groom depart for their honeymoon, and each recipient could then send on the photos to someone else using the 'third generation' mobile technology. The implications for PR are significant.

Will press reporting come under the law?

A law on privacy in the United Kingdom is widely predicted, but legislation would have to take account of emotion as well as fact. Emotional distress is notoriously difficult to measure and value; one reader might be much more hurt or angered by a given set of words and images than might another, according to his or her attachments, connections, temperament and so on. Maybe this is why the press has managed to become so intrusive over the years while lurking under cover of self-regulation.

The defence to complaints about reporting often rotates around talk of 'people in the public eye' as against 'ordinary people', the former being 'fair game' and the latter not. But it is observable that non-famous people can have their lives invaded by reporters, regardless of any such self-imposed strictures. And what exactly are the criteria for qualifying as someone who is a legitimate object of press enquiry?

Were it not for the cult of celebrity, all of this might seem fairly academic from a PR standpoint, but it is not. Ever more people want to be seen and heard in the mass media, and many, if not most, of them seem anxious to talk about their private lives, even to discussing them with others, through letters and studio exchanges. PR people have always tended to safeguard the private lives of their principals and clients, unless they are publicity agents. This new frankness and, in some cases, exhibitionism, is forcing some readjustments in determining issues of privacy.

All of which does not alter the certainty that we can expect a rich, continuing stream of people, such as pop music idols, sports professionals and show business personalities, who will ardently seek to 'reveal all' and thrust their carefully contrived lifestyles on newspaper readers. They at least must surely qualify for 'fair game' and cannot expect much sympathy for their alleged shock, anger, betrayal and so on when the papers report what they do not want reported, as against what they do. This is about freedom of the press, which is likely to be guarded ever more jealously in the years to come as a variety of people in the public eye seek to control content for their own purposes.

Sensitive to these controversies, the European Union is planning a uniform media code for the enlarged 25-member union of countries. The aim is press protection and community service through self-regulation that best fits regional cultures and conditions. At present there is widespread mistrust of the press in many parts of Europe; it is almost non-existent in some countries. 'Non-governmental media accountability systems' are primarily intended to establish and restore trust, or perhaps more correctly, questioning trust. Principal among these is a published code of conduct, which is accessible to everyone; the Alliance of Independent Press Councils of Europe has a Web site, which includes mention of ethical standards and issues.

> Press self-regulation assumes added significance when advanced technology applications threaten maintenance of reporting integrity. For instance, most major US newspapers forbid the alteration of news photographs. *The Los Angeles* Times (2 April 2003), reported on its front page that one of its photographers employed to cover the US/UK military invasion of Iraq 'acknowledged that he had used his computer to combine elements of two photographs, taken moments apart, in order to improve the composition'. The published photograph showed a British soldier cautioning civilians to take cover in the battleground near Basra. On close inspection it could be seen that some of the people in the background appeared twice. The photographer was dismissed.

Is our use of language getting in the way of communication?

How often this question is being asked, particularly among people who fear for the future of the English language, which is fragmenting. English, in one interpretation or another, is the most widely used language, by an estimated 1,900 million people. This is some six times as many as its native speakers, which may go some way to explain why, as never before, English-speaking peoples around the globe are developing their own discrete regional versions of the language, so that international understanding between them is becoming ever more uncertain. It is likely that there will be as many as six English languages by the end of the century, each sharing only modest similarities to the rest.

Of course languages evolve, supposedly to meet new needs and changing circumstances. How many nineteenth-century English words, for instance, have quietly slipped out of usage, to be replaced by many new ones? But we live in a time of hyperactive use of language. There is much creation of new language to suit the commercial or other needs of interest groups. PR people are encouraged to make up new words, whether they are necessary or not, because supposedly our language does not have sufficient words already available to convey the desired meaning satisfactorily. And yesterday's invention often becomes tomorrow's standard practice.

Just how many of these new words are really needed is questionable. Time was when many were dismissed as slang and maybe a good few of the new arrivals deserve that designation now. Also, new meanings are given to established words, like 'take' to mean interpretation. There is an insidious determination to use language in order to identify 'them and us', the 'insiders and outsiders'. This is not limited to IT argot, but is widely used in newspapers and broadcasting. Those who are not kept informed are deliberately left to speculate and forgo communication.

This may help to sell dictionaries, new and expanded editions of which proliferate, packed with words many of which sound horribly dated barely a decade later, so transient is their need. But does it *assist* communication, and are PR people doing themselves a service when they keenly adopt, or create, contemporary slang? Can we expect to see ever more insider language used in addressing individual publics, a kind of reassurance that the message is absolutely exclusive, just between you and I? It is a dismal prospect, but perhaps not irreversible. Maybe someone will rediscover the merits of the English language and adhere less to 'contemporese'.

The Plain English proponents fight an uphill struggle, for the odds are heavily against them. Could this be for another reason too, namely the desire to sound more important? This surely drives (another popular slang word that doubtless will be abandoned before long) all those customer service department replies, in which there is much mention of 'yourself', 'would' do this or that, 'due to the fact of' and similar pomposities. Might there even be a steely intention here to deliberately confuse, mislead, render every formal communication unintelligible? Could it be that nonsensical letters are carefully crafted to encourage recipients to make phone or e-mail contact, to enquire after the meaning?

Since PR is about communication and understanding, presumably it has more than a passing interest in the current use and abuse of the English language, particularly as the world 'shrinks'. PR people whose first language is English have an enviable opportunity, as the source of so much written and spoken output, to collectively exert considerable influence, for better or for worse. Unfortunately, the greater probability is that the current frenzied language invention and distortion will persist unabated, encouraged by commercial, cultural and technological interests.

Is McWorld a consequence of PR's international reach?

PR plays its part in the globalization of markets, which has been dubbed McWorld by those who object to what they perceive to be the consequent disorder and unfairly distributed costs. The commercial benefits of deregulation and greater trade are not in doubt, but outside the developed countries this process is often seen not as providing opportunities for a better life for all but as economic imperialism, amounting to exploitation and oppression.

McWorld is perceived to be entirely driven by commercial values that flourish where there is total economic independence of nation states and all commercial interests are privately held. Political and legal constraints are seen as obstructions to this process that must be supplanted, because 'the market must decide'. This is fine for the beneficiaries, but what of those who are not yet, cannot see when they might be or suspect they are exploited victims of McWorld?

This holds great interest for PR, because of one word: terrorism. It is clear that freedom of movement around the world combined with the growth in communications has fostered both the ability and desire to 'hit back' in ways that are potentially very destructive and bloody. Perceptions of disorder created by globalization are being met with disorder. Violence and anarchy are increasing, and this in turn is promoting more violence. So we see, for instance, hijackers and suicide bombers, in the names of democracy and various religions and beliefs, provoke retaliation using overwhelming 'firepower' by those for whom globalization is already working well.

The major consequence of globalization, however, is subtler: it is the growth of interdependence between peoples everywhere. This cliché has become a reality. The free movement of capital, people and goods – and terrorists – has resulted in a decline in regional autonomy, sovereignty of nation states and cultural differences and an increase in international collaboration, standardization of processes and greater use of fewer languages.

Just as PR is a key player in the promotion of world trade, so too it has a role in addressing these consequences: in explaining the more complex, generating meaningful understandings, squaring up to the really hard questions, providing the feedback that is needed to create greater harmony and lessen discord internationally. Half a century and more ago, the founding fathers of modern PR counted among their purposes the application of a balm to the wounds of society, with which to facilitate mutually beneficial understandings and collaborations, at whatever level and for whatever purpose, whether commercial or otherwise. They foresaw in communication a potentially great power that might bestow significant benefits on society at large. Now that communication has enveloped the world, PR people have the opportunity and challenge to prove them right as never before.

further reading

Black, S and Davis, A (ed) (2002) *Public Relations*, 3rd edn, Old Bailey Press, London.
Cutlip, S, Center, A and Broom, G (2000) *Effective Public Relations*, 8th edn, Prentice Hall, Englewood Cliffs, New Jersey.
Grunig, J and Hunt, T (1984) *Managing Public Relations*, Holt, Rinehart and Winston, Orlando, Florida.
Grunig, J et al (1992) *Excellence in Public Relations and Communication Management*, Lawrence Erlbaum Associates, Hillsdale, New Jersey.
Hart, N et al (1995) *Strategic Public Relations*, Macmillan, Basingstoke, England.
Kitchen, P et al (1997) *Public Relations: Principles and Practice*, Thomson Learning, London
L'Etang, J and Pieczka, M (1996) *Critical Perspectives in Public Relations*, Thomson Learning, London.
van Riel, C and Blackburn, C (ed) (1995) *Principles of Corporate Communication*, Prentice Hall, Hemel Hempstead, England.

index

To Wendy Curme, for her constructive criticism and unfailing encouragement

This book has been endorsed by the Institute of Directors.

The endorsement is given to selected Kogan Page books which the IoD recognizes as being of specific interest to its members and providing them with up-to-date, informative and practical resources for creating business success. Kogan Page books endorsed by the IoD represent the most authoritative guidance available on a wide range of subjects including management, finance, marketing, training and HR.

The views expressed in this book are those of the author and are not necessarily the same as those of the Institute of Directors.

First published in Great Britain in 2003 by Kogan Page Limited

120 Pentonville Road
London N1 9JN
UK
www.kogan-page.co.uk

ISBN 0 7494 3925 4

British Library Cataloguing in Publication Data

A CIP record for this book is available from the British Library.

Typeset by Jean Cussons Typesetting, Diss, Norfolk
Printed and bound in Great Britain by Biddles Ltd, Guildford and King's Lynn
www.biddles.co.uk

Everything You Should Know About Public Relations

Direct answers to over 500 questions

Anthony Davis